Film as social practice

This is the fourth edition of a classic student textbook which introduces film studies from a cultural studies perspective.

Film as Social Practice is distinctive in that it approaches the study of film as a social and cultural practice that does not end with the text. Rather than being examined as a set of canonical texts, film is examined as entertainment, as narrative and as cultural event. The focus is upon the cultural function of film.

This latest edition is fully revised and updated throughout, incorporating recent theoretical directions as well as updating the films referred to as examples or sites of analysis to include more recent and contemporary films.

This new fourth edition includes:

- New sections dealing with debates about spectacle versus narrative and with special effects among the 'languages' of cinema
- An extended treatment of sound and its contribution to cinema
- A new section dealing with the consumption of cinema and cultural identities
- A revised and updated account of the structure and condition of the global popular feature film industry
- An increased number of updated illustrations.

Graeme Turner is Professor of Cultural Studies and Director of the Centre for Critical and Cultural Studies at the University of Queensland, Brisbane, Australia. He has published many books on media and cultural studies including *British Cultural Studies: An Introduction, Understanding Celebrity* and *The Film Cultures Reader*.

Film as Social Practice

FOURTH EDITION

Graeme Turner

Routledge
Taylor & Francis Group

LONDON AND NEW YORK

First published 1988
by Routledge
2 Park Square, Milton Park,
Abingdon, Oxon OX14 4RN

Simultaneously published in the USA
and Canada
by Routledge
711 Third Avenue, New York,
NY 10017

Second edition 1993
Third edition 1999
This edition 2006
This edition 2009

Routledge is an imprint of the Taylor
& Francis Group, an informa
business

© 1988, 1993, 1999, 2006 Graeme
Turner

Typeset in Sabon by Keystroke,
Jacaranda Lodge, Wolverhampton

British Library Cataloguing in
Publication Data
A catalogue record for this book is
available from the British Library

Library of Congress Cataloguing in
Publication Data
Turner, Graeme.
Film as social practice / Graeme
Turner.— 4th ed.
p. cm. — (Studies in culture and
communication)
Includes bibliographical references
and index.
1. Motion pictures—Social aspects.
2. Communication. I. Title.
II. Series.
PN1995.9.S6T87 2006
302.23′43—dc22
2005030194

ISBN10: 0–415–37513–4 (hbk)
ISBN10: 0–415–37514–2 (pbk)
ISBN10: 0–203–96954–5 (ebk)

ISBN13: 978–0–415–37513–9 (hbk)
ISBN13: 978–0–415–37514–6 (pbk)
ISBN13: 978–0–203–96954–0 (ebk)

This is for Jessie
who missed out last time

Contents

CONTENTS

List of illustrations

Acknowledgements

For assistance with, and permission to reproduce, the illustrations in this book I would like to thank: John Fairfax & Sons; AAP; Time-Life; Fox/Columbia (Australia); Kobal Collection; Village Roadshow; Meg Labrum; the National Film and Sound Archive of Australia; the *Border Morning Mail* (Albury); Twentieth Century Fox; JBG Photo.com; Ronald Grant Archive; and Associated R&R Films.

Preface

This fourth edition of *Film as Social Practice* responds to the fact, first, that there have been significant shifts in the film industry's role within the multimedia marketplace, and second, that film and cultural theory have moved on appreciably since the previous edition. Film no longer stands alone as an industry, as it is increasingly embedded in a globalizing and convergent media. More people today watch film via their television set than in the cinema, and this book needed to report and reflect on the implications of this shift. Also, the character of the movies we see in our cinemas has changed significantly, as has the structure and operation of the industry itself. Consequently, the account provided of the current state of the popular feature film industry has been substantially revised in this edition.

This book looks at film studies from a cultural studies perspective, thus dealing with it in slightly different ways to most film studies textbooks, but there have been theoretical developments in both fields which it also seemed necessary to deal with at greater length in this edition. Among the new features of this edition is an increased focus on special effects, both as a component of the language of cinema and as a force driving the rise of the spectacle in contemporary cinema. The discussion of sound has been expanded, building on the development of research and debate around that issue in recent years. The debates around audiences and spectatorship which had come to the fore in the previous edition now need to be connected to the large body of work which looks at film in terms of its participation in the construction of cultural identities – particularly those of gender, race, and ethnicity. All the theoretical material has been updated throughout to reflect contemporary concerns. I have also updated the references to particular film texts, including recent popular films where possible so that the examples upon which I draw are likely to be familiar to the readers of this book.

It has not been possible to greatly expand the length of the volume, so the insertion of new material has had to be limited. However, I am confident that this fourth revision has again widened the range of ideas covered, and brought the ideas already dealt with up to date. It has retained its focus on film as popular culture, as among the representational forms and social practices of popular culture, while continuing to account for the changing trends in contemporary cinema. I hope the renovations made for this edition will refresh this approach and make it a more accessible and useful book as a consequence.

Graeme Turner
Brisbane, 2005

Introduction

In 1896 the French brothers Auguste and Louis Lumière became the first to project moving film to an audience. Like other pioneers in film, such as Thomas Edison in the USA, the Lumières imagined that their work with moving pictures would be directed towards scientific research rather than the establishment of an entertainment industry. Edison claimed that he decided to leave the movie industry as soon as its potential as a 'big amusement proposition' became clear, although his career makes this difficult to accept since he employed some cut-throat business practices. It is certainly true that when Edison ran his first 50 feet of film in 1888, the future he envisaged for moving pictures was more akin to what we now know as television; the emphasis was to be on domestic, information-based usage. However, despite the inappropriateness of the pioneers' initial objectives, it took barely fifteen years into the twentieth century for the narrative feature to establish itself – both as a viable commercial product and as a contender for the status of the 'seventh art', the new century's first original art form.

The history of film and of the ways in which it has been studied has already been written from a multitude of perspectives: as a narrative of key films, stars, and directors; as a story of ever-improving technology and more realistic illusions; as an industrial history of Hollywood and the multinational corporations which have succeeded it; as a cultural history, in which film is used as a reflector or index of movements within twentieth-century popular culture. Until relatively recently, film studies generally had been dominated by one perspective – aesthetic analysis in which film's ability to become art through its reproduction and arrangement of sound and images was the subject of attention. The first edition of this book, back in 1988, decisively broke with this tradition in order to study film as entertainment, as narrative, as cultural event. The book was intended to introduce students to film as a social practice, and the understanding of its production and consumption, its pleasures and its meanings, was enclosed within the study of the workings of culture itself. Pleasingly, this kind of approach to film – one which is comfortable with thinking of it as entertainment and popular culture – is far more widespread now, as I produce the fourth edition.

The academic area of film studies is now firmly established in colleges, schools, and universities around the world. However, while there has always been a theoretical and academic interest in film, it did not begin in the universities. When this interest expanded dramatically in the 1960s and 1970s, the move into the universities occurred, particularly in the USA, where film departments proliferated over that period. The success of these departments can be deduced from the fact that the place once occupied by literature in humanities or arts courses came under challenge by film during the 1970s and 1980s – just as the arts course itself was to come under attack from a wave of interdisciplinary fields such as communications, media studies, or cultural studies of one kind or another in the 1980s and 1990s.

Such challenges to the traditional literature or arts programme were, ironically, partly due to the defection of literature scholars who had moved into the area of film studies during this period. While this certainly resulted in more sophisticated understandings of film as a medium, the influence of attitudes developed in literary studies but applied to a popular and visual medium was not always positive. Many literary scholars brought with them assumptions which later film theory was to challenge: for instance, a high-culture suspicion of such popular cultural forms as mainstream movies, television, or popular fiction; an exaggerated respect for the single unique text (book or film) coexisting with a patronizing attitude towards commercial genre-styled films (westerns, thrillers, musicals, etc.); and a preference for films made from literary works. Interest in film in the 1960s and 1970s was rather narrowly circumscribed by the preference for modernistic, abstract films which bore greater similarities to literary works than to the mainstream of commercial feature film entertainment. Because film was seen to be analogous to literature, many of the things it did which literature did not were ignored. In particular, film's ability to attract millions of paying customers was disregarded because of aesthetic criticism of the most successful films. As a result it took some time to recover the need to understand the fundamental attraction of film-going itself: to understand the dreamlike separation from the everyday world that lies behind the shock we experience as we leave the cinema, or the lure of the luminous images on the screen.

At the time I wrote the first edition of *Film as Social Practice*, the arguments which dominated most texts on film theory revolved around the formalism–realism debate (that is, whether or not to talk about film by way of its artistic – *formal* – unity or by way of its specific relation to the particular world it is attempting to capture within its frames – its *realism*). The debate has a history as long as that of the medium itself, although its terms do keep changing. In their traditional form, rooted in arguments from the 1940s and 1950s, both the realist and formalist positions are aesthetic in that they are finally interested in evaluating how successful a film is as *art*, rather than as a social activity for its audience. The first edition of *Film as Social Practice* participated in a significant change in the kind of approach taken to film studies over the last couple of decades, and the movement away from a predominantly aesthetic approach is an important marker of that change.

It is now accepted that film's function in our culture goes well beyond that of being simply an exhibited aesthetic object. Popular film takes place in an arena where the audience's pleasure is a dominant consideration – both for the audience and for the film's producers. This does not necessarily mean that the audience is drugged or fed 'junk food for the mind'. The pleasure that popular film provides may indeed be quite different from that offered by literature or fine art; it is, however, equally deserving of our under-standing. Film provides us with pleasure in the spectacle of its representations on the screen, in our recognition of stars, styles, and genres, and in our enjoyment of the participation in the film-going event itself. Popular films have a life beyond their theatrical runs or their re-runs on television: stars, genres, key movies become part of our personal and shared culture, our identity. Film is a social practice for its makers and its audience: in its narratives and meanings we can locate evidence of the ways in which our culture makes sense of itself. Such is the view of film explored through these pages.

This is a short book and the following chapters cannot be comprehensive guides to the full body of film theory. Rather, they are a map locating those areas of film and cultural theory that will be of most use to students first encountering the study of film – as a set of texts and as a social practice. Suggestions for further reading and consideration will follow each chapter, and point towards issues or applications I have been unable to include within the body of the text. Chapter 7 presents a set of sample analyses or 'readings' of films in order to demonstrate the kinds of approaches outlined earlier in the book. The aim is not to define what each film is 'about', or what it means, but to show what kind of information is produced by each analytical method. Throughout the book, but especially here, I am concerned with the *readings* any film may invite, rather than *the reading* we might want to impose.

Students wanting to follow some of these arguments further, and who find the cultural studies-inflected approach of this book productive, can find further elaboration of its take on film studies, as well as a relevant collection of readings, in my companion reader *The Film Cultures Reader* (Turner 2002). The essays and book excerpts contained in the *Reader* are frequently cited in this book, and will provide a rich background to the film student who wants to learn a little more.

In choosing examples with which to illustrate the points made in this book, I have attempted to deal primarily with mainstream popular films which students may well have seen. Although there are references to some of the 'classic' films – *Metropolis* and *Citizen*

Kane, for instance – the focus of this book is on film's function within popular culture, rather than its more rarefied role as high art. This is a film text about movies *and* cinema, not just cinema alone. (Readers will note that such terms as film, movie, and cinema are used interchangeably throughout.)

In writing this book, I have received help and encouragement from a number of colleagues over the years, but the one who most deserves my thanks is Rebecca Barden, my editor at Routledge. Rebecca shepherded me through several editions of this book, always astutely and helpfully, before leaving Routledge to join the BFI. The partnership between author and editor can be a difficult one, but working with her has been a genuinely pleasurable collaboration. Much of the success of the previous editions of this book is due to her intelligence and professionalism. The task of completing this fourth edition, including that of seeking out some fresh illustrations, was taken on by Aileen Irwin, and I wish to thank her for so ably carrying on the tradition.

Chapter 1

The feature film industry

The feature film today

The cultural prominence of the feature film within Western cultures may have peaked in the 1930s, but it remains pervasive today. Indeed, in a reversal of the trend over the preceding thirty years, the 1990s witnessed a steady growth in the size of film audiences as the number of screens in use multiplied dramatically. Now, at the beginning of the twenty-first century, audiences seem to have stabilized largely around the late 1990s' levels, although they do fluctuate significantly from year to year in ways that more or less reflect the popular appeal of the films on release at the time. As I write this, in 2005, audience figures are down. Popular cinema in 2005, however, is very different from what it was in the 1930s. Now, popular film is rarely presented to its public as a single product, event or commodity. Rather, it is a kind of composite commodity, linked to 'The Making of . . .' DVD, the computer or video game, the range of action figures, or the theme park ride – all aimed at extending the purchase of film beyond the cinema walls. More fundamentally, the change in the nature of film as a cultural commodity reflects the hard industrial fact that film is no longer the product of a self-contained industry; today, it is most often merely one of a range of cultural commodities produced by large multinational conglomerates whose main interest is more likely to be electronics or petroleum or theme parks than the construction of magical narratives for audiences to enjoy on the screen.

Despite its specificity as a cultural experience, the contemporary feature film has had to respond to a great deal of competition from other media, and from other sources of entertainment. Over the last few decades, the growth of cable TV, the development of the VCR and the DVD, the adaptation of the computer to home leisure use, and the expansion of the attractions available via the Internet have exposed the feature film to a highly competitive multimedia marketplace. As film producers have competed for what was for some years a shrinking market, many changes in industry practices have occurred. First, the industry has concentrated its resources on the 'blockbuster' – the aggressively promoted big-budget movie with high production values, big stars, massive simultaneous release patterns and, increasingly, expensive special effects (Stringer 2003; Lewis 2003: 61). The amount of money invested in these productions is now massive, and this significantly increases the risk to their producers. As a result, the international industry – primarily Hollywood – has made fewer films and is thus increasingly cautious about *which* films to make. It is unfortunately the case that most of the blockbusters of today tend to be narratively conservative, featuring spectacular special effects and a limited group of established stars, and most often dependent on those elements for which an audience has already been established – the Tolkein novels for *The Lord of the Rings* series, or the previous *Star Wars* movies for *Revenge of the Sith* (2005). Jon Lewis (2003) actually talks of the distinction between 'marketable' and 'playable' movies: roughly, those which can be successfully promoted through their 'high concept' narrative or special effects, and those which audiences will actually enjoy and talk about afterwards. Even though the 1990s saw a number of quite modest productions succeed at the box office – these would include Hollywood productions such as *My Best Friend's Wedding* (1997) as well as non-American independent productions such as *The Full Monty* (which cost $US2.5 million to make and returned more than $US250 million at the box office in 1997) – this has happened less often in recent years. The success enjoyed by *Sideways* in 2005, for instance, is rare. At the same time, the amount of money invested in the chosen few major releases has continued to climb. *Titanic* set an industry record in 1997 by costing a monstrous $200 million, and the average production cost per film for Hollywood studios has risen from $US26.8 million in 1990 to $US55 million in 2000 – to which can be added another $27 million in average marketing costs (Wasko 2003: 22). Little wonder that it has become more and more difficult for independent producers to interest a major company in backing their film.

Of course, even this level of expenditure does not guarantee that a movie is a hit. Recent high profile (and expensive) flops include *Batman Begins* (2005, cost $135 million), *Troy* (2004, $190 million), *Sahara* (2004, $130 million), as well as slightly cheaper but heavily marketed features such as *Bewitched* (2005, $85 million). One of the effects of the increase in production expenditure and the consequent importance of marketing has been a change in the pattern of release for the big-budget blockbusters, which are now increasingly given a saturation release over their first weekend of exhibition in order to maximize the effect of their marketing budget. (Previously, it would have been more common to employ a 'platform' release, opening in a smaller number of major metropolitan sites before expanding into other markets.) It has become very important for films to perform on their first weekend, and Lewis has noted how the media's reporting on the cinema industry is now almost totally confined to the reporting of box office performance rather than anything to do with the content or narrative of the films themselves (Lewis 2003: 63). While such a release pattern maximizes the likely effect of advertising and other marketing activities, it also maximizes the costs; opening on as many as 500 screens simultaneously in the US alone raises the costs of supplying prints (Wasko (2003: 122–3) puts the cost of prints at around $3 million per film) and saturation releases demand saturation advertising (some industry estimates put the *Batman Begins* marketing budget at $100 million).

The high public profile generated for the blockbuster release has certainly ensured that going to see a film is still a major popular cultural event, the nature of which will be discussed in Chapter 5. But it is no longer a discrete event. Indeed, what were once ancillary markets for film – video, DVDs, and computer games – have in some cases become more important than cinema exhibition. In the US, home video is now a more lucrative source of income for the industry than cinema exhibition: in 2001, home video generated $118.7 billion in revenue (Wasko 2003: 125). When the DVD of *Spider Man* was released in 2002, it sold 7 million copies in one day; more than $125 million was spent on buying or renting the title on DVD or video on the opening day alone (Wasko 2003: 134). There are new ways, too, through which cinema is embedding itself in our daily lives. An example of this is the growing practice of 'product placement' – of contracting to insert a partner's products into an appropriate context on screen as a means of offsetting production costs. Toby Miller tells us that the 1997 James Bond film *Tomorrow Never Dies* 'broke new ground in product placement: Smirnoff,

Heineken, Avis, Ericsson, Gateway, BMW, Brioni, Omega and Visa were all party to payments that meant the film recouped its $100 million budget without selling a ticket, video rental, or an actual item of merchandise' (2001: 307). This has created something of a tradition as the Bond films have become a favourite location for product placement; Janet Wasko reports that the 2002 Bond film *Die Another Day* featured over twenty branded products onscreen: including Aston Martin, Jaguar, Thunderbird and Range Rover vehicles, Finlandia vodka, Bollinger champagne, and Norelco shavers. The product manufacturers also spent '$120 million on advertising that featured the film as well as their products in a campaign that included global television, print, radio and outdoor advertising, plus sweepstakes and other promotions' (Wasko 2003: 155).

The desire to watch a popular film is related to a whole range of other desires – for fashion, for the new, for the possession of icons or signs that are highly valued by one's peers. One of the ways in which such desires are satisfied is through the massive increase in merchandising – in the amount of products now licensed to individual films. The modern development of this revenue stream is usually seen to have begun with the marketing of the 1975 film, *Jaws*; merchandise connected with *Jaws* included a soundtrack album, T-shirts, plastic tumblers, a book about the making of the movie, the book the movie was based on, beach towels, blankets, shark costumes, toy sharks, hobby kits, iron-on transfers, games, posters, shark-tooth necklaces, sleepwear, water pistols, and many more. We have gone well beyond that today. The website for *The Lord of the Rings* movies lists the following categories of merchandise available on line: action figures, axes, audiobooks, battle games, board games, bobble heads, books, bows, bracelets, brooches, buttons and pins, calendars, caps and hats, card games, CD cards, chess sets, coins, clothing, costumes, DVD/VHS, earrings, figures, games, glasses, helmets, headdresses, jewellery, keychains, letter openers, lifesize standups, lighters, maps, masks, medallions, miniswords, mithril, movies, mousepads, mugs and cups, music, navel rings, necklaces, ornaments, party supplies, pendants, pewters, pewter figures, pipes, posters, puzzles, The One Ring, Rings of Power, other Rings, Secret Boxes, site products, statues/busts, stamps, sweaters, swords, tin boxes, tongue rings, toys, T-shirts, video-games, waterglobes, weapons, and weapon sets. Significantly, these are not only directed towards the traditional market for such merchandising: children. Adults are offered 'prestige' collectables such as highly detailed figurines, stone chess sets, elaborate jewellery, and even bridal gowns. Finally, taking us well beyond this, the tourism development strategy of a whole country – New Zealand – has attached itself to the merchandising around *The Lord of the Rings* as a way of cashing in on the fact that it was a primary source for the films' locations.

The growth in the movies' advertising budgets reflects not only the change in industry practice addressing concerns raised by the early 1990s' fall in audiences, but also the change in the nature of the audience's use of the cinema. At the peak of the feature film's popularity, audiences attended their favourite cinema as a regular night out – often more than once a week – and effectively regardless of what was showing. Going to *the movies* was the event, not going to *this particular* movie. That situation has now reversed itself as home-based competitors for the entertainment dollar have appeared – cable TV, VCRs, DVDs, video games, stereos, home computers – and as the increased mobility of the population – a result of the spread of private vehicle ownership – has multiplied the leisure-time choices available to any one individual. A film has to attract its own audience if it is to be successful. Hence the advent of what Justin Wyatt calls 'high concept' or what others have seen as the development of the spectacular nature of the cinema experience as a means of competing with the 'home theatre' or computer games. The resulting focus upon exploiting the magical appeal of special effects has also been a crucial factor in the spiralling cost of feature film production over the last decade.

As costs have risen, as big budgets for production and for promotion have become the norm, American domination of feature film production and distribution in the English-speaking world has become further entrenched – despite the recent trend towards so-called 'runaway' productions (that is, productions which have moved from an American base to cheaper production locations such as Canada and Australia). Only major companies can now afford current production and promotion costs. America is still the biggest

1 The sequel – a sign of a cautious industry: *Spiderman 2*

single market for feature films and it is one of the very few countries where locally produced films can recoup their costs without relying on foreign sales. Even Britain's population cannot support anything more than the most modest locally produced film. It does, however, provide a juicy market where an American film which has already covered its costs at home can be distributed cheaply in order to generate profits. The integration between the production and the distribution arms of the film industry in America means that foreign-made films find it very hard to reap similar benefits from the lucrative American market. For a foreign film to achieve mainstream distribution in the US it would need to be supported by a major distributor whose *own* films are the main competitors to any foreign product. It is clearly not often in the major's interests to support its competitors.

The film industry has been undergoing significant change for most of the last two decades. Where once it may have been a small-scale business run by enthusiastic entrepreneurs, it quickly became an oligopoly run by Hollywood studios. During the 1980s and the 1990s, they, too, had to sell out to other interests – in communications and electronics, mainly – as film became another victim of the large multinational media conglomerates' need to diversity. While the activities on the sound stages and the locations remain those of the craftsperson, the economic practices of the industry have become categorically those of big business. In order to better understand the changes I am referring to, we need to gain some idea of what the industry has been and how it reached its present set of practices, conditions, and objectives.

The establishment of the feature film

The feature film was not firmly established as the main attraction in the cinema until the introduction of optical sound with *The Jazz Singer* in 1927. Until then, the larger cinemas supported the features with an orchestra, vaudeville, or some other kind of live musical entertainment. A significant portion of the theatre-owner's costs went on providing such performances. After the establishment of the

2 The Hollywood blockbuster and its limitations: *Troy*

talking picture the practice of hiring supporting entertainment gradually disappeared from the industry.

Although it is tempting to see the development of sound and its application to the film industry as a natural, inevitable development, it is a temptation we should resist. First, the technology to produce sound was in existence well before it was applied. So we need to ask 'Why *then*?' Second, technological innovation does not produce a momentum all of its own. As Ed Buscombe (1977: 83) points out 'no new technology can be introduced unless the economic system requires it', and even then it will not be successful 'unless it fulfils some kind of need'. By 'need' he means some cultural, aesthetic, or political need, not just a perceived economic need. Changes in technology may be produced by individual inventors but their large-scale adoption depends on a wide range of other enabling cultural conditions. While the history of the feature film has often been written as a history of technological development, we need to be aware that even the term 'development' implies that by going from silent film to sound film we have made an advance. This implication, as we shall see shortly, depends upon debatable assumptions about what a film should be, including the assumption that it should be as 'realistic' as possible. There has been a great deal of argument over the industrial reasons for the introduction of sound. One view has it that the Hollywood majors were in financial trouble: audiences were declining and the mid-1920s expansion into the extravagant 'picture palaces' had saddled the industry with a string of venues which could return a profit only from the most popular of movies. Warner Bros, the first to use optical sound in a series of shorts and then in the musical *The Jazz Singer*, is claimed to have been facing bankruptcy anyway, and clinging to the hope of the talking picture like a drowning man (Sklar 1975). Douglas Gomery (1976) denies this view, saying that the studio was not bankrupt at all. He sees its achievement in the introduction of sound as a prescient business decision. At the time, Warners Bros was not one of the major companies and had trouble competing. What it needed was, in effect, a new product that none of the others had. Sound was that product.

Whatever the truth of the industrial history, there were some aesthetic and ideological conditions supporting the introduction of sound which deserve consideration. As Buscombe (1977) says, there has to be a specific need satisfied for a technological change to be successful. The need he identifies in the advent of sound is the need for the narrative feature film to become more realistic. The development of the moving picture from the still camera was a movement towards realism, towards the apparent replication of the experience of viewing life. Such an account argues that the camera itself is an apparatus that embodies a theory of reality, an ideology, because it sees the world as the object of a single individual's point of view. We claim to see and possess the world as individuals – a view not held before the Renaissance but increasingly demonstrated in nineteenth-century art and entertainment. As Steve Neale (1985: 22) argues, there is nothing natural or inevitable about this way of seeing or its instruments, such as the camera: 'Photography . . . constituted an enormous social investment in the centrality of the eye, in the category and identity of the individual, in a specific form of visual pleasure, and in an ideology of the visibility of the world.'

Neale argues that photography and the camera had a democratic effect. Just as film is more democratic than the theatre, photographs of loved ones were cheap and accessible equivalents of the family portraits in the rich man's gallery. However one views such arguments, it is clear that the increasingly realistic reproduction of the world offered by the camera must be embedded in the ideological and aesthetic systems of the nineteenth century.

The introduction of sound also facilitated the complication of realistic narrative in films. Here realism is not just an ideological position, but an explicit aesthetic – a set of principles of selection and combination employed in composing the film as a work of art. The reproduction of dialogue reconnected the feature film with real life, and the industry rapidly developed a system of conventions for shooting and cutting dialogue. For instance, the technique of shot–reverse shot over a continuous soundtrack was used to represent a conversation. (In this convention the characters speaking to each other appear on opposite sides of successive frames, each looking in the direction of the other.) Such conventions helped complete the evolution of the system we now use as we watch and construct a narrative feature film. These systems are analogous to those employed in the nineteenth-century novel, the epitome of realistic art. Certainly, the feature film, like the realist novel, sets out to construct a realistic world, to provide psychological depth for its characters, and to place itself within notions of real life. This series of objectives dominates the development of the narrative feature after the advent of sound.

In contrast to such ideological and aesthetic considerations, a persuasive explanation for the introduction of sound as an economic strategy relies on its effectiveness in reviving a dwindling cinema audience. In the US between 1927 and 1929, net profits for exhibition companies rose by 25 per cent; for production companies they rose a massive 400 per cent – this, despite the high cost of converting to sound in production and exhibition. However, one still has to resist such a simple cause-and-effect explanation in mapping cultural change. Colour provides a cautionary example of the failure of a new technology to hold an audience. Far from increasing cinema audiences, it proved to be a relatively costly and unpopular process until the introduction of colour TV. More on this later in the chapter.

It is undeniable that one of the effects of, if not the motivation for, the introduction of sound was the re-establishment of Hollywood's hegemony over world markets. Both the German and the Russian industries were aesthetically and culturally influential in the late 1920s and were looming as competitors in the quality of their films, if not in their ability to market them. Hollywood, being the first on the block with sound, outstripped these rivals. The advantage was reinforced by the development of a new genre, the musical, which to this day is still a quintessentially American form. The great virtue of the musical – apart from its obvious exploitation of sound – was that it could offer the pleasures of film and vaudeville at the same time. Many famous artists, never likely to share the same vaudeville bill, could be seen on the one screen. It was very difficult for foreign industries to compete with this.

A further industrial effect of the move into sound was that it changed the nature of the financial backing for the industry in the USA. To finance the transfer to sound, the film industry had to go outside its own boundaries, into the world of Wall Street bankers and into the communication industry – the location of sound technology. Although this may not have appeared to be such a dramatic move, its long-term effects on the evolution of the industry have been profound. While these effects may have been localized, the story of the feature film industry is inevitably tied up with American domination, and movements within the American industry affect all the others. To gain some understanding of this we need to take a further step back, into the period before the end of the silent feature film.

American domination of the feature film industry

The projection of moving pictures for commercial purposes began in France, and the French film industry maintained its dominance over the world market until the First World War. Pathé Frères was the world's largest film producer until this time, supplying up to 40 per cent of the films released in the United Kingdom, for instance, as against America's 30 per cent. Other national cinemas were also thriving. The Italians supplied 17 per cent of the British market before the war (note how little this left for British features) and Australia had a sufficiently strong industry to produce multi-reel features regularly.

With the onset of war, the French and Italian industries cut their production dramatically, as did the less important industries in Britain and Germany. America moved into markets hitherto dominated by other suppliers – not only in Europe but also in Latin America (previously dominated by the French) and Japan (previously Italian-dominated). The results were dramatic. American film exports rose from 36 million feet in 1915 to 159 million in 1916; by the end of the war the US was said to produce 85 per cent of the world's movies and 98 per cent of those shown in America. The control of the US home market was most important, because movies could now be confidently made for an American market and sold abroad for profit. From this point on there has been little incentive for American producers to tailor their product for other than an American audience.

The first twenty years of commercial moving picture exhibition saw a rapid development of feature production and exhibition worldwide, followed by the expansion and domination of US-based companies. As the audiences for the cinema reached saturation point around 1922, and as competitors for the audience's leisure time began to appear – radio and the motor vehicle, for instance – the pressure on the minor producers increased. American domination had expanded during the classic silent period – for good reasons, since they made their films well – to the point where other national cinemas found their very survival threatened. In Australia in 1914 the USA supplied around 50 per cent of the films shown; in 1923 it supplied around 94 per cent. In Britain, the local share of the market had dwindled from a peak of around 15 to 20 per cent to a mere 5 per cent in 1926.

Capitalizing on the insurance of a large home market, American companies used their new dominance to change the structure of the industry. Once, production of films, their distribution to cinemas, and the management of cinemas exhibiting them had been separate enterprises. As the American domination grew, it became apparent that control over the industry could be guaranteed if a company could produce, distribute, and screen its own movies. This change in structure, called *vertical integration*, began after the First World War. Throughout the 1920s Paramount, Loew's, Fox, and Goldwyn embarked on programmes of expansion, integration, and, most importantly, acquisition of first-run theatres in the major cities. Restrictive practices, such as Paramount's block booking, followed. Block booking enabled producers to extract agreement from exhibitors to take all their pictures in a total package, sight unseen, thus guaranteeing a screening for their product and making the exhibitor bear much of the risk for the film's success or failure. This practice was eventually outlawed in the US in 1948, and later in most other countries, but it exercised an important influence over the nature and conduct of the industry into the 1920s. It still survives in the way that old movies are sold to TV today.

One effect of vertical integration was to expand the capital base of the companies, as they drew investment from banks and communication companies in the push to expand. As this development continued, outside assistance became necessary, carrying with it affiliations, obligations, and responsibilities which rendered the movie industry vulnerable to movements in the financial markets during the Depression. Ultimately the industry became a hostage to these markets.

A further effect was to encourage the development and entrenchment of the studio system which had begun before the 1920s. The studio system was another method of control over the production and marketing of feature films. If studios could guarantee release for their pictures through their own distribution and exhibition network, it made economic sense to put the most popular actors on an exclusive contract and retainer as a kind of repertory company. The development of the star system, the identification of studios with certain kinds of film, and the studio's control over directors, were possible because the production companies could determine whether a film would ever be screened, and whether it would be in New York or Peoria. There was little future for film industry workers outside the studio system.

Finally, competitors like the smaller Warners studio were shut out of these structures, and this ultimately led to the series of decisions which brought sound to the feature film. (Also, sound further entrenched the studio system as it made location shooting more difficult and 'sound stages' in studios became necessary.) The coming of sound initially tightened Hollywood's grip on the world cinema market. However, this only served to foster the adoption of vertical integration in other countries, linking national productions with distribution and exhibition chains so as to counteract American and German competition. Both France and Britain adopted this strategy. Britain set up a link between distribution, exhibition, and local production companies by including British International and Gaumont in the two conglomerates – Gaumont British and Associated British. Such strategies were sufficiently successful for British companies to engage in some offshore involvements. British Empire Films bought into the Greater Union share of the distribution and exhibition networks in Australia, and British commercial interests have been a feature of the Australian industry structure since the 1920s.

It has been suggested that after the novelty of sound dissipated, the US share of the international market declined. Clearly, sound introduced the problem of translation, and the pleasure of sound was obviously going to be minimal if foreign-language subtitles were needed. So locally made films had an advantage in countries where English was not the national language. This factor did open up space for some foreign industries, many of which were already sheltering behind a quota system limiting the number of films which could be imported or, more ingeniously, requiring an exporting nation to reciprocate by distributing the local product in their home market.

The 1930s, then, while a period of classic film-making, was not the healthiest for the Hollywood studios. As the Depression deepened, movie attendances dropped (by 30 per cent in 1932), and some companies went into receivership as a result of the debts owed to bankers and the large corporations during the conversion to sound. Fox, RKO, and Universal were all in this situation, and the influence of the financial managers can be seen to expand during this period. Despite the involvement of such business acumen, audiences did not recover until the economy did, well into the 1940s. Within this shrinking market national cinemas showed signs of establishing themselves again, particularly in Britain through the documentary movement. However, the recovery of the European film industries was short lived. Once again it was interrupted by the outbreak of war.

During the Second World War, the US regained some of its lost markets; it also began producing films in other countries, notably in Latin America. The big shake-up for the industry, foreshadowed in 1938 in the first challenge to vertical integration, came after the war when the practice was outlawed by the US Supreme Court. Exhibition was separated from production and distribution by the ruling of 1948, providing a model for other countries to follow – although some did not do so until well into the 1970s. Distribution, it was quickly realized, is the pivotal point of the film industry, and most production companies were careful to retain their distribution arms while dissolving their formal connections with exhibition. Distribution – gaining access to the right cinemas in sufficient numbers and at the right time – is still the key to a film's success. Small national cinemas deal with this fact daily, as they try to find a suitable outlet for their films in competition with the big multinationals whose constant supply of product persuades the major exhibitors to deal more or less exclusively with them. Examples of chances missed – potential box-office hits being overlooked because they were made independently – are legion. When Australia's industry revived in the 1970s, the film which proved to be the catalyst – it showed Australian films could make money – could not find a distributor in its home country. *The Adventures of Barry McKenzie* (1972) eventually opened in a Melbourne cinema hired by the producers, and its successful run there had to be cut so that the exhibitor could meet its commitment to imported product. One of Britain's most successful post-war features, *Tom Jones*, failed to get a local circuit release initially, although it eventually went on to take one of the largest box-office grosses of 1963.

Since vertical integration was outlawed and the studio system declined, the role of the feature film has been under continual attack from new forms of entertainment, new financial constraints, and a fluctuating but mostly declining audience. Largely, it has successfully repelled these attacks to survive, if not always to prosper. Audience numbers recovered slightly during the 1990s and although they have not returned to the levels of the 1940s they have remained relatively stable. New formats such as home video and DVD have increased the commercial possibilities available to film producers, new markets have opened up for the international feature film industry in Eastern Europe and Asia, and new contexts of exhibition such as the multiplex have helped the cinema to experience something of a revival within Western popular cultures. That said, however, and while the feature film may have been the predominant form of entertainment for most of the twentieth century, there are very few periods when it has not faced a significant challenge. Consequently, it is to the alternatives currently in play, and to the feature film's response to its competitors since the Second World War, that we now turn.

New competitors, new strategies, 'new Hollywood'

As noted above, film audiences have been in decline for most of the last fifty years. In most Western capitalist countries the figures for attendances at the movies peaked in 1946 and the overall trend has been downward until quite recently. By 1953, when nearly half of all American households had a TV set, the US attendance levels had sunk to half the 1946 figures. Quota systems in Britain, France, and Italy made it more difficult for American producers to recoup losses overseas, although one response to this – making American films in foreign studios – did cut costs and evaded some of the more stringent restrictions.

Although this decline in film audiences began before television hit the largest market, America, television was obviously implicated in the complex of conditions which produced the trend. No one has yet satisfactorily explained why the decline occurred; but it is clear that film was already losing its cultural pre-eminence by the beginning of the 1950s and that television merely exacerbated this decline. Reasons so far offered for this trend range from the fanciful – the baby boom kept parents at home looking after their (presumably booming) babies – to the sensibly economic – that the industry's response of making bigger and more expensive movies to win back its audience initiated a cycle of events which ultimately deepened the crisis. Surveys of Hollywood's production in the late 1940s also support the view that the industry had lost its identification with 'middle America' and the pictures it was making were less commercial. Whatever the reason, the threat of television and the film industry's response to this threat seem to be crucial to this period of the industry's history.

The film industry responded to the threat of television in two main ways. Of these, the attempt to 'colonize' television by producing films for it has proved to be the more successful. The big media conglomerates which have prospered are those which have incorporated a TV production company, such as Gulf and Western's Paramount and Desilu. Television's enormous appetite for material meant that there was a large market to be developed and for the most part it was successfully developed by film producers. Warner Bros and Disney are examples of how successful the film industry's invasion of television can be.

The less successful response is perhaps the more interesting. The experience of the conversion to sound had led the film industry to form some misconceptions about the relationship between technological innovations and box-office returns (something we are seeing again in the current fascination with special effects extravaganzas). This, combined with the attempt to make movies better than ever (and thus better than television), produced some well-calculated, and some bizarre, innovations. A series of widescreen formats appeared in the early 1950s: Cinerama was introduced in 1952, Cinemascope in 1953. Neither idea was new: both dated from the 1920s. Cinerama used three projectors to screen images from three cameras on a curved screen in a specially equipped theatre. Cinemascope was cheaper and simpler, projecting its image onto an elongated screen, its dimensions not the prevailing 1.33:1, but 2.35:1. Both these screen formats have survived, and the normal size for projection screens is now wider than it was in the 1950s as a result of the success of these wide-screen formats. Neither process, however, was sufficiently dramatic to draw an audience single-handedly. Cinerama was expensive to shoot and screen, and was largely seen in a series of demonstration films with roller-coaster rides and car chases which exploited the realistic effect produced by the wrap-around screen. It did not make the transition to narrative features, the only way to build and hold an audience. Cinemascope was more successful but, paradoxically, the greater the success it had in carrying a narrative the less apparent was the technological innovation itself. It succeeded by becoming invisible rather than by appearing as a selling point.

Other attempts to build new experiences into the feature film during this period include 3D (necessitating special spectacles and two projectors operating simultaneously); and Aromarama and Smel-O-Vision (both dependent, presumably, on plots with strong smells). The latter two were gimmicks, involving a card impregnated with smells which had to be activated by the user at certain points in the film. Although these novelty processes are revived periodically,

3 3D movie viewers, 1952

their inherent silliness limited their impact on attendances. The only other venture to succeed was colour, but not without difficulty.

Coloured movie film is not a recent invention: several systems were in existence as early as 1900, and much silent film was tinted. Technicolor, the dominant producer–processor of coloured film stock for most of the 1930s and 1940s, was formed in 1915. One of the reasons why colour was not more widely used before the 1960s was the cost: some of the early processes were labour-intensive, early cameras were expensive, and Technicolor's eventual monopoly often irritated and restricted producers. Colour was used primarily for spectacles, epics set in the past, or for special effects in fantasies. It became more widely used, though, after sound and Technicolor's introduction of a new three-colour subtractive process in 1932 (Steve Neale (1985) goes into this in more detail). The first to use this process was Walt Disney in his cartoon series *Silly Symphonies*; other notable early users in the 1930s were Mamoulian in *Becky Sharp* and Selznick in *Gone with the Wind*. But it was not the dramatic breakthrough that sound had been, and although its use increased steadily from the mid-1930s into the mid-1950s, it had nothing like the revolutionary effect of sound. This is true even of the 1950s after Eastmancolor had broken Technicolor's monopoly, reduced costs, and opened up space for a range of such new colour processes as Deluxe which were mobilized in the attempt to revive cinema attendances. It was not until TV's conversion to colour in the 1960s that colour film finally became the conventional stock for feature film production.

On the face of it, this is odd. Surely, the aim of the film is to replicate reality as closely as possible. If the advent of sound increased the film's correspondence with 'the real world', why not add colour? Ed Buscombe (1977: 88) offers an explanation:

> [This may] seem rather strange if one supposes that the demand for realism in the cinema has always been merely a question of the literal rendering of appearances. We perceive the world as coloured, after all, and therefore an accurate representation of it should also be coloured. . . . But in fact it has never been a question of what *is* real but what is *accepted* as real. And when

it first became technically feasible, colour, it seems, did not connote reality but the opposite.

Colour was widely used in cartoons, musicals, westerns, and comedies where fantasy or spectacle were paramount. So, colour's function was not to create the illusion of the real, but to signify artifice, decoration, the cinema as storyteller. In *The Wizard of Oz*, colour is used in the fantasy world of Oz, while the 'real' world of Dorothy's Kansas home is shot in black and white. As colour became part of current affairs programmes and news reporting on television it lost its association with fantasy and spectacle. The special ways in which colour was seen are useful reminders of how conventionalized our readings of film can be. Now, since colour has lost many of its unreal connotations, it is hard to imagine that understanding of it. However, even now we can come across the residue of this way of seeing: black-and-white footage can still be used in documentary or in certain kinds of feature film (e.g. the Australian film *Newsfront*) as a guarantor of 'truth', the break into black and white signifying an amplification of the real. With such a history, then, colour never had much hope of reversing the decline in movie audiences in the way that sound had done.

The most recent attempt to use advances in technology to lure audiences into the cinema has been in the area of special effects, particularly computer-generated special effects. During the 1990s, the box-office success of a number of films which employed spectacularly convincing special effects – *Terminator 2* (1991) and *Jurassic Park* (1993) – encouraged a trend for movies which were marketed for their appeal as spectacle rather than as narrative. Disaster movies such as *Twister* (1996) and *Dante's Peak* (1997), comedies such as *Men in Black* (1997) and *Mars Attacks!* (1996), sci-fi apocalypse action epics such as *Deep Impact* (1998) and *Armageddon* (1998), and children's films like *Babe* (1995) and *Toy Story* (1995) were all marketed through trailers which promoted their spectacular visual effects rather than their content or storyline. Consequently, for a large part of the 1990s, the blockbuster and the special-effects movie were almost synonymous; even the success of *Titanic* seems to have been tied, in large part, to director James Cameron's use of computer-generated images to create the illusion of the sinking liner. In such films, the creation of the illusion itself becomes the explicit object of audience attention and admiration. More importantly for the purposes of the industry, the inherently spectacular and visceral nature of the experience of watching such films insistently recommends the pleasures of the cinema over those of television, home video, or other forms of entertainment. It is an expensive way to produce a film, however, and the audience's enthusiasm for the purely spectacular seems as likely to fade in this case as it did for the earlier gimmicks like Cinerama or 3D. As Peter Weir's *The Truman Show* indicated in 1998, box-office success could still be generated by a strong narrative; alternatively, and as the failure of *Batman Begins* indicated, whiz-bang special effects no longer guarantee an audience.

What I have been describing over the last few pages are changes which have occurred within the American film industry since the end of the Second World War, and the transformation of the studio system which followed. It has become customary for film historians to talk of the industry which emerged from these changes as 'the new Hollywood' (Schatz 1993; Balio 1996; Tasker 1996). While the term was coined initially to describe post-war Hollywood, it has increasingly come to refer to post-1970s American cinema and to the changing media environment within which it operated (Tasker 1996). We have already dealt with one of the key aspects of the new Hollywood: the studios' reliance upon a small number of big hits to generate their profits. This strategy was accompanied by the rise of the target market – the framing of advertising campaigns, release patterns, the casting of stars, and ultimately even the scripts so as to appeal to specific fragments of the total movie market (Schatz 1993: 8–9). This reflects the change in the composition of movie audiences over the decades since the Second World War. The family market that once sustained the industry has now all but gone, and in its place is a predominantly youthful market. The film industry now depends on pleasing the 14–24 age group. Going to the cinema is still a regular and highly valued leisure activity for this group, while the older middle-class audience, who were the new segment in the 1970s, are probably key contributors to the expansion of video and cable television. Market segmentation is the new premise; films either are aimed at a particular segment of the market – young women in the late 1990s, for instance – or are designed to contain within them attractions for a number of different market segments. The mass market has broken into smaller units, and the trend towards housing multiple cinema screens under the one roof – the multiplexes – reflects this. No longer can one film please the whole family (and the causes of this are not confined to the film industry), nor can one location expect to meet their overheads from the proceeds of exhibiting one film. A result has been the clearer definition of the new sub-genres, narratives developed for a specific segment of the market. *Star Wars* (1977) was perhaps the clearest example of the 'kidult' movie, aimed at two separate markets – the kids and their nostalgic parents – but there are plenty more: the *Harry Potter* films, for instance, or the revival of the James Bond and the Batman franchises. The teenage/young adult audience has dominated for several decades now, and is served by a wide range of styles, content, and social/ political attitudes: from *Porky's* (1982) and *Something About Mary* (1998), to *Ferris Bueller's Day Off* (1986), *Clueless* (1995), and *The Wedding Singer* (1998), to *Romeo + Juliet* (1996) and *Girl Interrupted* (1999).

Thomas Schatz has suggested that there are conflicting trends confronting the new Hollywood today: the success of the block-buster as an event and as a merchandising occasion; the low profitability of even successful special-effects blockbusters; the fragmenting of the market and the importance of the youth audience. He believes that there are now several tiers to the new Hollywood's production strategies, as the industry concentrates on producing three different classes of movie:

> the calculated blockbuster designed with the multimedia marketplace and franchise status in mind, the mainstream A-class star vehicle with sleeper-hit potential, and the low-cost independent feature targeted for a specific market and with little chance of anything more than 'cult film' status. The three classes of movie have corresponding ranks of directors, from the superstar directors at the 'high end' like Spielberg and

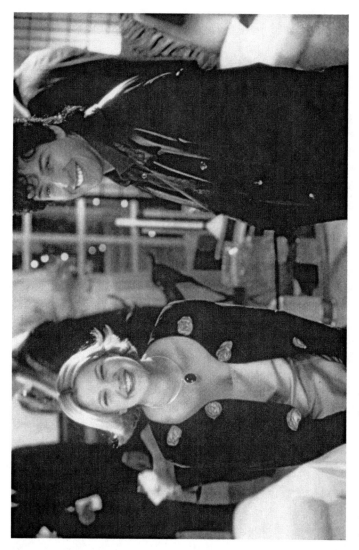

4 Drew Barrymore and Adam Sandler, *The Wedding Singer*

Lucas, whose knack for engineering hits has transformed their names into virtual trademarks, to those filmmakers on the margins like Gus Van Sant, John Sayles and the Coen brothers, whose creative control and personal style are considerably less constrained by commercial imperatives.

(Schatz 1993: 35)

Of course, not all of the three tiers enjoy the same level of investment, nor the same importance to the industry. But they do reflect an institutional response to changes in the make-up of the market.

This break-up of the mass market into smaller segments (which might be combined in the audience for specific films) followed an earlier segmentation which challenged, albeit only at the margins, the total market dominance of American popular film. The introduction of alternative 'art-house' cinemas throughout the Western world began in the 1950s and peaked in the 1970s. The art-house network took many different forms: in some countries it was subsidized by governments through such bodies as Britain's National Film Theatre, and in others it survived through subscriptions to 'seasons' from its patrons. It originally existed to screen non-American films – primarily European – and it contributed to the growth in respect accorded to the British and, more recently, the Australian film industries. In 1986, six out of the 'top ten' foreign films at the US box office were British. The art-house circuit is now more properly seen as a kind of specialist, non-mainstream, or repertory cinema which presents new films made by independents as well as offering retrospective glances at classics and constructing 'seasons', or groups of films from a particular country, director, or movement, which will run over a set period.

It is clearly a very different business from mainstream film distribution. An art-house film can open in one city, play it for weeks, and only then move to another city. Without a large advertising budget, films are dependent on critics' approval and recommendation by word of mouth from those who see them. The supply of 'art' films has diminished since the 1970s but this deficit has been more than met by the supply of films which are aimed at a mass audience but are either not American-made or for some other reason have not won the support of the major distributors. So, these days, a key function for the specialized film network is to provide outlets for all kinds of independents – from disillusioned American directors to mainstream but non-American films which may want to develop a case for major distribution. Many British, European or Australian films which have drawn mass audiences at home have been distributed through art-house or specialized cinemas in America. For most films made outside America, but still wishing to break into the lucrative American market, this is the best alternative after they have failed to convince a major distributor to take them on. Since it is very rare indeed for a major to take on a foreign film, it is also the most common method of distribution for independent films. It is a long way from the big profits that are available through the majors, however. *The Full Monty* was taken up by Twentieth Century Fox and went on to earn something like a hundred times its budget worldwide. The 1990s' success of independent American companies such as Miramax and New Line has provided another avenue, however, for independent, art-house, or non-American cinema to reach an international audience.

Initially, it seemed as if the rise of the multiplex would assist the fortunes of small and independent film-makers by increasing the demand for new product but as time has gone by this is less the case. Internationally, multiplexes became widespread during the 1990s and they represent the third major reconfiguration of the cinema as a space (after the invention of the silent cinema and the renovations required for the introduction of sound). These complexes can offer up to twenty-five choices of film at any one time, with high-quality sound systems and large screens. The quality of the cinema experience they provide has enhanced the audience appeal of the blockbuster while the multiplication of the number of available screens also enabled, at least in theory, the exhibition of a greater number of films. Distributors maintain that multiplexes have extended the life of individual films in their markets and they certainly dramatically affected box-office figures when they first came into the market. In the US, where the number of cinema screens doubled during the 1980s and has continued to grow ever since, attendance figures in 1997 increased by 12 per cent to hit their highest levels in 38 years; in Britain, where the multiplexes expanded throughout the 1990s, audiences increased by 13 per cent over the course of that decade. Initially seen as a highly risky move by exhibitors, the building of the multiplexes did play a substantial role in bringing audiences back to the movies, and in maintaining a range of profitable movie genres during a period in which studio investment has been dominated by the blockbuster.

However, it is also true that the extended reign of the blockbuster has taken its toll on the diversity of product once seen as the key benefit of the multiplex. As we have seen, there is an emphasis on maximizing the box-office take on the opening weekend of the big blockbusters. A corollary of this is the rapid decline of the box office in subsequent weeks, even for successful films. Exhibitors respond to this by multiplying the number of screens available to the blockbuster early in its run, and by shortening its run. The effect of these two strategies is to dedicate more of the many screens available at any one time to the top-grossing, big-budget, mass-advertised blockbuster and thus to edge out the less profitable features.

Fortunately, the rise of ancillary markets for the feature film has ameliorated the effect of such practices. As we have seen, video and DVD purchase and rentals can earn more for a film's producers than the box office: licensed merchandise, video games, and tie-ins with retailers or fast-food companies all play a part in returning a profit to the producer. Cable TV has also become a significant purchaser of cinema product. It requires an enormous amount of material to stay on the air, and channels which only screen movies are important buyers for films from both the majors and the independent production companies. One such organization, Home Box Office, had over 38 million subscribers in the US in 2004, it was available in over 50 other countries, and through its location in the TimeWarner stable of media businesses is connected to independent production companies such as New Line, conglomerates such as Warner Bros, and cinema exhibition and distribution networks. HBO is now a key target for film-makers who wish to support a minor theatrical release with all the extras the industry can offer in order to return a profit. The importance of HBO has begun, and will continue, to exercise some influence over the nature of film production and distribution in the US and, therefore, elsewhere.

Finally, too, we should note the growth of a trend towards so-called 'runaway productions'. Driven by the need to reduce costs, as well as by the potential made available by new technologies and the industry's increasing capacity to digitally modify the images on the screen – dramatically increasing the amount of 'blue screen' shooting (where actors perform in front of a blue screen to which backgrounds and settings will be added later) – a significant amount of Hollywood production now occurs outside Hollywood, and outside the US. Australia, Canada, and a number of European locations have become significant options for the industry as it attempts to speed up production while reducing costs. O'Regan and Goldsmith's *The Film Studio* (2005) outlines some of the looming implications of the selective globalization of film production for Hollywood and for national industries in the 'runaway' locations.

Spectacle versus narrative

What I have been describing above is a commercial industry that has undergone a number of significant changes in recent years. Many regard the overall effect of these changes as unfortunate in that they have shifted the focus onto the marketability of film projects and away from their unique qualities as narrative or spectacle or even as popular art. Nowhere has debate over this been more vigorous than in the discussion over Hollywood's use of special effects; in particular, as the use of computer-generated special effects extends beyond science fiction or fantasy into other genres – featuring in *Titanic, Gladiator* (2000), and *Forrest Gump* (1994), for instance – there are concerns about what might be the end point of such a development. Barbara Creed (2002), for instance, notes the widespread use of computer-generated imagery to represent not only monsters or aliens, but also 'real' people in such films as *Titanic* and *Eyes Wide Shut* (1999). In a discussion of the rise of the 'cyberstar', she asks whether there is a possibility that we will one day no longer need the real human star; in their place, we may have their computer-generated image, able to do everything their original could do (but at a fraction of the cost and without the tantrums or marriage breakdowns). This is only one area where concerns have been raised about contemporary cinema losing its soul, its human referent, and thus eventually its audiences. The most significant debate around such issues focuses on the increasing importance given to special effects, particularly CGI effects, in the marketing and promotion of the contemporary blockbuster.

As we saw earlier, it has become commonplace to suggest that Hollywood cinema now depends on the production of spectacle, rather than narrative, as a means of generating an audience for mass-marketed movies. Certainly, it is now routine to encounter newspaper reviews which describe the latest blockbuster as a special effects extravaganza which lacks a plot. Or, where there is a plot, it is in need of further development: many of the reviewers of the first two *Matrix* films found the plot but reported great difficulty in following it. The focus upon what illusions can be generated through new technologies certainly provides us with plenty of opportunities to marvel at what is on the screen, but, it is said, the capacity to develop strong and resonant stories may have atrophied as a result. Conversely, some such as Geoff King (2000) take issue with this in order to argue that the critics themselves underestimate how tightly the special effects are tied to the movie's narrative structure. In his discussion of *Jurassic Park*, for instance, King argues that even the most spectacular of special effects are still contained within 'the arc' of the narrative. Whatever the resolution of this debate, it is commonly acknowledged that the development of CGI technologies has dramatically expanded the potential for, and reduced the cost of, the integration of CGI into the representation of setting, action, special effects – even of character – in the movies. Therefore, it is argued that the marketing of Hollywood cinema has been dominated by the presentation of the spectacular rather than the meaningful: by the promotion of the visual effects available in the film concerned rather than the narrative concept which structures it or, even, the stars who appear in it.

It is not necessary to see all these as mutually exclusive categories, of course, nor are such distinctions particularly novel. There

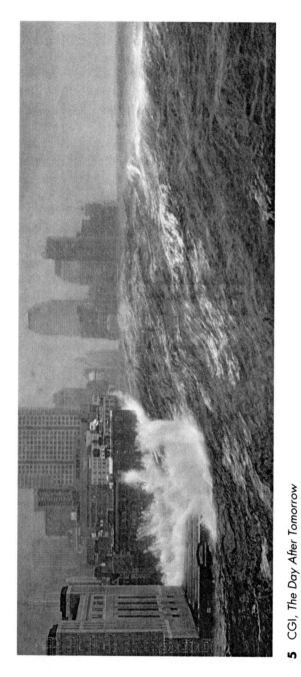

5 CGI, *The Day After Tomorrow*

have been previous instances in the history of film when new technologies exercised a similar, apparently magical, attraction. Tom Gunning's 1986 account of early silent cinema as 'a cinema of attractions' has been recalled recently by a number of writers as a means of reminding the field that the importance of spectacle to the contemporary popular cinema does have its historical antecedents. Gunning's account of cinema's history, when it was part of a vaudeville bill and when its performance was surrounded by other kinds of entertainment, is useful in nudging film studies slightly aside from its privileging of narrative as the necessary hook to consumption, on the one hand, and from overstating the novelty of current trends, on the other.

Michele Pierson's study of special effects, *Special Effects: Still in Search of Wonder* (2002), usefully places contemporary cinema's exploitation of the spectacle within a larger and much longer historical context. Drawing upon a wide range of research traditions and theoretical insights (film theory, film history, cultural history, cultural studies, and new media technologies), Pierson writes a cultural history of the public visual spectacle – not merely spectacle in the cinema – from the nineteenth century to the present. Spectacle, she argues, has always been there, and it has been integrated into screen cultures from the beginning. A benefit of Pierson's approach is its focus upon the specificity of the pleasures generated by the spectacle and thus implicated in the contemporary development of the spectacular potentials of CGI. So far, she argues, there has been very little scholarly treatment of special effects and thus very little information about 'the patterns of production and consumption governing the use of new technologies in relation to older cultural forms' (2002: 59).

Pierson's book is notable for the fact that she refuses to simply jump on the new technologies' bandwagon and argue that, once CGI arrives, everything has changed. *Special Effects* is clearly situated within a longstanding, continuing project for both film studies and cultural studies: that of understanding the specific pleasures of cinema as they shift and mutate in response to new systems of delivery and new formats of exhibition. This means, according to Pierson, that we must acknowledge contemporary cinema's reliance on 'the novelty of its attractions to capture and sustain the attention of viewers', and thus its inevitable investment in new technologies which can produce new spectacular experiences to sell to its audiences. On other hand, we must also recognize the audience's continuing 'emotional and intellectual attachment to the cinema – to the particular kind of experience it offers – that has continued to lure them away from the television set, the video or DVD player, the game console, and the computer screen'. There is still enough which is specific to this medium and its classic locations of consumption to require attention and explanation. Even if these locations have multiplied in ways that blur the boundaries between the cinema and 'the other spaces of consumption that surround it' (2002: 122), the experience of cinema shows no signs of disappearing altogether.

I share Pierson's view that despite regular warnings of doom for the film industry, the feature film still offers a distinctive set of experiences, pleasures, and social practices for its audiences. None of the competitors has been able to replicate these. That film has survived is due to its nature as a medium and its social usage by its audiences. Audiences enjoy going to the movies. To find out how, and perhaps even why, is the project for the rest of this book. We start by reviewing the study of film, prior attempts to analyse the nature of the medium, and its appeal for an audience.

Suggestions for further work

1   Those interested in knowing more about the cultural development of the movies in the US could read Robert Sklar's *Movie-Made America* (1975), and for a history of the American hegemony in film see Kristin Thompson's *Exporting Entertainment* (1985). For a challenging political economy of the industry, see Miller *et al.*, *Global Hollywood* (2001).

2   The development of colour processes is beyond the range of this book but is worthy of further study. Steve Neale's *Cinema and Technology* (1985) provides a detailed analysis of the development of these processes as well as reproductions of stills using the different processes.

3   How do you see the relationship between your national cinema and the American movie? It could be interesting to discuss this with others, and see if the problems outlined in this chapter have occurred to anyone else.

4   The development of the cinema has increased the sophistication of audiences; some TV producers have maintained that television advertising, for instance, has taught audiences to read films better and more quickly than ever before. Analyse a silent movie, and see what differences of convention and what differences in audience reaction you can locate between silents and talkies.

5   Discuss the attributes of a 'kidult' movie such as *Star Wars: Revenge of the Sith* or *The Lord of the Rings: The Fellowship of the Ring* or any of the *Harry Potter* films. What do you think is the attraction for the various age groups to such a film?

6   Do you think there is still such a thing as a 'youth' film? What would be the similarities or differences between, say, the teen films of John Hughes (*Pretty in Pink* and *Ferris Bueller's Day Off*), the 'gross-out' comedies of the 1990s (*Wayne's World*, *Something About Mary*), *Romeo + Juliet*, and the Eminem vehicle *8 Mile*?

7   For further work on film history, Allen and Gomery's *Film History: Theory and Practice* (1985) and Cook's *A History of Narrative Film* (1981) are both useful.

8   The recent history of the changes in ownership of the major Hollywood producers is both complicated and volatile. For a discussion of the way in which Hollywood became caught up within processes of globalization, see the Introduction and the essays in Part I of Albert Moran's edited reader *Film Policy: International, National and Regional Perspectives* (1996), especially Tino Balio's 'Adjusting to the global economy: Hollywood in the 1990s'. Also see Balio's 'A major presence in all the world's important markets: the globalization of Hollywood in the 1990s', in Turner, *The Film Cultures Reader* (2002).

9   Turner's *Film Cultures Reader* also has a section dealing with the analysis of film technologies – colour, sound, and special

effects. Discuss the issues raised in the essays by Stephen Prince on realism and digital technologies (2002: 115–28) and by Barbara Creed on the likely rise of the 'cyberstar' (pp. 129–34).

Chapter 2

From seventh art to social practice – a history of film studies

Early aesthetic approaches

The beginnings of motion-picture exhibition can be found in vaudeville, music-hall, amusement arcades, fairgrounds, and travelling shows. It commences almost simultaneously in France, Britain, and the USA. Commercial development of the technology began almost immediately after the first exhibitions. The French pioneers, the Lumières, sold their commercial interests to Charles Pathé in 1900, and this paved the way for large-scale commercial development and for initial domination by French film production. In France, the audience for the medium spread across the classes, but it remained working class for some time in the USA and Britain. In the US it began in penny arcades ('penny gaffs' in Britain) and in vaudeville houses as featured support to live acts, but within the first decade of exhibition it had moved into store-front theatres in, primarily, working-class neighbourhoods across America. In Australia, the travelling picture show man was also important, bringing his films to country towns and projecting them in local halls or marquees. In all cases, it was a medium that went as directly to its audience as possible.

The first films were not structured narratives, but brief one-shot recordings of everyday scenes, such as the Lumières' famous film of workers leaving their factory at the end of a shift. The models provided by vaudeville skits (performed in the same locations as the pictures were projected in) soon revealed what could be done with the addition of some fictional or comic structure. The brevity of these early films – some lasted for less than a minute – fitted music-hall 'sight' gags rather well, and the link between the feature film and vaudeville was often explicit and direct.

The French producer George Méliès is usually credited with the development of the narrative feature film, and he commenced commercial production in 1896. His most important contribution was to free 'screen time' (the amount of time taken to project the film on to the screen) from 'real time' (the amount of time actually taken to perform the actions or complete the events depicted on the screen). We take it for granted now that a screen representation of a war which lasted five years does not actually take that long; early feature film, however, did not immediately grasp the possibility of intervening between the reality being filmed and its representation on the screen. Joining separate pieces of film – editing – made this intervention possible. The use of *editing* was pioneered by Méliès, and it enabled the film-maker to orchestrate the sequence of images on the screen rather than allowing this to be dictated by the subject matter itself. Méliès is also credited with the invention of other practices which made it possible for narratives to be structured – that is, speeded up, slowed down, in short, composed – with some economy. Such techniques as the *fade-out* (the disappearance of the image into black) as a method of transition or closure, and the *lap-dissolve* (a fade-out coinciding with the gradual superimposition of a new image) as a more elegant method of transition, have assisted all narrative film-makers since. They are early examples of the development of techniques which became formalized into a system of conventions that determines both film-making practice and the audience's 'decoding' or understanding of the narrative as they watch it. We will talk more about these conventions and this process of decoding in later chapters.

The date of the first narrative feature film is a perennial source of nationalist argument: England, France, the USA, and Australia all have contenders. What *is* clear is that within ten years of the beginnings of production and exhibition in Europe and America, the feature film industry had established the concept of the narrative feature and the means of composing it through shots and editing, and the first western had been produced (*The Great Train Robbery* (1903)). This immediate success and rapid development are perhaps less surprising than the rapidity with which this form of mass entertainment came to be seen as a new aesthetic form, a companion to sculpture, painting, or literature: the 'seventh art'.

In 1915, two events occurred which are worth linking in that they represent a kind of turning-point for the place of film within Western cultures. D. W. Griffith's *Birth of a Nation* was released to an extraordinary popular and critical response; in its epic scale (it was the longest feature so far) and the personal quality of its vision seemed to lie the potential of great art. The same year, 1915, also saw the publication of Vachel Lindsay's *The Art of the Moving*

Picture. Whereas prior to *Birth of a Nation* movies had been the subject of middle-class condescension, Lindsay, an American poet, used his intelligent, prescient, and clearly polemical book to stake film's claim to the status of the seventh art form. With very little in the way of existing feature films to support his position, Lindsay announced his intention of convincing the cultural institutions of America that the 'motion picture is a great high art'. Lindsay was not the only one to hold such a view, and much of the theory which succeeds him for the next forty or fifty years happily accepts this proposition. While the legal and governmental discussion of film concentrates on issues of class, entertainment, and morality, much early film theory argues over the definitions of, or prescriptions for, the aesthetic characteristics of film.

Griffith's next film, *Intolerance* (1916), failed to repeat his popular and critical success and thus he lost some of his pre-eminence in the US as the film 'artiste'. However, his influence spread beyond America and was particularly strong in the 1920s in Germany and Russia. There, state-funded film industries were producing films into which 'the film-maker as artist' was clearly inscribed. German expressionism and Soviet montage were fashionable and respected as developments of film's aesthetic potential, and came close to challenging Hollywood's leadership in the formal development of the silent feature. There seems to have been a strong prejudice against local films among the American intelligentsia in the 1920s, and a strong preference for the more 'expressive' (that is, more clearly the statement of an artist) films from Europe.

The 'expressive' use of film is usually defined as the reshaping of the raw material printed on celluloid, using images of the real world to 'make a statement'. The images become something else: art. Like the nineteenth-century novel, the expressive film sets out to create *its own* world rather than simply reproduce the one we know. Possibly the most important of the figures exploiting the potential of film as an expressive art at this time was the Russian exponent of montage, Sergei Eisenstein.

Eisenstein is an influential figure, and a customary starting-point for histories of film technique and film theory. As a theorist, Eisenstein is notable for attempting to understand the language of film. As a film-maker, he used editing as his major tool to transform exposed film into a statement. According to his theory, the meaning of film is produced by the audience's contrasting or comparing the two shots which make up a montage (the physical joining together of two separate shots by splicing the film). Eisenstein was not interested in simply reproducing the reality he had filmed; he wanted to use the images he had filmed to create something new. As he saw it, two film pieces of any kind, placed together, inevitably combine into a new concept, a new quality arising out of the juxtaposition. That new quality is constructed by the viewer. So, one shot of a face, followed by another of a loaf of bread, might create the idea of hunger through the *combination* of shots. The meanings generated by montage are more than the sum of their parts, and the editing technique which produces montage is the basic structuring technique behind film composition.

The idea that film simply recorded or reproduced images of the real world came under attack here. Instead, film was proposed as a medium which can *transform* the real, and which has its own language and its own way of making sense. And as far as this went, it was accurately understood. Montage *does* work as Eisenstein suggested; as a tool of Soviet education it was effective, its didacticism a political benefit. An irony is that its most common use in contemporary capitalist societies now is in advertising; this irony is lessened a little by the fact that it is also widely used in rock-music video clips. As we shall see, however, when we deal with subsequent critiques of Eisenstein and montage, it is only one way of communicating through film, not the basis of its language.

Eisenstein was not alone in his rejection of any view of film that would relegate it to the category of a simple recording agent. A number of theorists argued, in fact, that the very *limitations* of film as a recording agent were the factors which determined its artistic potential. Although many such positions are expressive, the extreme aestheticism which underlies them separates them from Eisenstein. When sound comes to the movies in 1927, such theories emerge in something of a rush. Rudolph Arnheim's *Film as Art* (1958, first published in 1933) is only one such argument which sees the silent film as a superior medium for aesthetic purposes; for Arnheim, the silent film's inability to reproduce the world entirely realistically is the source of its artistic potential. The idea that art is an imitation of the real, a conventional literary and aesthetic tenet, is denied in order to propose film's special qualities as an art form. A by-product of such arguments was an attack on the 'lust for the complete illusion' of sound and colour on the movie screen. Realism and art were thus placed in opposition to each other, with the silent film being given the status of art while the sound film was dismissed as crass and vulgar.

Such approaches as we have been examining in the last few pages are usually considered under the label of 'formalism' in film histories. Formalist approaches see a film's forms of representation (its specific manipulation of vision and sound) as more important in the production of meaning than its 'content' or subject matter. The dubious distinction between form and content is thus blurred by the assertion that the form is the content. Formalism is an approach which examines the film text for its own intrinsic interest, without necessitating reference to its realism or its 'truth' to some version of the real world. Formalism is opposed to any view of film as the *capture* of the real world; instead it proposes film as a *transformation* of the real.

Realist approaches

The coming of sound to the feature film reinforced the trend towards greater realism of narrative form and structure which was already becoming apparent in the silent film. Sound was held to enhance greatly the illusion of reality. Further, within the individual film, the use of dialogue of some complexity and detail now made possible greater intricacies of motivation, more psychological versions of character, and complexities of tone such as irony or sarcasm. As pointed out in Chapter 1, the changes which followed the advent of sound were incorporated into the narrative feature's progressive imitation of the classic nineteenth-century novel, with its individualistic delineation of character, social world, and notions of personal and moral conflict.

6 Eisenstein's *Battleship Potemkin*

If expressive or formalist views of film dominated the European silents, the advent of sound contributed to the conditions which favoured a revival of realism in European cinema after the Second World War. A further contributing factor may have been the brief burst of social realism in Hollywood films of the early 1930s (*Smart Money* (1931), *The Public Enemy* (1931), or *Scarface* (1932)) – a mode quickly scotched by the industry's self-censorship mechanisms. However, a key factor in the post-war interest in realist film may well have been the success of the documentary movement in the 1930s and 1940s, initiated in the UK and led by John Grierson. The movement became known beyond the UK as documentary units were set up in Canada and Australia with Grierson's assistance, and later as wartime documentaries were made and shown. Now it is the most developed form of film-making after the narrative feature and probably the most respected.

This respect was won early. Under Grierson's leadership, the documentary film was seen to offer a social service in dealing with problems and issues of national importance (at a time, it may be said, when there was an unusually high degree of consensus about what was important). At the same time it offered itself as an aesthetic object: Basil Wright and Harry Watt's *Night Mail* (1936), for instance, has been representatively described as an 'aural and visual poem to man, machine, and the work they perform' (Sobchack and Sobchack 1980: 345). The documentary movement had a profound influence on British film, particularly the products of Ealing Studios, during the next thirty years. Britain's achievement of a reputation for 'quality' during the 1960s, a reputation largely drawn from the modes of documentary realism employed in films such as *This Sporting Life* (1963), has had an influence on the social realism in Hollywood films since. British television is probably the major beneficiary of this tradition, though, with the realist docu-drama (*Days of Hope, Boys from the Blackstuff*) becoming recognizable as a British genre. The social impact of film is also reinforced by the documentary movement, pushing aesthetics to one side in the face of social movements and upheavals that make art film seem a little self-indulgent. Such an effect is also reinforced by the major realist movement of the period, the 'neo-realism' of the post-war Italian directors, Rossellini, de Sica, and Visconti.

Neo-realist films look like documentary: they have a grainy, under-lit look, rather than the evenly lit, glossy image of the classic fictional film of the period. Neo-realists distrusted the use of narrative as a contrived structuring device; they often dispensed with actors and replaced them with 'real people' under the assumption that this would be more true to life, and they made extensive (for the time) use of location rather than studio shooting. The movement distanced itself as far as possible from the staged confections of previous Italian films – the epics and the sophisticated farces called 'white telephone' films – and dealt with social and political issues affecting everyday life in occupied and post-war Italy. For Italians in the mid-1940s, everyday life was a more than sufficient subject, and the aim of the neo-realist cinema was to deal with it as directly as possible – to capture 'the illusion of the present tense', as one director put it (Cook 1981: 391).

Neo-realism is a film movement – a body of films loosely directed towards similar formal or social ends – as well as a theory of what the cinema should be as an art form. Although the movement died out within five or six years, its influence has been profound in suggesting what relations film might have to the real world. Its influence on the French New Wave of the 1950s and 1960s is widely acknowledged, and there are a number of significant Hollywood directors who admit to its influence. Industrially, it exposed new acting styles and revealed the greater possibilities of location shooting.

We have been talking about European films and film theory at a time when Europe was not the dominant force in world feature film production, distribution, or exhibition. The 1930s and 1940s are the heyday of Hollywood, of the star system. The war's gutting of the competing European cinemas of France, Italy, Germany, and Britain had once again left the market open to American domination. Yet much film theory of the time ignores Hollywood, and concentrates on the realist aesthetic being developed in Europe. Eventually, as we shall see, it is through the arguments around realism that the renovation of interest in Hollywood and in American popular film occurs.

Bazin

André Bazin is the next key figure. Through his writings and his involvement with the French journal he founded in 1951, *Cahiers du Cinéma*, Bazin is seen as a centre of realist approaches to film. Although he never developed his position in fully argued form, he has been extremely influential. Firstly, he consigned Eisenstein to the past. In contrast to Eisenstein, who saw the intrinsic nature of film lying in the *combination* of shots, Bazin saw the intrinsic quality of film in the *composition* of the shot itself – its specific representation of the real world. For Bazin, it is the real world which is the subject of film art. For Eisenstein, shots were only raw material, the 'fragments of reality' constructed into art through montage. Bazin found montage too manipulative, too distorting of the real, too much of an imposition of the film-maker upon the viewer. Instead, as he saw it, the shot and, particularly, the long uninterrupted take allow the viewer to scan the frame, to read and interpret what it represents.

Bazin looked to the movement and arrangement of elements within the frame or the shot in order to examine how meaning might be generated. The movement and placement of figures, camera position, lighting, set design, the use of deep focus, all merit greater attention from this perspective. Significantly, all these features also enhance the illusion of reality and thus constitute the 'art' of the film. For Bazin, the real and the aesthetic were not separable. As Brian Henderson (1971b: 397) has said, for Bazin 'film art has no overall form of its own, but that of the real itself. Bazin has a theory of the real, he may not have an aesthetic.'

The term used to describe the arrangement of elements within the frame or the shot is *mise-en-scène*. The term itself has been more influential than Bazin's wider theories, possibly because it inspired the rejection of Eisenstein's claim to have established montage as the basis for a grammar of film composition. Further, the notion of *mise-en-scène* is useful in that it allows us to talk about the way in which elements within a frame of film, or a shot composed of many consecutive frames, are placed, moved, and lit. Since significance can be communicated without moving the camera or editing – for instance through a character moving closer to the camera or throwing a shadow over another's face – the concept of *mise-en-scène* becomes an important means of locating the process through which such significance is communicated. It is also widely used as a means of analysis of visual style in particular films or groups of films. Today, montage and *mise-en-scène* are no longer seen as mutually exclusive terms, but are contained within a notional grammar of film language.

The shift from montage to *mise-en-scène* can be seen as a shift towards an emphasis on visual style. Most importantly, emphasis on the interpretative role of the viewer in *mise-en-scène* prefigures a reorientation in film theory. It eventually results in a revaluation of popular film; more significantly, it begins the movement away from an examination of the relations between film and reality and towards an examination of the relationship between film and the viewer.

Auteurs and genres

Auteur theory is usually credited with having given the feature film an 'author'. Instead of being a co-operative industrial project, a film became identified with its director, who was seen as its ultimate creator. This is something of a distortion of the *auteur* position, but an understandable one because the *auteur* theory *does* attempt to insert an author – in the literary, expressive sense – into films which had hitherto been regarded as the faceless, standardized products of a studio system. As such it is an odd theory to discuss while charting the decline of aesthetics; nevertheless, in my view, that is where it belongs.

A polemical article by French film-maker François Truffaut, published in *Cahiers du Cinéma* in 1954, marks the beginning of *auteur* 'theory'. Although its specific points were almost entirely enclosed within industrial and political conflicts in the French film industry at the time, it led to a position which was aesthetic in that it argued for the necessity of a personal vision or style in a director's films; even some films produced under the most industrialized conditions (Hollywood) were held to bear the mark of an artist/*auteur*.

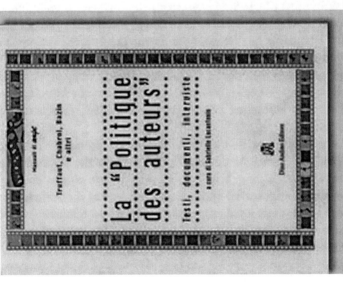

7 *Auteurs* and genres – Bazin, and the publication which started it all: *La Politique des Auteurs*

As such, the theory invoked artistic standards while at the same time, paradoxically, rescuing a large body of popular films (Jerry Lewis comedies, for instance) which had been consigned to the cultural junk heap by critics and theorists alike.

Since American film was the chief beneficiary of the *auteur* theory, it is not surprising that it caught the imagination of American film scholars more than any previous approach. The controversy which it provoked peaked in the 1960s, and helped to build a stronger film culture in academe. Andrew Sarris (1962–3) complained about the lack of a decent intellectual context in which the auteurist debate could take place. As he saw it then, 'film scholarship remains largely an amateur undertaking' devoid of the 'most elementary academic tradition'. Auteurism was possibly a key factor in changing this situation, as it did help to usher in a tradition of director-dominated film teaching which was essentially modelled on literary studies – and it is not hard to see why.

Before following this trail further, a cautionary note. We are not dealing with a homogeneous body of theory here; nor does it cross national or ideological boundaries without modification. So the following summaries of its repercussions may appear a little contradictory. Nevertheless, they are contradictions we need to explore.

On the one hand, then, auteurist theories gave films authors and thus bound them even more closely into a literary/aesthetic mode of analysis. On the other hand, since Truffaut was using the American cinema as a club with which to beat his French antagonists, American films which had been dismissed as predictable and formulaic were recovered. Genre films in particular – westerns, musicals, thrillers, gangster films – were now deemed to be interesting. The range of material considered by film theorists thus widened, so that Hollywood movies were now accepted, but only so that they could be dealt with in oddly inappropriate ways. Discussions of the newly respectable Hollywood directors revolved around the construction of a 'canon' of their best works (a body of 'classical' works held to be the best of their kind and therefore worthy of study). This was a critical practice which precisely paralleled the dominant modes of literary criticism of the time, and it produced similar results – the canon of film greats which now decorate film courses around the world. Popular film was thus incorporated into an alien critical tradition.

Only further reading can fully uncover the complexities of the auteurist debate; suffice here to stress a number of important aspects of its influences on film studies. Firstly, in one of its manifestations, *auteur* film theory followed on from the interest in *mise-en-scène* to concentrate on visual style – on the way in which films were composed and constructed for the viewer. Many auteurist critics uncover a stylistic 'signature' in the visuals which they attribute to an author/*auteur*, and this has become a customary critical practice.

Another strand interested itself in film genres. 'Genre' is a term appropriated from literary studies and used to describe the way in which groups of narrative conventions (involving plot, character, and even locations or set design) become organized into recognizable types of narrative entertainment – westerns or musicals, for instance. Auteurist critics realized that these sets of conventions were used by audiences as well as film-makers. Therefore they must exercise some determining power over what a director could and could not do if, for instance, she or he wanted to make something which an audience would recognize as a western. The constraints of the genre limited the ways in which any authorial signature might be inscribed, let alone detected. The genre was also seen as a convention to be *challenged* by many directors. Inevitably, work had to be done on defining the genre in order to understand its variations.

Such work revealed how dynamic genres are, how they continually change, modulate, and redefine themselves; genre emerges as the product of a three-way negotiation between audiences, film-makers, and film producers. This raised an issue which became prominent later: the role of the film as a commodity – a marketable product sold to an audience through, among other things, its genre. More significantly, these enquiries began a long series of revaluations of the notion of genre, the study of the relationships between audiences and movies, and a better understanding of the pleasure of the familiar and predictable in popular entertainment – partially qualifying the hitherto conventional privileging of the novel, the unique, and the original. Further discussion of this aspect is to be found in Chapters 4 and 5.

Lastly, and in yet another configuration, some *auteur* theorists moved away from their grounding in literary/aesthetic modes of analysis entirely, and embraced those of linguistics, anthropology, and semiotics. This is an early clue to the future of film studies, which increasingly became a site for the application of theories developed in other disciplines. The common element between linguistics and anthropology was the group of theories under the umbrella term of 'structuralism'. Structuralism accepts that films are produced by film-makers, but it also reminds us that film-makers are themselves 'produced' by the culture. So structuralist theory has been very useful in reconnecting film with the culture it represents. It has also offered ways of looking at film as a set of languages, a system for making meaning, and has thus furthered our understanding of what the medium is. We will talk more about this in later chapters.

The institutionalization of film studies

Although writing about the movies has been a familiar aspect of popular culture since the beginning of the twentieth century, it is only relatively recently that journals and magazines which deal with film on an academic level have become established. Even in the 1960s, many influential articles were published in journals which were not devoted to film at all: Sarris wrote much of his auteurist criticism in *The Village Voice*, while the *New Left Review* was a location for much screen criticism in the UK. In Australia, much of the agitation for the support of the film industry had to go on through the mainstream press, the newspapers, and magazines such as *Nation*. Predictably, growth in film scholarship and publishing accompanies the gradual encroachment of academic institutions upon the study of film and ultimately into teaching its practices too. The *Star Wars* series' director, George Lucas, is a sign of the times – a graduate of a film school, not the product of an industry.

The typical film department to emerge out of the expansion of the 1960s and 1970s is easily characterized: it was American, an offshoot of an English literature department, dominated by young staff with an auteurist outlook who preferred European films to

Hollywood films. Featured on its courses were a few Hollywood directors: John Ford and Alfred Hitchcock might share the semester with Eisenstein, Fritz Lang, and the European modernists. The characterization is not without some validity. Film departments grew out of recognized disciplines that already had an established aesthetic viewpoint which fitted well with auteurism. The modernism of much contemporary European film – its symbolism, its reflectiveness, its overall literariness – enabled such departments to treat films as literature with pictures. It was a method of analysis and an institutionalization that is still in the process of transformation.

It has been argued that the late 1960s offered slightly more adventurous fare for mainstream cinema, tapping a younger, more visually literate audience (the 'TV generation') whose assumptions about film were not literary/aesthetic at all. Films such as *Bonnie and Clyde* (1967) or *The Graduate* (1968) demanded a relatively sophisticated audience, and got it despite the critics (who hated *Bonnie and Clyde*). It is true that this period sees some rejuvenation of interest in feature films at a number of levels and although it does not produce dramatic changes in the box office, apart from the freak boom year of 1968, a wider film culture of some variety and sophistication gradually came into being. (The growth of the art-house and specialized cinemas discussed in Chapter 1 is implicated in this development.) This has affected academic study of film. Bill Nichols wrote in 1974 that 'whereas no more than a few years ago' film journals tended not to deal with theory at all, at the time of writing '*Film Quarterly, Film Comment, Cinema, Women and Film, December, The Velvet Light Trap*, and *Jump Cut* have published an appreciable body of formal criticism, joining the English magazine *Screen* and the French journals *Cahiers du Cinéma* and *Cinéthique*' (Nichols 1976: 7). The revival of Australian cinema coincided with the growth of a new audience, a new awareness of film as cultural capital and the importance of a popular cinema, and the launching of such journals as *Cinema Papers* and the *Australian Journal of Screen Theory*. It could be argued that it was in such ventures rather than in the academic institutions that film culture was most dynamic. From the new journals a reorientation of film studies could be abstracted: they presented a view of film as a means of communication, a set of languages, a system of signification – not just the seventh art.

Film as social practice

The key to this change of approach has already been mentioned: the insertion into film studies of methods taken from other disciplines, including linguistics, psychoanalysis, anthropology, and semiotics. Some of these 'disciplines' were themselves hybrids, already crossing traditional disciplinary boundaries. The structuralism used in Peter Wollen's 1972 work on genre, for instance, employs concepts from linguistics and anthropology which are ultimately aimed at understanding the nature of the human mind.

In such instances, film is not even the final target of enquiry, but part of a wider argument about *representation* – the social process of making images, sounds, signs, stand for something – in film or television. Odd as this might sound, what emerges is a body of approaches to film that is rich when applied to film but which is not confined to the analysis of film. In effect, film theory becomes part of the wider field of disciplines and approaches which came to be called 'cultural studies'.

The cultural studies influence on film theory was not particularly direct at first. Cultural studies initially analysed how social meanings are generated through culture – a society's way of life and system of values as revealed through such apparently ephemeral forms and practices as television, radio, sports, comics, film, music, and fashion. The influence of a variety of British interventions – the establishment of the Centre for Contemporary Cultural Studies at Birmingham or the popular culture course at the Open University – and the support of French theorists such as Barthes and Althusser generated research into the function, practices, and processes of culture. 'Culture' came to be redefined as the processes which construct a society's way of life: its systems for producing meaning, sense, or consciousness, especially those systems and media of representation which give images their cultural significance. Film, television, and advertising thus became prime targets for research and 'textual' analysis. Within this research, culture is seen to be composed of interconnected systems of meaning. So one might begin by examining comic strips and wind up talking about codes of dress within urban subcultures. Inevitably, film became involved in such discussions; if, for example, one was examining the ways in which a youth subculture defined itself – through fashion, for instance – the role of fan magazines, the music press, and television might become very important. To follow the function of the fan magazines one might also need to know about their subject matter – film, television, music. Accordingly, in order to understand better how film might be part of the cultural systems under analysis it became necessary to enquire more closely into film itself as a specific means of producing and reproducing cultural significance.

Some of these enquiries looked very familiar: for example, historical studies of the industry and its institutions. Other projects looked unlike anything that had come before, partly on account of the apparently oblique angle of approach. For example, research into television became a major item on the cultural studies agenda. Rejecting American research which looked for behavioural evidence of television's effect on its audiences, cultural studies approaches turned instead to the analysis of the television message – 'reading' the audience's response from the specific sound and images on the screen. Clearly, there was potential for overlap between the methods used to do this and film analysis. Television analysis had borrowed some of its assumptions from film theory in the first place. Film journals broadened to include television and theorists moved freely between one medium and the other. A publication outlet for many of the innovative materials being taught at the Open University was provided by its link with the British Film Institute. Film was examined as a cultural product and as a social practice, valuable both for itself and for what it could tell us of the systems and processes of culture. Ironically, this enclosure of film within the culture – a reduction of its importance as a practice in some ways – has resulted in a greater understanding of its specificity as a medium.

Although film studies are established in institutions around the world, we are now at a crucial stage in their development. Film is revealed as not so much a separate discipline as a set of distinct social practices, a set of languages, and an industry. As we shall see in Chapter 5, the focus upon the audience, and upon the conditions within which the consumption of film takes place, has become increasingly important. Indeed, the interest in the context of consumption has loomed as a primary focus for the contemporary analysis of the feature film. As Toby Miller puts it, the analysis of the text or the audience must today be 'supplemented by an account of *occasionality* that details the conditions under which a text is made, circulated, received, interpreted, and criticized, taking seriously the conditions of existence of cultural production' (2001: 306). The current approaches to film come from a wide range of disciplines – linguistics, psychology, anthropology, literary criticism, political economy, media studies, and history – and serve a range of political positions – Marxism, feminism, and nationalism, among them. But it has become clear that the reason we want to examine film at all is because it is a source of pleasure and significance for so many in our culture. The relations which make this possible – between the image and the viewer, the industry and the audience, narrative and culture, form and ideology – are the ones now isolated for examination by film studies, and by this book.

Most recently, we have seen a proliferation of what have come to be called 'screen cultures' – cultural formations built around the consumption of texts and processes delivered through visuals on a screen: video games, DVDs, home computer games, and the continual development of new modes of access to visual entertainment through digital and online media. Film now must consider its institutional position in relation to these new visual cultures, and how the practices of production and consumption around the film screen might or might not converge with other screen formats. Significantly, feature films are now most often consumed, in one format or another, through the TV set. The division between film and other media – especially television, as we have entered the era of the widescreen plasma TV 'home theatre' – is less clear now than it has ever been. Films are available via celluloid, CD, DVD, videotape, and downloads from the Internet. It is notable that the most venerable American professional association for those working in film studies – the Society of Cinema Studies – has recently changed its name to become the Society of Cinema and Media Studies. A mode of film studies which is dominated by a focus on the singular text consumed in a cinema is looking more and more anachronistic. That said, the communication structures employed within the feature film remain fundamental to how this burgeoning visual culture makes sense and attracts our attention. An understanding of the specific technologies, languages, and grammar of the cinema, then, is even more important today as it provides the foundation for an increasing field of representation in popular culture.

We can now begin to deal with some of the specifics that go to make up such an understanding. In Chapter 3 we start with the 'languages' film uses to produce meaning and pleasure.

Suggestions for further work

1   This chapter offers a very brief overview. Many of the articles referred to and positions summarized in it can be found in collections discussing film theory, such as Bill Nichols's foundational two-volume *Movies and Methods* (1976 and 1985), Mast, Cohen, and Braud's *Film Theory and Criticism* (1992), and Stam and Miller's companion and anthology (1999 and 2000).

2   How much of a difference can you see between montage and *mise-en-scène*? Look at some television advertisements and see if you can: (a) isolate both styles of filming/editing, and (b) distinguish different effects pursued by both.

3   Examine the film reviews in your quality dailies or weeklies and see if you can determine their underlying theoretical assumptions. Is any one approach dominant? Why do you think this is so?

4   How convinced are you of the analogy drawn between English literature departments and film studies departments? What are its limits? Has the growth of communications or cultural studies or visual cultures programmes made any difference?

5   If possible, it is worth looking at the films which are used to support the various theoretical positions. For example, try

examining *The Battleship Potemkin* in order to understand the virtues of montage and expressive film-making; or look at *Metropolis* or *The Cabinet of Dr Caligari* for expressionist film-making; or, finally, examine a series of John Ford westerns to see how far the requirements of the genre and the personal qualities of a director can be separated.

6   The key movement we have examined is away from the film–reality relationship and towards the film–audience relationship. Do you see why that might be important? It is worth reading Brian Henderson's article (1971b) 'Two types of film theory' for what he has to say on this topic.

7   Further reading: John Caughie's *Theories of Authorship* (1981) remains a good collection of articles dealing with *auteur* theory and related issues. Jim Collins *et al.* (eds) *Film Theory Goes to the Movies* (1993) demonstrates what happens when a film studies aesthetic deals with some popular blockbusters, as do a number of the contributions to Stringer's *Movie Blockbusters* (2003). For a more recent take on the changes that have occurred around the disciplinary formation and academic institutionalization of film studies see Gledhill and Williams (2000) *Reinventing Film Studies*, and the introductory chapter to Turner (2002) *The Film Cultures Reader*.

Film languages

The title of this chapter may require explanation. Film is not, of course, a language but it does generate its meanings through systems (cinematography, sound editing, and so on) which work like languages. To understand how this idea might help in our analysis of films, and to understand the limits of this idea, we need to go back to some very basic principles. The first step is to see film as communication. The second step is to place film communication within a wider system for generating meaning – that of the culture itself.

Culture and language

Notoriously difficult to define neatly, culture, as I intend to discuss it here, is a dynamic process which produces the behaviours, the practices, the institutions, and the meanings which constitute our social existence. Culture comprises the processes of making sense of our way of life. Cultural studies theorists, drawing particularly on semiotics, have argued that language is the major mechanism through which culture produces and reproduces social meanings. The definition of language developed in this tradition of thought goes well beyond that of the normal definition of verbal or written language. For semioticians such as Roland Barthes (1973), 'language' includes all those systems from which we can select and combine elements in order to communicate. So dress can be a language: by changing our fashions (selecting and combining our garments and thus the meanings that culture attributes to them) we can change what our clothes 'say' about us and our place within the culture.

Ferdinand de Saussure is commonly held to be the founder of European semiotics. He argued that language is not, as is commonly thought, a system of nomenclature. We do not simply invent names for things as they are encountered or invented; thus the Bible story of Adam naming the objects in Eden cannot be an accurate account of how language works (whatever else it might be). If language simply named things, there would be no difficulty in translating from one language to another. But there is difficulty, because cultures share some concepts and objects but not others. The Eskimos have many words for snow, since it has great significance within their physical and social worlds; Australian Aboriginal languages have no word for money as the function that money serves does not exist within their original cultures; and every viewer of westerns will know that American Indians were supposed to be unable to comprehend the concept of lying (i.e. their language did not enable them to 'think it' or 'talk it'): hence the formula 'white man speak with forked tongue'. Even cultures which share the same language are not made up of precisely the same components, and so Australians, Americans, and Britons will attribute significance to the components of their worlds in different ways. The language system of a culture carries that culture's system of priorities, its specific set of values, its specific composition of the physical and social world.

What language does is to construct, not label, reality for us. We cannot think without language, so it is difficult to imagine 'thinking' things for which we have no language. We become members of our culture through language, we acquire our sense of personal identity through language, and we internalize the value systems which structure our lives through language. We cannot step 'outside' language in order to produce a set of our own meanings which are totally independent of the cultural system.

Nevertheless, it is possible to use our language to say new things, to articulate new concepts, to incorporate new objects. But we do this through existing terms and meanings, through the existing vocabularies of words and ideas in our language. A new object might be defined by connecting it with existing analogous objects – as is clear in the word 'typewriter' – or new ideas will interpellate themselves by trying to redefine current terms and usage – as feminism has done in its attack on sexist usage. Individual utterances are thus both unique *and* culturally determined. This apparent contradiction is explained by Saussure's useful distinction between the *langue* of the culture (the potential for individual utterances within a language system), and the *parole* (the individual utterance composed by choices from the *langue*). The distinction roughly corresponds to that between language and speech, and it reminds us that, although there are vast possibilities for originality in the *langue*, there are also things we cannot say, meanings that cannot be produced within any one specific language system.

All of the above is as true of film 'languages' as it is of verbal language, although the connection to film may seem a little distant at the moment. The operation of language, however, provides us with a central model of the way culture produces meaning, regardless of the medium of communication.

Language constructs meanings in two ways. The literal, or denotative, meaning of a word is attached to it by usage. It is a dictionary style of meaning where the relation between the word and the object it refers to is relatively fixed. The word 'table' is widely understood to refer to a flat topped object on (usually) four legs upon which we might rest our dinner, books, or a vase, and which has variants such as the coffee table and the dinner table. The denotative meaning is not its only meaning (in fact, it is doubtful that anything is understood purely literally). Words, and the things to which they refer, accrue associations, connotations, and social meanings, as they are used. The word 'politician', for instance, is not a neutral word in most Western cultures. It can be used as a term of abuse or criticism, or even as a sly compliment to someone who is not actually a politician but who manipulates people with sufficient subtlety to invite the comparison. The word can have specifically negative con- notations because it can mobilize the negative associations attached to politicians. This second kind of meaning, the connotative, is interpretative and depends upon the user's cultural experience rather than on a dictionary. It is in connotation that we find the social dimension of language.

Images, as well as words, carry connotations. A filmed image of a man will have a denotative dimension – it will refer to the mental concept of 'man'. But images are culturally charged: the camera angle employed, his position within the frame, the use of lighting to highlight certain aspects, any effect achieved by colour, tinting, or processing, would all have the potential for social meaning. When we deal with images it is especially apparent that we are not only dealing with the object or the concept they represent, but we are also dealing with *the way in which they are represented*. There is a 'language' for visual representation, too, sets of codes and con- ventions used by the audience to make sense of what they see. Images reach us as already 'encoded' messages, already represented as meaningful in particular ways. One of the tasks of film analysis is to discover how this is done, both in particular films and in general.

We need to understand how this language-like system works. Methods which deal only with verbal or written language are not entirely appropriate. So it is useful to employ a system of analysis which began with verbal language but which has broadened out to include those other activities which produce social meaning. The work of all these activities is called 'signification' – the making of significance – and the method is called semiotics. Once we understand the basic premises of semiotics we can apply them to the particular 'signifying practices' of film: the various media and technologies through which film's meanings are produced.

Semiotics sees social meaning as the product of the relationships constructed between 'signs'. The 'sign' is the basic unit of communication, and it can be a photograph, a traffic signal, a word, a sound, an object, a smell, whatever the culture finds significant. In film, we could talk of the signature tune of the shark in *Jaws* or the face of John Travolta as a sign. They signify, respectively, a particular version of 'shark-ness' (those meanings constructed around the shark in *Jaws*) and 'John Travolta-ness' (again, the mental concepts and meanings, both from within and outside a specific film, which are constructed around John Travolta). We can also talk of the way different signifying systems (sound, image) work to combine their signs into a more complicated message; the helicopter attack, musically accompanied by 'The Ride of the Valkyries', in *Apocalypse Now!* is such a case.

Theoretically, the sign can be broken down into two parts. The *signifier* is the physical form of the sign: the image, or word, or photograph. The *signified* is the mental concept referred to. Together they form the sign. A photographic image of a tree is a signifier. It becomes a sign when we connect it with its signified – the mental concept of what a tree is. The structure of the sign can be represented diagrammatically like this:

SIGNIFIER	SIGNIFIED
SIGN	

To extend this, let us refer back to our earlier example, of fashion as a language. When we change our garments to change our 'look', what we are doing is changing the signifiers through which we represent ourselves. We change our fashions (signifiers) to change what we mean to others (the signified). Our social identities are signs, too.

Signifiers carry connotations. Semiotics has enquired into advertising to show how the selection of signifiers with positive connotations (water-skiing, relaxing by a pool) is used to transpose these associations on to an accompanying advertised product, such as cigarettes. Signifieds, too, accrue social meanings. You will react to a picture of Bill Clinton in terms of opinions you already hold about his controversial personal life as well as about his political career. Such a picture mobilizes a second, less literal, chain of cultural meanings through the specific signifiers used, and the ideas we already have of Clinton himself.

It is with this second level of meaning that we will be most concerned in this book, because it is where the work of signification takes place in film: in the organizing of representation to make a specific sense for a specific audience. Semiotics offers us access to such activity because it allows us to separate ideas from their representation (at least, theoretically) in order to see how our view of the world or of a film is constructed. It does this by closely analysing a film (or a view of the world) as a 'text', a set of forms, relationships, and meanings. Those wishing to follow semiotic theory a little further can find a good introduction in Fiske (1982), but for the moment a definition of the three terms, 'signifier', 'signified', and 'sign', is all that is necessary to understand the following chapters' application of semiotics to film.

Film narratives have developed their own signifying systems. Film has its own 'codes' – shorthand methods of establishing social or narrative meanings; and its own conventions – sets of rules which audiences agree to observe and which, for example, allow us to overlook the lack of realism in a typical musical sequence. (When a singer is accompanied by an orchestra, we do not expect to find it in the frame just because it is on the soundtrack.) At the level of the signifier, film has developed a rich set of codes and conventions.

When the camera moves to a close-up, this tends to indicate strong emotion or crisis. At the end of love scenes we might see a slow fade or a slow loss of focus, or a modest pan upwards from the lovers' bodies – all coy imitations of the audience averting their eyes but all signifying the continuation and completion of the act. The shot–reverse shot system (see Illustration 8) is a convention for representing conversation. The use of music to signify emotion is conventional, too, as there is no real reason why the orchestra should build up to a crescendo during a clinch. Slow-motion sequences are usually used to aestheticize – to make beautiful and instil significance into their subjects. Slow-motion death scenes were in vogue during the late 1960s and early 1970s in films such as *Bonnie and Clyde* (1967) and *The Wild Bunch* (1969); the aim was not simply to glamorize death but to mythologize these particular deaths – injecting them with added significance and power. Slow-motion love scenes both aestheticize and eroticize. Genres are composed from sets of narrative and representational conventions. To understand them, audiences must, in a sense, bring the set of rules with them into the cinema, in the form of the cultural knowledge of what a western or a musical is. The role of the audience in determining meaning cannot be overestimated.

Shot 1   Shot 2

The spatial relations are reversed in the successive shots, as if to 'extend the boundaries' of the frame to include both parties to the conversation. The alternation of shots tells us they are speaking to each other.

8 The shot–reverse shot system for representing conversation

Film as a signifying practice

Film is not one discrete system of signification, as writing is. Film incorporates the separate technologies and discourses of the camera, lighting, editing, set design, and sound – all contributing to the meaning. No one system for producing meanings operates alone in film. Michael Keaton's performance as Batman is constructed through (at least) the portentous soundtrack, the choice of camera angles (he is consistently shot from below, exaggerating his size and power), the spectacular art direction, the lighting, and the interrelationships between all of these.

It is now time to qualify the analogy I have so far drawn between film and language. Written and spoken languages have a grammar, formally taught and recognized systems which determine the selection and combination of words into utterances, regulating the generation of meanings. There is no such system in film. Film has no equivalent to syntax – no ordering system which would determine how shots should be combined in sequence. Nor is there a parallel between the function of a single shot in a film and that of a word or sentence in written or verbal communication. A single shot can last minutes. In it, dialogue can be uttered, characters' movements and thus relationships can be manipulated, and a physical or historical setting outlined. This may be equivalent to a whole chapter in a novel.

If there is a grammar of film, it is minimal and it works like this. Firstly, each shot is related to those adjacent to it. As we watch a film we often defer our understanding of one shot until we see the next. When we see a character addressing another offscreen, our view of the significance of those words may have to wait until we see the following shot, depicting the person being addressed. Secondly, unlike the grammar of written language which is to a large degree explicitly culturally regulated, relationships between shots in a film have to be constructed through less stable sets of conventions. Much depends not only on the audience's 'competences' (their experience of, or skill at, reading film), but also on the film-maker's ability to construct any relationships which are not governed by convention.

The construction of a relationship between shots can be the first moment in understanding a narrative film. But the process is not as simple as it sounds. Readers will remember that Chapter 2 dealt with a major theoretical argument about exactly how this process worked – through constructing relationships between shots (montage) or through constructing relationships within shots (*mise-en-scène*). We know that these are not mutually exclusive and that both kinds of relationships are constructed by film-makers and interpreted by audiences. Both terms occur later in this chapter, as we move to a survey of the basic signifying practices employed in film production.

The signifying systems

The following survey will not be a full taxonomy (I do not talk about titles or produce a complete list of special effects, for instance), but it will provide a basis for work now and further reading later.

The camera

Probably the most complex set of practices in film production involves the manipulation of the camera itself. The film stock used, the angle of the camera, the depth of its field of focus, the format of screen size (for example, Cinemascope or widescreen), movement, and framing all serve specific functions in particular films, and all require some degree of explanation and attention.

Chapter 1 mentioned the different 'meanings' of colour and black-and-white film during the slow establishment of colour processing as the norm for feature film production. We can generalize from this to point out that different kinds of film stock with their differing chemical attributes and consequent visual effects are enclosed within different sets of conventions. Often black-and-white film stock is used to signify the past: it has been used to simulate the documentary in the Australian film *Newsfront* (1976) and in Spielberg's *Schindler's List* (1993), as well as suggest a nostalgic perspective on the past in Woody Allen's *Manhattan* (1979). At the moment, black and white is sufficiently unusual to have some power as a special effect; music videos and television commercials from time to time make use of the process to give their texts a high fashion or avant-garde look. Film stock which is particularly fast – that is, it can shoot in conditions where there is little light – tends to be grainy or of poor definition (slightly blurred), and thus reminds us of newsreel or old documentary footage. Most films try not to look like this. The aim now is to capitalize on the vast superiority of film's clarity of definition when compared with that of domestic video tape or broadcast television. Developments in film stock have had a significant impact on cinema history. The celebrated *Citizen Kane* (1941) achieved revolutionary clarity and depth of field (the whole image, from the foreground to the far background, was sharply in focus) by pushing the film stock to its limit and by experimenting with lighting methods. The Australian film revival of the 1970s was assisted by Kodak's development of a new film stock which produced sharp definition in the harsh sunlight as well as in deep shadow.

The positioning of the camera is possibly the most apparent of the practices and technologies which contribute to the making of a film. The use of overhead, helicopter or crane shots can turn film into a performance art, exhilarating in the perspectives it offers the audience. Much of the appeal of Ridley Scott's classic *Thelma and Louise* could be seen to come from the spectacular use of the camera and it can be a major component of the visual style of special effects movies such as *Spiderman*, *Batman Begins*, and *The Matrix*. Less dramatic manipulation of camera angles also has an effect on the experience and meaning of a film. The camera can be directed either squarely or obliquely towards its subject, with rotation of the camera possible along its vertical axis (panning), its horizontal axis (tilting), or its transverse axis (rolling). If a camera is, as it were, looking down on its subject, its position is one of power. In *Citizen Kane*, a confrontation between Kane and his second wife Susan is played in a shot–reverse shot pattern which has Susan (or the camera) looking up to address Kane in one shot and Kane (or the camera) looking down to address Susan in the next shot. Susan is oppressed and diminished by the camera angle while Kane's stature is magnified. In this sequence, the manipulation of camera angles is the major means by which the audience is informed about the changing relationship between the two characters.

Camera angles can identify a shot with a character's point of view by taking a position which corresponds to that which we imagine the particular character would be occupying: we see what the character would be seeing. In *Edward Scissorhands* (1990), Edward's struggle to get his peas on to his scissors and then to his mouth is shot as if the camera was his mouth. An extreme example of such a point-of-view shot is in Hitchcock's *Spellbound* (1945), where the camera adopts the point of view of a character who is about to shoot himself; when the gun fires, the screen goes blank. Point-of-view shots are important for motivation and also for controlling aspects of the audience's identification with the characters. The fact that the audience is under pressure to 'see' from the point of view of the camera has been exploited in varied ways. In the shark film *Jaws*, we are given numerous shots of the victims from the underwater point of view of the shark. The confusion caused by our discomfort with this alignment, and our privileged knowledge of the shark's proximity to the victim, exacerbates the tension and the impression of impotence felt by the audience, and enhances our sense of the vulnerability of the victims. The tactic is widely used in teen slasher films like *Scream* (1996), with the camera frequently adopting the point of view of the attacker as she or he closes in on the unsuspecting victim, usually from behind. The height of the camera and its distance from its subject can also have an effect on the meaning of a shot. A conventional means of narrative closure is to slowly pull the camera back so that the subject disappears into its surroundings. This technique can enhance the ambiguity of emotional response, or invite the audience to project their own emotions on to the scene, or serve as a distancing device. It can do all of these because it signifies the withdrawal of our close attention – the end of the narrative. The end of *Shakespeare in Love* (1998), for instance, deals with the fact that the lovers are now to be separated for ever by, among other things, the long shot of the heroine on the broad expanse of beach producing a gradual process of reflection and closure.

Panning the camera along the horizontal axis imitates the movement of the spectators' eyes as they survey the scene round them. Very often such a movement is connected with the point of view of a character. The prelude to the gunfight in a western is often a slow pan around the streets to check for hidden gunmen, or to register the cowardly townsfolk's withdrawal, as well as to prolong the suspense and maximize our sense of the hero's isolation and vulnerability.

Rolling the camera gives the illusion of the world, either actually or metaphorically, being tipped on its side. This is sometimes done as a point-of-view shot, to indicate that the character is falling, or drugged, or sick, or otherwise likely to see the world oddly. It is also used in stunt and special-effect photography, and occasionally for comic effect. It can be extremely sinister and unsettling, as in the slight degree of roll in the initial sequences of *The Third Man* (1949) where the first pieces of the puzzle of Harry Lime are introduced, or during the intense dramatic confrontations between Alex and Dan in *Fatal Attraction* (1987). Camera roll most clearly indicates a world out of kilter one way or another.

The apparent movement of the camera, as in a close-up, can be accomplished through the manipulation of particular telephoto lenses, or what is commonly called the zoom lens. The actual forward or lateral movement of the camera apparatus is referred to as tracking or dollying, and it is often used in action sequences or as a point-of-view shot – the gunfighter walking down the empty street, for instance. As a point-of-view shot it can be very effective in enhancing audience identification with a character's experiences. A chase scene through a city street shot in this way can have a physical effect: it reproduces many of the perceptual activities involved in the experience and is thus convincingly 'real'. Alterations in focus have a signifying function. Most films aim at a very deep field of focus in which everything from the foreground to the far background is clear and sharp. Variations from this can have specific objectives. A soft focus on a character or background may pursue a romantic or lyrical effect, and was widely used in the romantic comedies during the 'classic period' of Hollywood; if we look at movies from the 1930s and 1940s we can see how routinely the female romantic lead is shot in such a way. In such situations, then and now, a halo around the star's face, created through the manipulation of focus or lighting, or

9 The glamour shot: Nicole Kidman

by placing vaseline or gauze on the lens, gives an exaggeratedly glamorous and dream-like effect. 'Rack' focus is used to direct the audience's attention from one character to another. This is accomplished by having one face in focus while the other is blurred, and using the switch in focus from one to the other for dramatic or symbolic effect.

The composition of images within the physical boundaries of the shot, the frame, requires close attention, and the function of the frame in either enclosing or opening out space around the images on the screen is also important. Figures and other elements can be moved around within the frame to great effect. As Charles Foster Kane moves towards Susan in their argument at Xanadu, his shadow falls over her, signifying domination. In another scene in *Citizen Kane*, Kane is defeated but the audience gradually apprehends the strength of his resistance as he moves from the background to the centre of the foreground, dominating those on either side of him. At times, the frame takes part in, rather than simply containing, the narrative. In the opening sequence of *The Searchers* (1956), the titles and credits give way to an apparently black screen over which appears the title 'Texas, 1868'. Then the image changes as a door opens to reveal that the black screen was a dark interior, the homestead, and through its door we look out on to the desert. The juxtaposition of an image of the wilderness with the enclosed domestic world of the homestead initiates a chain of contrasts which are thematically and structurally central to the film.

Lighting

It could be said that there are two main objectives to film lighting; the first is expressive – setting a mood, giving the film a 'look' (as in the Merchant–Ivory haziness of *The Talented Mr Ripley* (1999) or the techno-futurist sheen of *The Matrix* (1999)) or contributing to narrative details such as character or motivation. In *The Searchers*, again, there is a moment when John Wayne's Ethan Edwards turns to the camera and reveals the degree of his obsessions: the shadow of his hat has obscured his face, with the exception of one shaft of light reflecting from his eye. The effect is sinister and alarming. A whole film can be lit in an expressive way: the gloomy darkness of Ridley Scott's classic *Blade Runner* (1982) is an index of its moral and spiritual decay and the uncertainties which dog its plot line (which characters are the replicants?). The blue-grey of gleaming technology and electric light is the dominant tone, alleviated only by the sickly pink of flesh tones and the bright red of lipstick. When the hero and heroine escape into the open country the sudden rush of natural colours is important in overwhelming the audience's understandable scepticism about their future. This film owes a lot to expressionist films shot in black and white (such as *Metropolis*), as well as to the Sam Spade *films noir* of the 1940s, where a similar chiaroscuro lighting was used as an index of hidden, dark motives at work within the characters. The mode has been picked up for use in more recent *films noir* such as *LA Confidential* (1997), as well as becoming the house style for television's *Law and Order* franchise.

Realism is lighting's second objective. This is by far the most common and least apparent aim of film lighting. If it is successful, the figures are lit so naturally and unobtrusively that the audience do not notice lighting as a separate technology.

The basic equipment used to light sound stages or film sets includes a main light (the key light), which is usually set slightly to one side of the camera and directed at the figure to be lit; the fill lights, which remove the shadows caused by the key light and mould the figure being lit in order to add detail and realism; and the back light which defines the figure's outline and separates him or her from the background, thus enhancing the illusion of a three-dimensional image. In conventional high-key lighting, we view a brightly lit scene with few shadow areas, as the fill lights mop up any shadows left by the key light. Much expressive lighting, however, aims at exploiting shadows, and at lighting only part of the screen to give a sense of ambiguity or threat. This is called low-key lighting: it makes much less use of fill lights, and thus has sharp, deep shadows. Low-key lighting will often move the key light from its conventional position to one side of the figure so that only half the face is visible, or it will increase the angle so that the face is lit from below and acquires a distorted, threatening aspect.

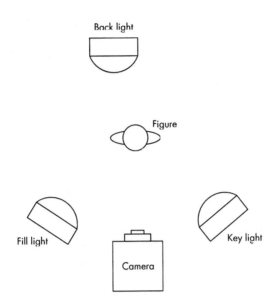

10 A conventional three-point set-up for high-key lighting

In general, high-key lighting is realist, while low-key lighting is expressive. These are conventions, which work only because we let them. But they are important constituents of the meaning of a shot and in many cases of an entire film. It is worth noting how lighting picks out and emphasizes elements within the frame, and how this appears to be a natural means of directing the audience's attention to one feature of the frame while obscuring others. This is particularly so during long takes, where a character can move in and out of shadow, into dominant or dominated positions, simply by moving from one regime of lighting to another.

Sound

Surprisingly little attention has been given to the role of sound in the cinema. Dialogue can seem less important to us than the image, and in many cases seems to be used to 'fix' the meaning of the image rather than to motivate the image itself. Yet, as the quality of sound recording and its reproduction in the cinema have improved, researchers are slowly turning towards developing a better understanding of sound's contribution to the signifying system. At the most obvious level, the movie soundtrack enhances realism by reproducing the sounds one would normally associate with the actions and events depicted visually; this is referred to as 'diegetic' sound (that is, sound that is motivated by actions or events contained within the narrative). We expect to hear the sound of breaking glass when we see a window smash on screen, and we expect the words uttered by the actors to synchronize with the movement of their lips. The cinema's illusion of realism has become quite dependent upon the diegetic use of sound. Other kinds of sound can serve narrative functions, of course; music, for example, in the musical genre can mark key narrative moments or even advance plot lines. More generally, music is routinely used as means of providing accompaniment to a film's dramatic or narrative high points, and it was in fact the first form of sound to be introduced into the cinema.

However, sound has many other, more subtle and contingent, signifying functions. It can be used as a transitional device, linking sequences together. *Citizen Kane* often concludes a speech begun in one scene after the visuals have taken us on to the following scene. The overlapping sound binds what is an episodic and disjointed narrative together. David Lean has used sound cleverly to accomplish the transition from one location to the next: in *A Passage to India* (1984) he uses the sound of a medical instrument being thrown into a steel bowl as the cue for a cut to the coupling of two train carriages. The sounds of the clashing metal bind together as one sound which welds the two shots together. Music plays an increasingly important contextual role in soundtracks today. It can be used as an important component of the construction of the world of the film, as a source of atmosphere, or as a reference point to the relevant subcultures in a teen film like *Mean Girls* (2004) or the more adult fare of *Jackie Brown* (1997). Unlike the realist, diegetic use of sound, however, music in films is usually non-realistic (and non-diegetic) in that we rarely see its source in the frame or even within the world of the film.

Simon Frith (1986: 65) argues that the reality music 'describes/refers to is a different sort of reality than that described/referred to by visual images'. He says music amplifies the mood or atmosphere, and also tries to convey the 'emotional significance' of a scene: the 'true "real" feelings of the characters involved in it'. He calls this the 'emotional reality' of film music, and its aim is to deepen the sense of the film's realism, to give it an emotional texture otherwise lacking. It is this kind of contribution that Ry Cooder's music makes to *Paris, Texas* (1984), for instance. Further, Frith sees film music as assisting in the construction of the reality of time and place, the world of the film. He uses the example of the music in *Zorba the Greek* (1964), which is responsible for much of that film's successful construction of 'Greekness'; we could point to a similar function for the music in *My Big Fat Greek Wedding* (2002).

A further aspect of music's signifying function within film is its capacity to invoke whole areas of cultural experience. The cultural background audiences bring to such films as *8 Mile* (2002) or *Pulp Fiction* (1994) is crucial to their response to what they see and hear. That cultural background specifies a range of musical, as well as cinematic, contexts that privilege certain kinds of meanings and pleasures; audiences recognizing the references to these meanings and pleasures are thus inscribed into the world of the film. In these days of Dolby stereo and music-packed soundtracks, the careful construction of the music track plays an important function in pulling the major segment of the audience, teenagers, into the cinema in the first place, as well as producing identification and enjoyment once they go inside. The close relationship between the world of the music video clip (so often resembling a feature film on fast-forward in its rapid montage of narrative images) and that of the teen movie is evidence of how much of the same popular cultural space is occupied by music and film. These days, soundtracks are compiled with the soundtrack CD, as well as the film narrative, in mind. A new category of person has appeared in Hollywood, the soundtrack producer, whose job is to pack the soundtrack with the right mix of contemporary popular music for the film's target demographic.

Theme songs offered at crucial moments can dominate the competition between signifying systems. Whitney Houston's performance of *I Will Always Love You* is probably the most memorable element of *The Bodyguard* (1992), but it is probably hard to recall quite which scene it accompanies. The nostalgia that permeates *The*

Big Chill (1983) is saved from becoming cloying and sentimental by the continuous vitality of the music track. Certain instruments, too, become temporarily identified with particular effects: the synthesizer soundtrack enhances the strangeness of *Blade Runner* and the same technique was used in television's *Miami Vice*.

Frith's final point is probably his most important. Music and images have a lot in common as media of communication: they are not understood in a direct, linear way by the audience, but irrationally, emotionally, individually. Lévi-Strauss (1966) says that the meaning of music cannot be determined by those playing it, only by those listening to it. Barthes (1977) notes that it is impossible to describe music without adjectives – that is, it must be understood in terms of its subjective effect rather than through a dictionary of meanings. Correspondingly, its effect can be profoundly personal. Film music, like the image, can have physical effects: it sends shivers down the spine or makes one tap one's feet. It has been said that film music 'feels for us', by telling us when a powerful moment is happening and indicating just what we should feel about it through the mood of the music. Simon Frith describes this phenomenon more accurately and less contemptuously:

> one function of film music is to reveal our emotions as *the audience*. . . . Film scores are thus important in representing *community* (via martial or nationalistic music, for example) in both film and audience. The important point here is that as spectators we are drawn to identify not with the film characters themselves but with their emotions, which are signalled pre-eminently by music which can offer us emotional experience *directly*. Music is central to the way in which the pleasure of cinema is simultaneously individualised and shared.
>
> (Frith 1986: 68–9)

So the convention of music swelling at the point of a romantic clinch is not manipulation but recourse to even more direct means of communicating with the audience.

It is important, however, that we do not fall into what has become a familiar trap of regarding the use of sound in the cinema as reducible to the music soundtrack. Today, sound of all varieties has become one of the key visceral pleasures in the cinema experience, and it also plays a more active narrative role than was previously the case. Gianluca Sergi (2002) argues that in contemporary cinema, since what he describes as the beginning of the 'Dolby era' (the mid-1970s, when the first economically viable stereophonic sound system was developed for the cinema), sound has become a more aggressive component of the movies' signifying system. Sergi argues that contemporary film sound demands to be considered more carefully for its contribution to the meanings and pleasures of cinema. Importantly, he reminds us that sound is not just a music score; rather it includes diegetic and non-diegetic effects, music, dialogue, and (significantly) silence.

Sergi points to a number of changes in the production of sound over the last thirty years that have significantly changed how sound contributes to the feature film. The introduction of stereophonic and thus multilayered sound allowed producers to build the movie soundtrack with dozens of tracks, layered into a complex architecture. Among the consequences of this was the capacity for this multilayered sound to be projected into the cinema from a number of different directions; Sergi suggests that this has allowed sound to be strongly foregrounded at certain points in the cinema experience – as when we hear the spaceship coming from behind us before we see it on the screen. Sound budgets have increased, more sound personnel are employed, and the reproduction of sound within the cinema has improved to the point where there is minimal distortion even at high volume. These developments have allowed more emphasis on enabling audiences to 'feel' as well as hear the sounds, as in the basso rumbling announcing the arrival of that spaceship at the back of the cinema or in the ricocheting bullets spraying around Batman and bouncing around the cinema space. Further, and rather than merely providing ancillary support to the realism of the image, today's soundtracks can provide us with the sound of something we may not even see – Sergi's examples include the crushing of bone or vigorous sexual activity – and thus provide information and generate responses in their own right.

Mise-en-scène

Among the confusing aspects of film theory is the use of *mise-en-scène* as a term to describe a theory about film grammar, a shooting and production style, and – as in this section – a shorthand term for 'everything that is in the frame' of a shot. We have already talked about the way in which the camera contributes to the *mise-en-scène*. In this section I want to emphasize the importance of those other aspects of the image: set design, costumes, the arrangement and movement of figures, the spatial relations (who is obscured, who looks dominant, and so on), and the placement of objects which have become important within the narrative (the murderer's gun, the secret letter, the reflection in the mirror).

We learn much, unconsciously, from the *mise-en-scène*. When we recognize the interior of a dwelling as middle class, bookish, and slightly old-fashioned, we are reading the signs of the décor in order to give them a set of social meanings. The film's construction of a social world is authenticated through the details of the *mise-en-scène*. Further, the narrative is advanced through the arrangement of elements within the frame; characters can reveal themselves to us without revealing themselves to other characters, and thus complicate and develop the story. The practice of watching a murder thriller involves the scanning of the frame to pick up the clues in the *mise-en-scène*. *Psycho* (1960) exploits this by offering us red herrings in the form of point-of-view shots which suggest that Norman's mother is still alive.

In films of epic proportions such as *Gladiator*, the plethora of information contained within the frame can itself be spectacular. The *mise-en-scène* in such cases is not necessarily only narratively significant, but is rather a performance of cinema, a celebration of its ability to trap so much of the world in its frame. The Coliseum sequences in *Gladiator* are spectacular for the comprehensiveness of the illusion they create – of the size of the crowd, of the details of the stadium and the ancient city. These shots display themselves for our pleasure, celebrating the scale of the images, the density of their detail, the impossibility of comprehending them fully during their brief time on the screen. Many historical films work like this, using their *mise-en-scène* to celebrate the power of the medium to recreate the real so overwhelmingly and thus, presumably, so authentically.

This is a large topic and one in which there are many subdivisions. Yet it is probably better to discuss the importance of *mise-en-scène* through an example, and I do this in Chapter 7 in a discussion of the opening sequences of *Butch Cassidy and the Sundance Kid* (1969).

Chapter 5 includes a discussion of the signifying function of the star, but it would be remiss not to mention it here. The star has a function outside a particular film which is only partly incorporated into that film. Actors do not just represent characters, becoming invisible themselves. Rather, characters become visible through actors and it is always important to understand those specific meanings of individual performers which become part of the characterization. Stars can be sufficiently meaningful as to require the bare minimum of 'character' in the narrative; they are watched for their own sake, not for their representation of a scripted character. The bodies of particular female stars have been important draw-cards for male audiences; few, perhaps, went to see Marilyn Monroe movies solely for her characterizations. It is possible that this is less common today, or at least, the phenomenon may be less gendered; the female audience's response to Brad Pitt's shirtless appearance in *Thelma and Louise* or in *Fight Club* (1999) comes to mind here. Even for 'character' actors, such as Meryl Streep, however, the audience still comes to see Meryl Streep perform (that is, do what Meryl Streep does) rather than to see Meryl Streep submerge herself. Finally, the star's face is part of the *mise-en-scène*. The spectacle of the face of a Jack Nicholson, a Cate Blanchett, or a Hugh Grant is a cinematic event in itself for particular film audiences, and one could be forgiven for thinking occasionally that characterization was only a pretext for bringing this spectacle to the screen.

Editing

Here we move back towards the realm of montage, the construction of the relationship between shots. We should not underestimate the importance of editing. The famous Kuleshov experiments present a powerful case for its centrality. These experiments juxtaposed a single shot of an actor with a plate of soup, then a woman in a coffin, and then a girl smiling. The audiences seeing the three sequences identified the actor's expression (which never changed) as hunger, sadness, and affection, respectively. Despite this demonstration of its power, montage is not so widely used now. It occurs most frequently as a means of representing a mood – cuts to shots of the sea, mountains, or crowded city streets – or for narrative 'ellipsis' – where sections of the narrative need rapid summarizing rather than full dramatization. In some cases the two functions are combined. In *Butch Cassidy and the Sundance Kid*, the period between the gang's escape from the US and its arrival in South America is summarized in a series of stills depicting the group's enjoyment of the pleasures of New York City. This fills a gap in the narrative and evokes a carefree mood which is abruptly terminated by their arrival in primitive Bolivia.

As realism became the dominant mode of feature film production, editing was required to contribute to the illusion that the film was unfolding naturally, without the intervention of the film-maker. Now editing is more or less invisible, seamlessly connecting shots so as to give the illusion of continuity of time and space. There are exceptions to this – action sequences, highly dramatic moments – but in general the craft of the editor in realist films is to remain invisible and knit the shots together according to realist aesthetics. The search for realism, in fact, has produced occasional avant-garde films which do not use editing at all; some of the late Andy Warhol's films eschewed editing in order to let the cameras record reality without any mediation. Some directors claim to 'edit in the camera', that is, to shoot scenes sequentially and cut the action at the appropriate moment for the transition to the next shot. This is both difficult and unusual.

There is a multitude of editing techniques. We have already mentioned two major ones – the fade-out and the dissolve. There is also 'the wipe', in which one image replaces another preceded by a demarcation line moving across the screen. The most frequent method these days is the simple cut from one shot to the next. As with most simple techniques, it requires great skill to do this well.

Various transition devices can be used or invented to soften the cut and make it less sudden or disorientating: overlapping sound from one shot to the next; the use of motivations in the first shot which take us to the next (such as an action shot where the viewer wants to see its conclusion). Most realist films avoid sudden cuts unless they are to be exploited for dramatic effect. A sudden cut produces surprise, horror, and disruption, so it tends to be saved for moments when such an effect is required. The shower sequence in *Psycho* derives its effectiveness from the fracturing and prolonging of the action – a nightmare effect produced by the rapid editing together of numerous angles of perspective on the murder. Again, in *Psycho*, when the murderer-mother is about to be revealed, the camera tracks in on the back of her chair. When the chair is spun around, revealing her skeleton, a cut is made to a close-up of the skeleton's face. The sudden cut exacerbates the audience's shock.

There are many editing conventions which assist the filmmakers and the audience to make sense of the film. I have already mentioned the shot–reverse shot convention. Other conventions include the use of short establishing shots above a new location to place the narrative within a physical context; and the observation of an imaginary line across the film set which the camera never crosses so that the viewer is given a consistent representation of the spatial relations between the actors and their surroundings (this is called the 180° rule). Skilful editors can use the timing of their cuts either to enhance the energy of the action, or to slow it down. Action sequences can take on greater drama and complexity if cuts occur within moments of high action; as a car is about to crash, for instance, we might go to several successive and separate views of the same moment. Alternatively, a cut in a moment of relative stasis can slow down action, retard the narrative, and open up ambiguities. A thoughtful character, considering his or her future, may be shot from several positions in order to expand the moment and instil significance into it.

The speed, pace, or rhythm of editing is important too. Documentary film tends to use fewer edits than narrative film, and social realist films tend to imitate this in the pacing of their editing. Many feature films pursue an identifiable rhythm throughout their length, and single scenes can be dramatically affected by the pacing and rhythm of the editing. It is easy to demonstrate this through an example. In *Mad Max II* (1981; *Road Warrior* in the US), there is a chase scene in which Max's large tanker truck is pursued by the followers of the villain, Humungus. Max has a shotgun with two bullets and a passenger, the 'feral kid' – a wild 10-year-old child. During a desperate battle with the arch-enemy Wes, who has climbed on to Max's truck, the shotgun bullets roll out of the broken windshield onto the bonnet. Although Wes is knocked off the truck and disappears, Max still needs those bullets. He sends the feral kid out onto the bonnet after them while the chase continues at high speed. The music soundtrack dies down to be replaced by the sound of the wind in the child's face, and a heartbeat. At regular but gradually accelerating intervals, there is a series of cuts from the bullets on the truck's bonnet back to the child's face. Rhythmically we cut back and forth from the child to the bullets, from the child to the bullets, from the child to the. . . . Wes's maniacal face appears over the front of the bonnet, screaming in full close-up, and the return cut to the feral kid has him screaming too: a terrifying moment. The surprise at Wes's appearance is all the greater for the expectations set up by the rhythmic alternations between the shots of the child and the bullets. The combination of the alteration in soundtrack and the skill of the editor has achieved this dramatic effect.

This point is important. Film is a complex of systems of signification and its meanings are the product of the combination of these systems. The combination may be achieved through systems either complementing or conflicting with each other. No one system is responsible for the total effect of a film, and all the systems we have just been surveying possess, as we have seen, their own separate sets of conventions, their own ways of representing things.

Special effects

When the first edition of this book was written in 1988, special effects were regarded relatively instrumentally; that is, they were subordinated to the narrative and seen as merely technical contributors to the finished film. That is no longer the case, and the primary reason for this is the development of new technologies – especially those involved in computer-generated special effects. This, as readers will no doubt realize, is relatively recent. Michele Pierson (2002: 77) tells us that the first completely computer-generated sequence in a feature film was in *Star Trek: The Wrath of Kan* (1982), the first completely computer-generated character was in *Young Sherlock Holmes* (1985), the first morph occurred in *Willow* (1988), and the first computer-generated main character was in *Terminator 2* (1991). Since then, CGI has been used extensively within the *mise-en-scène* in (for example) *Titanic, Forrest Gump, Gladiator,* and the *Matrix* movies, as well as in the production of character, such as the extraordinary hybrid CGI/humanoid Gollum in *The Lord of the Rings* movies.

Much of the writing about special effects which has responded to the development of CGI, and in particular to its widespread take-up by Hollywood as a way of attracting audiences to blockbuster projects, has made the point, in one way or another, that there are at least two kinds of functions for special effects in the movies. One is to simulate the appearance of something that actually exists (or once existed) in the natural world or in photographic or cinematic representations of that world but which is not easily available to the film-maker. Typically, this would cover the use of CGI to create the crowds in *Gladiator* or the passengers sliding down the vertical deck as the *Titanic* sinks or the complex alien worlds in *Star Wars: Revenge of the Sith* (2005). Pierson refers to this as a 'simulationist' tactic and it deploys special effects to produce what Stephen Prince (2002) calls 'perceptual realism' – something we are prepared to accept as real in the context of the narrative. Before the development of CGI, this would have covered the bulk of all special effects used in the modern feature film.

The second function is to exploit the spectacle of the effect as an end in itself. At one level, audiences appreciate the spectacle on the screen as a discrete pleasure. This appreciation might have an aesthetic dimension, as in the case of what Pierson calls the 'techno-futurist' aesthetic motivating the audience's fascination with the role played by CGI in such sci-fi fantasy productions as *The Matrix*

Reloaded (2003), for instance. This appreciation may also be the result of, simply, the audience's demand for novelty. Pierson reminds us that this impulse has always been among the pleasures cinema can provide – in what she describes as 'the search for wonder', cinema audiences have always sought the magical and the spectacular. What we are now witnessing as a 'distinct form of cinema spectacle' in the present day can actually be traced back to Gunning's 'cinema of attractions' in the silent era – a performance of the 'wizardry of the movies themselves' (Pierson 2002: 107).

Pierson argues that the different functions served by special effects also reflect different kinds of audience relations to the film narrative. That is, there will be points even in quite conventional films where the spectacular display of movie wizardry will be the focus of attention and a source of pleasure in its own right. The morphing of the terminator in *Terminator 2* is one such moment. The pleasures of gaining mastery over the narrative are suspended, Pierson suggests, in response to an aesthetic interest in the cinema effect. She also argues that we can locate 'effects sequences' in many blockbuster films where the attention is primarily directed to the display of new kinds of effects, and suggests that in particular many of the sci-fi films made in the early 1990s (when such effects were becoming available) 'exhibit this self-conscious show-casing of a new type of effects imagery' (2002: 125).

As we have seen, Geoff King (2000) has taken issue with the view that the narrative is displaced or suspended by such 'effects sequences', but there are others who argue that it is important to accept the different kinds of relations between the audience and the text that come into play when such spectacular deployments of special effects technologies occur. Angela Ndalianis (2000) argues that the current use of CGI in the feature film constitutes a convergence of theatre, film, and computer graphics in order to create 'an illusory magical environment in which audiences act and spectate at the same time' – that is, they are both in the world of the narrative and outside it, appreciating the quality of its spectacular visual realization.

Certainly, such an account would seem to accord with the industrial determinants which have recently facilitated the deployment of these new technologies. The rise of the special-effects spectacular has been motivated by the need for the film industry to compete with other visual media such as television. Television may have the capacity to match film in its delivery of the pleasures of narrative but is far less competitive in its capacity to provide the pleasures of spectacle. The contemporary redevelopment of the cinema as a site of spectacle – widescreen formats, improved sound reproduction, and so on – is also part of this competitive strategy. Interestingly, too, the focus upon spectacle has helped to multiply the formats through which film can be re-purposed and exploited – theme-park rides, computer games, and so on – as well as to assist in translating the film across language and cultural boundaries (King 2000: 21–2). So the return to the cinema spectacle has its roots both in the fundamental nature of the appeal of the cinematic experience and in the contemporary political economy of the media industries.

Reading the film

The complexity of film production makes interpretation, the active reading of a film, essential. We need to, and inevitably do, scan the frame, hypothesize about the narrative development, speculate on its possible meanings, attempt to gain some mastery over the film as it unfolds. The active process of interpretation is essential to film analysis and to the pleasure that film offers.

But films are not autonomous cultural events. We understand films in terms of other films, their worlds in terms of our worlds. 'Intertextuality' is a term used to describe the way any one film text will be understood through our experience, or our awareness, of other film texts. The construction of heroic endurance around Bruce Willis's character in the *Die Hard* films is of course completely implausible without our understanding of the cinematic convention that allows heroes to miraculously discover reserves of strength no matter how battered or injured they may seem. The films remind us of the relevance of this convention by slightly parodying it at various points. Willis is particularly skilled at performing parody and

11 The techno-futurist aesthetic: *The Matrix Reloaded*

heroism at the same time, something he has been called upon to do in a wide range of roles beginning with his early TV performances in *Moonlighting*. Rather than reducing our enjoyment, such a strategy sets up a knowing, ironic complicity between the audience and the narrative that enables us to take conscious pleasure in its acknowledged excesses. Similarly, our toleration for the slasher/horror film plot line that seems to compel all likely female victims of serial killers to take showers and leave the door open is at least partly generated by our acceptance that in order to experience the pleasure of being shocked we need to suspend our disbelief.

Films are also produced and seen within a social, cultural context that includes more than other film texts. Film serves a cultural function through its narratives that goes beyond the pleasure of story. To examine this we leave behind the problem of film languages and approach film through the category of narrative. However, many of the points made in Chapter 7 derive from this account of signification in film and will further demonstrate the processes surveyed in this chapter.

Suggestions for further work

1   This chapter does not present an exhaustive survey of the language-like activities which contribute to signification in film. Further reading should include some other introductory books on film theory and analysis which may give a more detailed account of these practices. Examples of such texts include James Monaco's *How to Read a Film* (1981), the Sobchacks's *An Introduction to Film* (1980), and any of the many editions of Bordwell and Thompson's *Film Art: An Introduction* (1986). These are all useful texts, but do not approach film in the social manner of this book. Further reading in semiotics might be fruitful, too. A good introduction can be found in Robert Stam *et al.* (eds) *New Vocabularies in Film Semiotics* (1992).

2   It is essential for any account of film to be conversant with the basic production practices. Attempts to produce a film of one's

own, no matter how primitive, or a visit made to a local film production unit, no matter how humble, will be of great assistance to anyone interested in the medium. Try to organize this, individually or as a group.

3 Building on the idea that a film is made up of a number of contributing systems, examine a scene from a film of your choice and try to break it down into its constituents. Try to determine just what has been the contribution of each element. Then propose a change in *one* element – the lighting, for instance – and see how that might change the meaning generated.

4 Examine the work of one system within a film of your choice – editing, for example. Is there an observable pattern in it? Can you detect any principles behind it? What is the nature of its contribution to the film as a whole?

5 What other language-like activities can you think of besides those mentioned in the chapter (dress, gesture, the discourse of film)? Does rock music, too, for instance, have a set of languages? How useful do you find this analogy of language in dealing with film as a communicative practice? What are the limits of the analogy?

6 Can you isolate a 'special-effects sequence' in a film you have seen recently and discuss the kinds of response it generates – whether it is received primarily as spectacle, whether it is fully integrated into the arc of the narrative, or whether it is a mixture of both?

Film narrative

The universality of story

Feature films are narratives – they tell stories. Even films based on real events will fictionalize them in order to produce drama, to telescope time, to avoid being filled up with too many minor characters, or simply to be more entertaining. Even in the current welter of special-effect movies, feature films are usually summarized by their plots – in their first 'treatment' (or outline of the script idea), in the advance publicity, in the TV guide, in reviews, and in conversations. Films may differ from other kinds of narratives – literary fiction or television drama, for instance – in the medium used and the representational conventions. They do, however, share with literary fiction and television drama the basic structure and functions of narrative. Much work has been done in the field known as 'narratology' on exactly what constitutes the structures and functions of narrative. The researchers' conclusions are of great use to students of the feature film.

Narratology is a large field of study. Those who have entered debates about the function and nature of narrative within primitive and modern industrialized societies include anthropologists such as Claude Lévi-Strauss, folklorists such as Vladimir Propp, semioticians such as Roland Barthes, and British cultural studies theorists such as Stuart Hall. The reason for the breadth of interest is narrative's universality: some societies may have no equivalent to the novel, but all societies tell stories. Story-telling can take many forms – myths, legends, ballads, folk-tales, rituals, dance, histories, novels, jokes, drama – and can be seen to serve many apparently different social functions, from entertainment to religious instruction. It seems that story-telling is part of our cultural experience, inseparable from and intrinsic to it.

What is clear is that the world 'comes to us' in the shape of stories. From the earliest days of our childhood, our world is represented to us through stories told to us by our parents, read to us from books, reported to us by friends, overheard in conversations, shared among groups at school, circulated around the playground. This is not to say that all our stories *explain* the world. Rather, story provides us with an easy, unconscious, and involving way of constructing our world; narrative can be described as a means of 'making sense' of our social world, and sharing that 'sense' with others. Its universality underlines its intrinsic place in human communication.

Not only is narrative common to all cultures, but there is evidence that there are structural similarities between the tales, stories, and legends produced by different cultures. The narrative structure found in the folk-tales of one culture can recur in another, suggesting that there is something universal in the structure as well as in the function of narrative. Vladimir Propp (1975) analysed a group of Russian folk-tales in order to see if they shared common properties. What he found was that all of them, no matter how widely they differed in their surface details (characterization, setting, plots), shared certain important structural features. The most basic of these were the functions of various sets of characters and actions within the tales. First, he reduced the range of different characters to a maximum of eight character roles. These are not separate characters, since one character can occupy a number of roles, or 'spheres of action', as Propp calls them, and one role may be played by a number of different characters. They are:

1   the villain
2   the donor (provider)
3   the helper
4   the princess (or sought-for person) and her father
5   the dispatcher
6   the hero or victim
7   the false hero.

All characters and 'spheres of action' which occur in folk-tales are accommodated by this list. This group of characters then participates in the limited set of narrative units or functions which make up the tale. From his analyses, Propp concluded that:

1   Functions of characters serve as stable, constant elements in a tale, independent of how and by whom they are fulfilled. They constitute the fundamental components of a tale.

2   The number of functions known to the folk-tale is limited.
3   The sequence of functions is always identical.
4   All folk-tales are of one type in regard to their structure.

We might understand the implications of this if we follow it a little further, into the basic structure he proposed for all folk-tales. Propp outlined a list of thirty-one functions, themselves organized in broader narrative groups indicating their place in the development of the plot:

1   A member of a family leaves home.
2   A prohibition or rule is imposed on the hero.
3   This prohibition is broken.
4   The villain makes an attempt at reconnaissance.
5   The villain learns something about his victim.   ⟩ PREPARATION
6   The villain tries to deceive the victim to get possession of him or his belongings.
7   The victim unknowingly helps the villain by being deceived or influenced by the villain.
8   The villain harms a member of the family.
8a   A member of the family lacks or desires something.
9   This lack or misfortune is made known; the hero is given a request or command   ⟩ COMPLICATION
     and he goes or is sent on a mission/quest.
10   The seeker (or the hero) plans action against the villain.
11   The hero leaves home.
12   The hero is tested, attacked, interrogated, and as a result receives either a magical agent or a helper.   ⟩ TRANSFERENCE
13   The hero reacts to the actions of the future donor.

14 The hero uses the magical agent.

15 The hero is transferred to the general
   location of the object of his mission/quest.

16 The hero and villain join in direct combat.

17 The hero is branded.

18 The villain is defeated. > STRUGGLE

19 The initial misfortune or lack is set right.

20 The hero returns.

21 The hero is pursued.

22 The hero is rescued from pursuit.

23 The hero arrives home or elsewhere and
   is not recognized. > RETURN

24 A false hero makes false claims.

25 A difficult task is set for the hero.

26 The task is accomplished.

27 The hero is recognized.

28 The false hero/villain is exposed.

29 The false hero is transformed. > RECOGNITION

30 The villain is punished.

31 The hero is married and crowned.

Not all stories will have all of these functions. But, Propp argues, they *will* be composed from this list, and *only* from this list. Furthermore, they will all follow the order outlined. In some cases, sequences might be repeated – as in the struggle unit. The story outline is probably recognizable. The stereotyped cartoon plot involving the moustachioed foreclosing landlord, the widowed mother, and the heroic son is apparent in the first seven functions, for instance.

While there has been argument about the comprehensiveness of Propp's 'morphology' of the elements of folk-tales, his work has been extremely influential. In particular, there have been numerous applications of Propp's specific conclusions (and his more general idea of uncovering a 'grammar', or set of compositional rules, of narrative construction) to areas other than folk-tales. Although there is a limit to the parallels that can be drawn between the cultural productions of primitive folk-cultures and modern post-industrial cultures, Propp's work has been applied to mass-produced narratives in contemporary Western cultures. Much popular film and TV can be found to be structured according to Propp's principles. There have been a number of morphological analyses of films – for example, of *Sunset Boulevard* by Patricia Erens (1977) and of *North by North-West* by Peter Wollen (1976) – as well as more general discussions of Propp and the feature film (Fell 1977). John Fiske (1987b) has looked at programmes such as *The Bionic Woman* and *The A-Team* and found an extraordinary degree of correlation between Propp's functions and the narrative structure of the TV series. We can easily demonstrate a degree of fit between Propp's categories of 'spheres of action' and characterization in film, too. A list of the main characters in the original *Star Wars* movie fits Propp's eight spheres of action quite neatly:

The villain	Darth Vader
The donor	Obi-Wan Kenobi
The helper	Han Solo
The princess	Princess Leia
The dispatcher	R2-D2
The hero	Luke Skywalker
The false hero	Darth Vader

We need not make too much of this as a way of understanding *Star Wars*, although it might flesh out vague claims about the film's fairy-tale, fable-like quality. It does suggest, however, how applicable to film studies much of the work on the cultural function and structural characteristics of narrative could be. At the very least, it underlines the possibility that the modern feature film and the primitive folk-tale serve similar functions for their respective audiences. It is to the function of narrative that we turn next.

The function of narrative

The fact that narrative is universal should alert us to at least two possibilities. The first is that narrative might be a property of the human mind, like language; the second is that narrative might serve an essential social function which makes it indispensable to human communities. At least one theorist, the anthropologist Claude Lévi-Strauss (1966), has attempted to relate the characteristics of myth and legend back to the perceptual mechanisms of the brain. So far, there is no way of proving or disproving such a proposition. It is, however, possible to examine the ways in which narrative might serve some social function. Lévi-Strauss, again, provides a useful starting-point here.

Lévi-Strauss (1955, 1966) examined the nature of myths and legends in ancient and primitive cultures. From them he believed he could unravel the structures of meaning and significance which differentiated one cultural system from another. Like Propp, Lévi-Strauss discerned common structures in myth which crossed cultural boundaries. However, unlike Propp, he also saw a degree of cultural specificity in the particular transformation of these common structures. What all cultural myths, all primitive narratives, had in common was the function they served for the society. Myths, he argued, were used to deal with the contradictions in experience, to explain the apparently inexplicable, and to justify the inevitable. Within myths, contradictions and inequities which could not be resolved in the real world were resolved symbolically. The function of myth was to place those contradictions – between humans and his natural environment, for instance, or between life and death – as part of natural existence. Myths negotiated a peace between men and women and their environment so that they could live in it without agonizing over its frustrations and cruelties.

So a body of mythology which attributes the vagaries of the weather to the particular dissatisfactions of a god (or gods) 'explains' those vagaries. The function of such a mythology is not necessarily to describe *accurately* our relation to a god or gods (although we cannot categorically rule that out either); rather, its essential function is to represent that relationship in such a way that those who have to can live within it. The notion mentioned earlier – that narrative makes sense of the world – is explicit in myth and ritual.

Lévi-Strauss suggests that a feature of mythologies is their dependence upon 'binary oppositions', a two-term conflict. One of the ways in which humans understand the world is through dividing it into sets of mutually exclusive categories – land and sea, man and woman, good and bad, us and them. These are binary oppositions and they divide up and thus structure our understanding of the world. They can do this because they are one way of determining meaning. Meaning is a product of the construction of differences and similarities; in this case, placing an object on one side of an opposition rather than on the other. This binary pattern is logically supported by the fact that we define things not only in terms of what they *are*, but also in terms of what they are *not*. 'Man' means 'not woman', 'not boy', and so on. We define things by aligning them with what they are like, and by separating them from what they are not like. Because this means we are placing things in already existing categories, already opposed to other categories, oppositions can 'breed', producing further transformations of the same binary principle.

In the following example we can see why feminist attacks on constructions of gender difference are so well aimed. Assuming male and female are opposites means that, automatically, women *are* what men are *not*; if the male is strong, then the female must be weak, and on it goes:

male	strong
female	weak
rational	emotional
reliable	unreliable

With the gradual proliferation of items under these headings we can see the accretion of negatives on the female side as a necessary product of the assumption that male and female are opposites. To continue with the chain is to end up with good (male) versus bad (female). Ultimately, of course, all patterns of opposition – and thus their possibilities for meaning – are produced by large overarching categories like 'nature' and 'culture'. (Men, for instance, in our culture are seen as physical, comfortable outdoors, and 'natural', while women are seen to be indoor creatures, emotional, and in need of protection from nature. Men are 'nature', women are 'culture'.) Lévi-Strauss saw this perceptual and linguistic concept repeated in the structure and process of narrative itself, in its dependence on conflict and binary oppositions. Patterns of opposition can be traced quite easily through narrative and we will explore this notion a little more fully later on in this chapter.

Structuralism and narrative

The theories we have been looking at so far fall into the general area of structuralist approaches. Structuralism has been very powerful in its influence on narrative theory. Its main virtue is that it is most interested in those things that narratives have in common, rather than in the distinctive characteristics of specific narratives. Structuralists look at films, for instance, to see how they fit into or help to define a genre, style, or movement. As a result, what they notice tends to be a component of all narrative, or the narrative systems of a particular medium, rather than the features of a particular narrative. This may be a weakness when looking closely at one text, but for understanding the nature of the medium of film it is very useful indeed.

What we can glean from structuralist approaches is an idea of how narrative works. Of course, we already know that narrative is set in train by the establishment of some kind of conflict. Most films start by establishing the lines of conflict which will determine or motivate the events and actions of the story. Binary oppositions can be useful here because often the conflict is between a pair of opposing forces which are mutually exclusive. The hero is faced with a threat, a challenge, or a need which has to be met or satisfied. Those forces which will inhibit the meeting of the threat or challenge, or satisfaction of the need, are seen to be in opposition (enemy-like) to the viewer, who identifies with the hero. So a simple binary system is set up in which we measure good and bad through the determining category of the good hero.

More usually, however, we see the 'world' of the film as itself made up of conflicting forces, loyalties, or value systems. The problem of the film (and its hero) is to resolve or opt for one side of this opposition. The conflict can be quite stark and uncompromising in, say, the characteristic opposition between homesteaders and Indians in a traditional western. This is how such an opposition looks and note how comprehensively this can structure the film in all its signifying systems – the visual imagery surrounding the Indians, or the tendency to emphasize the white's family but not the Indian's, for instance – and note also how the basic set of oppositions breeds others):

homesteaders	Indians
white	red
Christian	pagan
domestic	savage
helpless	dangerous
weak	strong
clothed	naked

(Of course, this opposition, too, could be boiled down to a governing one – that of culture versus nature.) The opposition here cannot be resolved unless one or the other side withdraws or capitulates. The hero usually operates as someone who can understand both sides of the pattern: he is usually strong, not weak; dangerous, not helpless; and is often associated with the red man as well as the white. His role then is to mediate the opposition. In the classic western *The Searchers*, John Wayne's Ethan Edwards enacts vengeance on the Indians for the murder of his relatives (indices of his identification with the homesteaders' side of the oppositions) but with savagery, a lack of respect for the law, and (in the final act of scalping) a specific invocation of the Indian. By crossing the opposition, he 'resolves' it by killing his counterpart, Scar. We can see that the resolution is not one that could survive outside the narrative as a model for solving disputes, but that is precisely narrative's function – to resolve *symbolically* what cannot be *actually* resolved.

In a different example the conflict is resolved by the main character repudiating one side of the opposition and opting for the alternative. The problem for Roberta (Rosanna Arquette) in *Desperately Seeking Susan* (1985) is that she has a fascination for something she is not, for Susan (Madonna). The conflict between her life and Susan's could be represented as follows:

Roberta	Susan
conventional	unconventional
bourgeois	anti-bourgeois
suburban	urban
married	unmarried
sexually submissive	sexually aggressive
boring	exciting
constrained	free

The conflict is localized in Roberta's relationship with her bathroom-spa salesman husband, Gary. When she rejects him and his values in favour of a less secure but more exciting future, the opposition dissolves; it loses its ability to generate conflict. This film mounts an unusually strong attack on suburban marriage and will be the subject of a more detailed reading in Chapter 7.

The key idea here is that the oppositional conflict in narrative is not just a feature of narrative structure but is interwoven with the full range of meanings generated by the film as a whole. The binary structure produces not only the bald outline of a narrative but its specific images too; we see the specific opposition motivating key images in the film – Ethan framed between the desert and the homestead in *The Searchers*, Roberta wearing Susan's pyramid jacket in *Desperately Seeking Susan*. A pattern of opposition, once set up, produces both structure and discourse – the movement of the plot and the specific means of its representation in sound and image.

An alternative way of explaining the structure of narrative is to look at it as a process. Todorov (1977) sees narrative beginning in a stable point of equilibrium, or what he calls a state of 'plenitude' – when things are satisfactory, peaceful, calm, or recognizably normal. This equilibrium or plenitude is then disrupted by some power or force which results in a state of disequilibrium. This state can be resolved only through the action of a force directed against the disrupting force. The result is the restoration of equilibrium or plenitude. But, and so we see that the process is not entirely circular, the second stable point is not entirely the same as the first. Conversely, in some films the equilibrium at the end may be achieved through the recognition that we cannot change or affect the power of the disrupting force at the beginning. In the differences between beginning and end, we have the movement of narrative. Even in films such as *Terminator 2*, where the protagonist ends up almost exactly where he began, the state of equilibrium is radically changed by his having served the group which escapes through his self-sacrifice.

Todorov's explanation is usefully simple. It is easy to chart, particularly since most films allow their disruptions to occur near the beginning. *Scream* begins with the most graphic of the film's many murders, performed while the victim is talking to the murderer on the phone. While the characters in *Alien 3* (1992) take some time to realize that the alien is among them, the audience has been aware of this almost from the beginning. *Jaws* opens with a group of teenagers having a party on the beach (the moment of plenitude); two leave for a moonlight swim, the girl throwing off her clothes as she leads the way. Almost as soon as she is in the water, we meet the opposing 'force' of the shark, and she is attacked. The shark, and the commercial forces which collaborate in its disruption, continue to harass the community until opposed through the combination of Brody, Hooper, and Quint, and a variety of more or less useless machinery. The shark's eventual defeat is the product of chance, but the audience's relief helps to mask the fact that the attitudes which allowed swimmers on to the beaches, unwarned, still exist. The 'plenitude' restored is one that is marginally different in that the immediate threat (the shark) is gone and the police chief is vindicated, but its fragility is revealed by the promotional legend eventually employed in *Jaws II* (1978) – 'Just when you thought it was safe to go back into the water . . .'.

Narrative process could be represented diagrammatically like this:

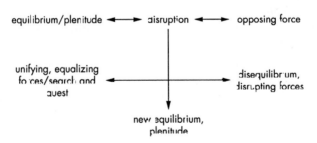

This process has an ideological dimension; that is, it carries a burden of social and cultural meanings which need analysis, and we will look at this in Chapter 6. For the moment, though, it is important simply to understand the fact that there is a common structural process in narrative which has a determining effect on what we see on cinema screens. Despite its immense variety and difference in forms, narrative is something we can describe. We need to consider now what differentiates one narrative from another.

Codes and conventions

When we want to deal with bodies of films, film movements, or even a single text, we need to look at the specific relations established between one film and the whole context in which it is viewed. This context will include other films as well as the full range of media constructions, advertising strategies, and so on, that frame the particular film. This is ultimately a social context. The satisfaction an audience finds in a film does not emerge from the narrative alone. At the simplest level, film narratives are viewed within a context that is both textual and social. From the social context, connections can be implied between a film and social movements – *Rambo* and Reaganism, for example – or between a film and contemporary events – *Jaws* as a Watergate film, *The Fly* (1986) as an AIDS allegory, or the remake of *The Quiet American* (2002) which implied strong parallels between Vietnam and the war in Iraq and was in fact embargoed from release by a cautious studio for some time after 9/11. As we shall see in Chapter 6, this can oversimplify the relationship between film and society.

For now, however, we need to be aware that the myths, beliefs, and practices preferred by a culture or group of cultures will find their way into those cultures' narratives where they can be reinforced, criticized, or simply reproduced. It is possible to apprehend social change through shifts in thematic or formal trends in narrative over time. For example, in the nineteenth-century novel, narrative closure was often provided through the use of marriage as a mechanism which symbolized the education of the character(s) and the final achievement of their lives. Usually this marriage indicated that all the problems within the relationship were now solved. This was not a direct reflection of social attitudes, of course. Whatever the existential reality of marriage in Victorian times (and there are plenty of accounts which reveal that the novels did not accurately depict, let alone reflect, a social fact), ideologically it was central to the society. Today, our films are unlikely to use marriage as such an uncomplicated mechanism for closure. Even in a film as conventional as *Bridget Jones's Diary* (2001) it is not marriage that provides closure, but a comic–romantic clinch that is promptly unravelled in the sequel. In a number of films during the late 1970s to the early 1990s, the abandonment of the marriage was presented for the same automatic approval from the audience as marriage once was. Roles identified with such actresses as Jill Clayburgh or Jane Fonda in the films *An Unmarried Woman* (1978) and *Nine to Five* (1980) represented marriage as a domestic trap which is limiting and boring, and even sexist. Many contemporary films, from the discomforting drama of *American Beauty* (1999) to the comedy star vehicle *The Banger Sisters* (2002), also depict marriage as a limiting and constricting institution. The meaning of marriage in Western societies, and thus its capacity to happily close off a narrative, has been altered by shifts in traditional attitudes to gender relations and in the ideologies which support them.

Again, this change is not reflected by film in any simple way, nor is the change evenly distributed. Indeed, the career of such a film as *Thelma and Louise* (1991) reveals deep unease, in the audience and the producers, about the female behaviour the film depicts. *Thelma and Louise* is reputed to have been screened to a preview audience to test two alternative endings: the existing one, and a more optimistic version in which Thelma and Louise escape. Apparently, the preview audiences opted for the 'harder' ending, where the women are emotionally supported by the freeze frame and the music track but narratively punished for their deeds by dying, presumably, on the floor of the Grand Canyon. Even this ending, however, provoked bitter media critiques for its alleged advocacy of 'female violence towards men' (*not* something we encounter in many Hollywood movies!). Given such reactions, it is hard not to see the

12 Susan Sarandon and Geena Davis: *Thelma and Louise*

reception of the film as enclosed within contemporary ambiguities and uncertainties about the kinds of power available to women in our society.

With *Thelma and Louise*, the problem was not so much the idea of women 'striking back', one suspects; rather it was the way in which it was handled that offended some critics. This highlights the fact that the social dimension of film narrative is not necessarily found at the deep structural levels explored by Todorov, Propp, or Lévi-Strauss. Rather, it occurs at the level of discourse – the ways in which the story is told, inflected, *represented*. This discursive level is also the location of cultural specificity – where we can differentiate the dominant discourses of one culture from those of another.

This is not to launch us into the hunt for cultural specificity in mainstream film. But it does alert us to the social influence on film, an influence which is most active in establishing the sets of codes and conventions which make communication possible. At the most elementary level we understand the societies depicted in films through our experience of our own society. As we watch a film and understand it, we look at gestures, listen to accents, or scan a style of dress, in order to place characters within a particular class, taste group, or subculture, for instance. And if the gestures, accents, and styles are not those of our society, we understand them through our experience of them in other films or by way of constructing analogies between the film's society and our own. All of these 'clues' are codes – systems by which signs are organized and accepted within a culture.

The dominance of Hollywood and its corporate successors has meant that film does not always exploit cultural differences as actively as some other forms of narrative. There is a high degree of cross-cultural coding where audiences agree to accept an imported system of meaning for the purposes of enjoying the film. So if audiences accept the gung-ho invocation of America that they find in many American films – from the *Lethal Weapon* series to more overt examples such as *Black Hawk Down* (2001) – this does not mean that they are being traitors to their own countries or necessarily accepting an American version of patriotism. It has become a way of coding the dominant filmic representation of certain definitions of duty, honour, and masculinity. An upper-class British accent linked with a certain style of dress and behaviour is coded to read 'comic Englishman' in many Hollywood films; in Britain, it is seen as a characteristically American view of the British. Even the coding of Hollywood, while accepted for the purposes of entertainment, will be subject to further definition and mediation by other cultures.

Narrative events can themselves become 'coded': in film we accept that a knock on the head can cause amnesia, and that a further knock can cure it. Such cases exemplify an even more complex and conscious system of coding communication and representation: that of conventions. Conventions are like codes, systems which we all agree to use. 'Manners' are conventional – a system of constraints on and expectations of behaviour that is aimed at organizing social interaction to particular ends. In the cinema, we have learned to use a wide range of conventions which organize the film and which greatly assist the film-maker and his or her attempt to communicate. At the simplest level, it is conventional for us to accept ellipsis in film – the omission of non-essential parts of the story in order to avoid matching screen time with real time. So when a character gets into a car in one shot, and in the next has arrived at his or her destination, we understand that this is a convention, a shorthand method for getting a character from A to B without wasting screen time. It is conventional that films are realistic only within certain unspoken limits: they do not try to imitate the full complexity of life if this would hold up the narrative unnecessarily. For example, characters going somewhere by car in a big city can usually find somewhere to park immediately – something we know is highly unlikely but which we agree to accept in order to continue the narrative. No one really wants a twenty-minute sequence showing the hero looking for a parking space. When we talk of popular films as 'realistic', then, we do not necessarily mean they are like 'real life'; we mean that we have in a sense agreed to respond to their codes and conventions – their established systems of narration – as if they *were* like real life.

The clearest example of a conventional narrative system was established within classical Hollywood cinema (Bordwell 1985). Even now, within most mainstream Hollywood productions, audiences expect to encounter a plot centred around a main character played by a star; driven by a consistent set of cause and effect relationships; employing a double-plot structure which links a heterosexual romance with another sphere of action (adventure, business, crime, for instance); and which uses the romantic clinch as the sign of narrative closure. Departures from such conventions within contemporary Hollywood cinema are usually seen as especially realistic and 'confronting' (*Silence of the Lambs*, 1991; *The Accused*, 1988), as especially 'arty' (*Being John Malkovich*, 1999), or as fantasy (*Pirates of the Caribbean*, 2003).

Conventions have built up around the representation of the female in films. Particularly in Hollywood film since the adoption of colour, the female is shot in a different way to her male counterpart. There is more emphasis on individual parts of the body, even to the extent of cropping out the head or face; more attention to the moulding produced by lighting; and a greater use of *mise-en-scène* for display. Hollywood film has turned the female form into a spectacle, an exhibit to be scanned and arguably possessed by the (male) viewer. Although the conventions of the 'halo' and the 'soft-focus' effects (achieved through veiling the camera or spreading vaseline on the lens) defy reality, they are widely accepted in representations of women. In films we are offered an impossible image of female beauty as the object of male (and even female) desire. This convention is no longer seen to be as 'natural' as it used to be. Laura Mulvey (1975) has argued that narrative film necessarily places all viewers (male and female) in the position of the male voyeur and that this is a direct result of narrative film's conventions rather than an incidental by-product.

Certainly, the male body has never been displayed in the same ways as the female body or to the same degree, although it is possible to argue that certain male stars today, such as Antonio Banderas, Brad Pitt, Nicholas Cage, or Bruce Willis exploit their bodies as spectacles. Miriam Hansen's work on Rudolf Valentino and the female audience for silent cinema (1994) demonstrates that this would not be the first time Hollywood exploited the male body as an object of the desire within its narratives. Yvonne Tasker's *Spectacular Bodies* (1993) talks of the increased visibility of the muscular male (and, also, female) bodies in contemporary Hollywood action films but it is still accepted that, in general, men are not usually employed as secondary characters who exist simply as spectacles of desire in the way that 'starlets' are still used in a typical James Bond film, for instance. Impossible images of femaleness can only exacerbate the already highly constructed view of women most Western men pursue. Conventions of representing the female in film are examples of the dialectic action of film upon society, in that the production of such images has made it more likely that further examples of such images will continue to be produced until the convention itself is overturned. This has been an object of concern to feminists and increasingly to cultural studies over many years, and rightly so.

The breaking down of such conventions relies upon audiences understanding that they are, in fact, conventions. That such an understanding is possible is an important reminder that all the parties involved – film-makers, audiences, critics – are very well aware of the working of conventions. Many films will themselves operate as a series of comments upon conventions – sometimes invoking a convention only to break it. In *Raiders of the Lost Ark* (1981) Indiana Jones is pursuing his abducted partner through a bazaar when he is suddenly confronted by a giant Arab wielding a scimitar. Up to this point, the film has shamelessly and self-consciously exploited every convention of the action adventure serial, milking every situation for its dramatic potential in order to offer as many 'thrills' as possible. In this scene, the Arab is grinning and chuckling in threat and challenge, and the crowd draws back in expectation of a battle. Similarly, the audience. We are given medium close-ups of the Arab, and he is a convincing threat. When we cut to Indiana Jones he looks irritated, preoccupied; he pulls out his revolver, shoots the Arab in the most offhanded of ways, and then resumes his search. The expected battle turns to burlesque as the conventional expectations of a fair fight to the death are comically overturned.

Raiders of the Lost Ark, of course, manages to have it both ways: while it sends up the conventions of action adventure movies at particular moments, it also works within them for the bulk of its narrative. Working against the conventions which frame the representation of women in film, however, is not nearly so easy. As we have already seen in relation to *Thelma and Louise*, these conventions have their social origin in how women are generally seen and valued within the community. The social construction of the feminine rules out most of the possibilities we might suggest as avenues for changing the representational conventions in film. For women to take on more power within the narrative (that is, becoming the one who drives the action forward) is to risk being seen as masculinized – the so-called 'phallic woman'. For women to resist acting as the object of male desire is also to reject most of the codes and conventions which structure them as attractive, sexual, beings. The trend towards the muscular heroine (Demi Moore in *GI Jane*, 1997, or Linda Hamilton in *Terminator 2*, for instance), exhibiting what Tasker calls 'musculinity' (1993: 3), can be seen as an erasure of the female body rather than a redesigning of its potential for power. It becomes, that is, masculine and powerful rather than feminine and powerful.

There are many examples, however, which would seem to indicate a shift in women's role within the Hollywood narrative system – which changes their meaning for male as well as for female viewers. Consequently, there is a growing critical literature dealing with the new, narratively powerful, Hollywood heroine (Creed 1993; Tasker 1993, 1998; Brunsdon 1997; Bruzzi 1997). Carol Clover (1992) has argued that low budget horror–slasher films relied upon a powerful feminine heroine for many years before a similar trend was discernible in mainstream popular films. In relation to these mainstream films, Sigourney Weaver's Ripley in the *Alien* trilogy is most often seen as naturally powerful and commanding, without becoming 'masculinized' or asexual. Geena Davis's Charley in *The Long Kiss Goodnight* (1996) explicitly deals with the apparent incompatibility between power and maternity. Frances McDormond's performance in the Coen brothers' *Fargo* (1996) broke most of the existing conventions: her character was unassuming and domestic, narratively powerful but not 'musculine', folksy rather than sexy or charismatic – and pregnant. It is not difficult, however, to find contradictory examples which demonstrate that conservative ideologies of gender remain in place. The negative side to the narratively active heroine is apparent in films which depict

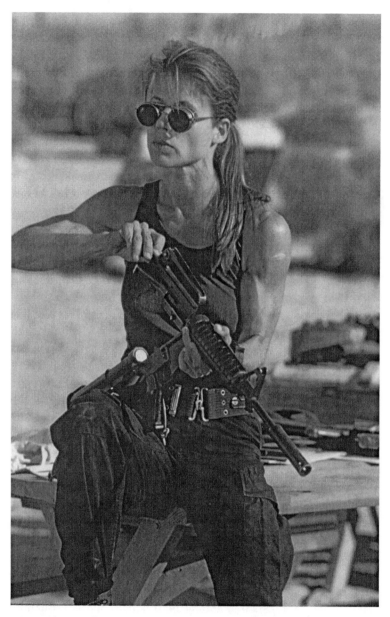

13 Linda Hamilton in *Terminator 2*: a sign of new constructions of female power?

female power as pathologically threatening: in *Fatal Attraction* (1987), *The Hand that Rocks the Cradle* (1992), *Single White Female* (1992), *Basic Instinct* (1992), and *Body of Evidence* (1993), the powerful, self-possessed woman is insane, obsessive, and needs to be destroyed. A slightly modified version of this can turn up even in more formulaic action spectaculars – such as Halle Berry's Ginger in *Swordfish* (2001). Despite such instances, however, it is certainly the case now that there is at least a competing set of minor conventions at work which problematize the traditional representation of women in the cinema; among the consequences, one might say, is Quentin Tarantino's celebration of Uma Thurman as a full-blown martial arts heroine in his *Kill Bill* movies.

Within popular film generally, of course, it is never easy to challenge or disregard existing conventions. Popular films need their shorthand, their accustomed routes, to operate effectively. Once accomplished, however, the breaking of a convention can itself become conventional. *The Searchers* is a film which follows the search for a lost child kidnapped by Indians. A familiar plot line in westerns, it has a surprise twist in *The Searchers*. When the child is found she does not want to return. This break in convention has spawned a number of movies which are, as Stuart Byron (1979) has pointed out, precisely similar to *The Searchers* in structure and in the key fact that the object of rescue does not wish to be rescued. A group of films from the 1970s – *Taxi Driver* (1976), *Close Encounters of the Third Kind* (1977), *Star Wars*, and *The Deer Hunter* (1978) – all use this convention. In another example, over the last two decades action films which involve an all-powerful killer of some kind – an alien or a particularly demented murderer – have given their villains a 'second wind'. Typically, after the villain has been dramatically and bloodily 'killed', the camera moves off to (usually) the threatened couple who comfort each other with the knowledge that it is all over. But, of course, it is not. The villain – often made even more repulsive by supposedly mortal wounds – returns for one last attack, a reprise performance of incremental mayhem, so that the hero or heroine must find yet another still more cataclysmic way to exterminate them properly. This became fashionable, particularly, in the mid-1980s and early 1990s: *Cape Fear*

(1991), *The Terminator* (1984), *Terminator 2* (1991), *Predator* (1987), *Dead Calm* (1989), and *Fatal Attraction* (1987) are just some of the films which come to mind as employing this strategy. Rather than surprising us, this convention is now so familiar that we have built it into our expectations, deliciously waiting for the surprise attack we know must eventuate and which is now signalled by the hero (and usually the heroine) turning his (or her) back on the apparently vanquished villain/monster/alien.

What we have been describing, then, is a dynamic system of conventions, rather than one that resists change. At its best, it works to give us a great deal of pleasure in our mastery of the conventions, and at its simplest it enables us to recognize what we see on the screen as pictures of reality. It is a system that makes possible the most interesting method of classifying films: that of genre, to which we turn next.

Genre

One of the ways in which we distinguish between different kinds of film narratives is through genre. Borrowed from literary studies, where it is used to delineate the difference between satire and comedy, tragedy and farce, and so on, the term 'genre' has become a useful tool in film analysis. In film, genre is a system of codes, conventions, and visual styles which enables an audience to determine rapidly and with some complexity the kind of narrative they are viewing. Even the musical accompaniment to the titles can indicate to an audience whether the film fits into broad generic categories like the comedy or the western. Finer discriminations develop as the film continues, involving the recognition of a visual style perhaps, or a recognizable set of moral and ideological values which will be inscribed into such genres as detective thrillers.

What genre does is recognize that the audience watches any one film within a context of other films, both those they have personally seen and those they have heard about or seen represented in other media outlets. This aspect of genre, *intertextuality*, polices the boundaries of an audience's expectations. It can tell them what to expect or it can deliberately mislead them by offering expectations that are not going to be met. In general, the function of genre is to make films comprehensible and more or less familiar. Even parodies or criticisms of a genre depend on the audience's recognition of and familiarity with the target. The choice of a black sheriff in the Mel Brooks spoof western *Blazing Saddles* (1974) is comic only if one is aware of how radical a departure this is from the conventions of the genre. Sometimes parodying of genre can be risky, however. Reviews of *Starship Troopers* (1997) suggested that its difficulty in reaching its audience was in part due to its slightly obscure relation to the genres of the space adventure and the teen romance; some audiences couldn't decide if it was a parody or just plain unconvincing.

A genre often includes specific narrative expectations – recurrent settings, set-piece sequences of action (the shoot-out, the car chase) – so that the task of resolving the film's conflicts can be deferred on to the genre. The western's final confrontation between opposing forces is almost ritually represented as a shoot-out. Through the management of the shoot-out (who wins and how) the film-maker 'closes' the film. Similarly, sci-fi films which routinely pit humans against machines lead to a resolution where human ingenuity (or some other dimension of specifically human behaviour) rather than brute force is used to defeat the machine's technical superiority. Generic conventions assist closure, confirming it as a textual force, and sharing some of the film's responsibility for articulating an individual resolution.

Genres depend on the audience's competences and experience: on the skills they have developed in understanding films and the body of similar experiences they can draw upon. Although many films fail because they are too predictable and too much bound by the limits of the genre, many others fail because they are simply not comprehensible. One of Francis Ford Coppola's few commercial disasters was *One from the Heart* (1982). Promoted with the tag line, 'When Francis Ford Coppola Makes a Love Story . . . Don't Expect Hearts and Flowers', it mixed genres unpredictably as well as moving frequently between fantasy and reality. As a result, and despite Coppola's reputation as a director (*The Godfather* (1972) and its sequel *The Godfather Part II* (1974) both won three Oscars and *Apocalypse Now!* (1979) won two Oscars), the film irritated and confused its audiences, who soon stopped coming. Films need to encourage expectations that they can satisfy; or if they fail to satisfy them there must be a plausible reason and a reward for the audience in the final denouement. A mystery thriller, for instance, will offer many possible resolutions to the problem it sets up as a way of misleading the audience until the appropriate moment to reveal the killer. Audiences accept this. As long as the real culprit is revealed in a satisfying and convincing manner, the audience can forgive the deception. But a film which arbitrarily ushers in a solution without the support of a generic convention or without foreshadowing is in danger of offending and irritating audiences. Contemporary viewers of Fritz Lang's *Metropolis* usually react in this way to the contrived ending of the film.

It is easy to make genre sound like a deterministic threat to creativity. It is true that all popular media, not just film, have to deal with the familiar and the conventional more than do, say, painting or poetry. The individual perception is not given the privileged place in the popular arts that it is in more elite forms like literature. Instead, there is a pleasure in the familiar, in recognizing conventions, and relishing their repetition and restatement. Nevertheless, there is innovation and originality in genre films, and the best examples can achieve a very complicated and delicate balance between the familiar and the original, repetition and innovation, predictability and unpredictability. Producers of popular film know that each genre film has to do two apparently conflicting things: to confirm the existing expectations of the genre, and to alter them slightly. It is the variation from the expectation, the innovation in how a familiar scenario is played, that offers the audience the pleasure of the recognition of the familiar, as well as the thrill of the new.

Genres are dynamic. They change. Christian Metz (1975) has argued that genres go through a typical cycle of changes during their lifetime. In his view, the genre evolves through a classic stage, to self-conscious parody of the classics, to a period where films contest the proposition that they are part of the genre, and finally to a critique of the genre itself. It is a little early in the history of film to be certain of such propositions but there is certainly evidence that

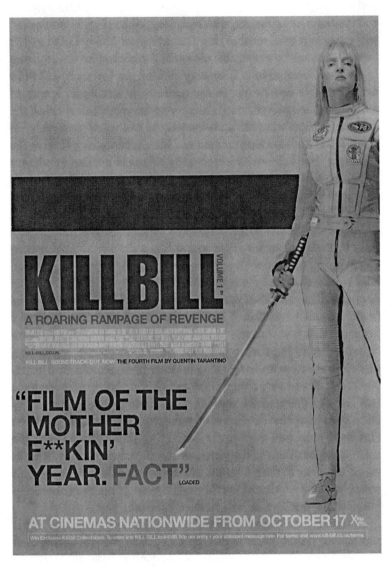

14 Genres and stars: the key elements in movie posters – *Kill Bill*

such a genre as the western has evolved and exhibited the kind of dynamism we are discussing.

In his *Six-Guns and Society* (1975), Wright examines the kind of cyclical development Metz argues is characteristic of film genres. He employs the combination of the methods of narrative analysis we have already met in this chapter: he uses the notion of myth associated with Lévi-Strauss, the use of oppositions as a means of describing narrative structure also developed by Lévi-Strauss, and describes a 'deep' narrative structure in the same terms as Vladimir Propp. Wright argues that the western genre goes through a thematic and approximately chronological change from what he calls the 'classic' western (*Shane* (1953), *Dodge City* (1930), *Canyon Passage* (1946), and *Duel in the Sun* (1947) are among his examples) to the 'transitional' western (*High Noon* (1952), *Broken Arrow* (1951)) and finally to the 'professional' western (*Rio Bravo* (1959), *The Professionals* (1966), *The Wild Bunch* (1969), and *Butch Cassidy and the Sundance Kid* (1970)). He acknowledges a further variation on the 'classic' western which he calls the 'vengeance' western and which includes films such as *Stagecoach* (1939) and *One-Eyed Jacks* (1960). The transition he describes reorients the hero in relation to his society, and reflects, according to Wright's analysis, social and political shifts in America over the period concerned. Briefly, the changes represent American society as inadequate, the heroes as more isolated, and all parties as less effective at resolving problems (in the professional western, death often resolves the narrative problem for heroes who are basically antisocial). The development is, Wright argues, not merely one internal to the film texts; there is clearly a broader social and political dimension involved as well.

Finally, to bring this discussion of genre to a close, it is important to emphasize that genre is the product of at least three groups of forces: the industry and its production practices; the audience and their expectations and competences; and the text in its contribution to the genre as a whole (see diagram on p. 124).

For the industry, there is often enormous market pressure to repeat successful versions of popular genres; hence the rash of sequels we are seeing these days. Within the industry, films are often conceived in terms of genre, marketed through their associations with other films within the genre, and produced with an eye on the conventional limits of the genre. *Romancing the Stone* (1984) was a film which, in a sense, was made possible by the success of *Raiders of the Lost Ark*, which itself allowed its audience to understand its genre by carefully referring to the serial adventure film throughout its length. Genre is one of the determinants of the audience's choice of a film, not only in terms of whether or not they possess the competences to appreciate that genre, but in terms of which kind of film it is they want to see, and whether the specific example of that general kind of film (say, a comedy) suits their taste – is it a teen comedy like *American Pie* (1999) or an adult romance like *Sleepless in Seattle* (1993)? Or, to pick up this last example, among the ways that *You've Got Mail* (1998) specified its audience was through repeating the pairing of Tom Hanks and Meg Ryan that had been so successful in *Sleepless in Seattle*. Finally, the film itself indicates how it is to be understood through its own signifying systems by its intertextual links with other films.

Chapter 5 will discuss the specific roles of the audience in greater detail but it is worth suggesting here that audiences make genres as much as film-makers do. Also, genre can be as much of a challenge to directors as a restriction on them. While it may tend to restrict audience hypotheses about a film to the 'how' rather than the 'what', it enables complex narratives to be told in a minimum of screen time, actually enhancing the capacity of the medium to deal with complex and sophisticated material. Its familiarity, on the other hand, offers the many of us who want it the pleasure of seeing the predictable happen in unpredictable ways.

Narrative and narration

Before leaving the subject of narrative, however, I need to acknowledge an alternative approach to those emanating from structuralism. Work within the cognitivist tradition, particularly *Narration in the Fiction Film* by David Bordwell (1985), shifts the focus onto the process of narration, proposing a much more active model of the film viewer. The use of the term 'viewer' is significant here. Rather than approach film through the idea of spectatorship, which implies a passive consumer unconsciously positioned by the film text, this group of theorists examines the active viewer consciously making sense of film texts. Some, such as Stephen Prince (1996), suggest that a great deal of this activity is available to us as empirical information. 'Questions about how people process, interpret, and respond to cinematic images and narratives', says Prince, are empirical questions 'or at least incorporate an empirical dimension which can be investigated by observing the behaviour of real viewers' (1996: 72).

Bordwell, more characteristically, insists on recognizing the importance of perception and cognition in understanding our relation to film texts. The cinema depends upon certain physiological characteristics of our 'visual system'. First, the retina's inability to follow rapidly changing light intensities and thus its tendency to view a light flickering very quickly (more than fifty flashes per second) as a steady one; second, the phenomenon known as 'apparent motion when the eye sees a string of displays as a single moving one' (1985: 32). In terms of cognition, Bordwell emphasizes the importance of prior knowledge and experience. This can involve what he calls *schemata*, organized clusters of knowledge which guide the hypotheses we make about the world, and the inferences we draw from what we experience. Schemata assist in all perceptual or cognitive processes, and, Bordwell argues, they play an important part in story comprehension as well.

When Bordwell moves into discussing the viewer's activity with film, he starts with the viewer's perceptual capacities, their prior knowledge and experience, and only then deals with the 'material and structure of the film itself' (1985: 33). Engaging with the film text, he operates in a distinctive manner, arguing that the narrative film is made so as to encourage the spectator to 'execute story-constructing activities'. It does this by presenting cues, patterns, and gaps that shape the viewer's application of schemata and the testing of hypotheses (1985: 33).

The usefulness of Bordwell's approach is demonstrated when he sets out to describe narration in the 'classical' Hollywood film. To give the flavour of this kind of approach, this is how it begins:

> The classical Hollywood film presents psychologically defined individuals who struggle to solve a clear-cut problem or to attain specific goals. In the course of this struggle, the characters enter into conflict with others or with external circumstances. The story ends with a decisive victory or defeat, a resolution of the problem and a clear achievement or non-achievement of the goals. The principal causal agency is thus the character, a discriminated individual endowed with a consistent batch of evident traits, qualities, and behaviors. Although the cinema inherits many conventions of portrayal from theater and literature, the character types of melodrama and popular fiction get fleshed out by the addition of unique motifs, habits or behavioral tics. In parallel fashion, the star system has as one of its functions the creation of a rough character prototype for each star which is then adjusted to the particular needs of the role. The most 'specified' character is usually the protagonist, who becomes the principal causal agent, the target of any narrational restriction, and the chief object of audience identification.
>
> (Bordwell 1985: 157)

While this may contain echoes of structural accounts, the elaboration of narrational strategies which follows produces quite different information and elicits different expectations of the audience's activity. While many of the strategies he deals with are straightforward representational techniques – the use of the wipe, or the flashback, for instance – others are characteristic, normative, methods of story construction. Bordwell, for instance, examines the importance of the principle of causality in the narrational construction, and the usefulness of the processes of 'retardation', the withholding or deferring of information essential to narrative development, which temporarily put the viewer's expectations and schemata to work against their gaining control of the story. Similarly, he shows how the structure of the individual scene moves through set phases: the expositionary phase which defines time and space; the middle section where characters pursue their goals; and the final section where closure is produced at the same time as aspects of the plot line lead directly to the next scene. It is a slightly taxonomic exercise, difficult to quote from or to compress, but the result is a very useful guide to the kinds of operations performed by film-makers and by audiences in their engagement with the film text. It is to the audiences we turn next.

Suggestions for further work

1   Apply Propp's categories to a popular genre film and see how closely (or not) they fit. This might be used to introduce a discussion of just how closely one should draw the analogy between folk narratives and film narratives.

2   Look at the opening of a narrative feature film for, say, ten minutes and see if you can map the central patterns of opposition. Then compare this map with the final resolution at the end of the film. Does this process tell you much about the film's structure?

3   I mentioned plot conventions in this chapter – the blow on the head which causes amnesia, for instance. How many other such conventions can you name? If it is difficult to do this, it is because the conventions have become so effectively naturalized that we are unconscious of them.

4   Further reading: David Bordwell's *Narration in the Fiction Film* (1985) and *Making Meaning* (1989) are both very useful books on narrative theory. Other, post-structuralist accounts include Seymour Chatman's *Story and Discourse* (1978) and Rimmon-Kenan's *Narrative Fiction* (1983). Gamman and Marshment (1988) and Penley's *Feminism and Film Theory*

(1988) are good collections of feminist critiques, dealing with the representation of women in Hollywood. A useful and accessible account of genre theory and of specific genres is Thomas Schatz's *Hollywood Genres* (1981), and a more recent account of Hollywood genres can be found in Steve Neale and Murray Smith (eds) *Contemporary Hollywood Cinema* (1998).

5   Examine a contemporary teen comedy or teen slasher–horror film and see if you can develop a list of generic codes and conventions that are activated within it – and perhaps even suggest to which films they refer.

Chapter 5

Film audiences

It is customary for our society to see the media, generally, as a group of technologies which are unusually blatant in their devotion to the delivery of profits to the few through the exploitation of the many. 'No one ever went broke underestimating the taste of the public,' as the cynical phrase goes, and this perception is most comprehensively applied to the major means of mass entertainment: film and television. In neither medium, however, is it simply true that audiences are at the mercy of a knowing and cynical group of entrepreneurs who churn out the latest money-spinner in the easy assurance of inevitable success. Fortunes are still spent and lost in making movies. The top-grossing twenty movies in any one year will be the survivors of a field numbering in the hundreds – from American producers alone. Even those movies which we might come to recognize as classics are not guaranteed to make money (*Citizen Kane*, usually held to be an American classic, lost money at the box office). Movies might be made by actors, directors, and producers, but they are ultimately made successful by audiences. Promotions of various kinds intervene in the process, but why one film will catch an audience's imagination while another will not is still a mystery to the industry, to audiences, and to theorists alike. Nevertheless, film is, as Christian Metz (1982: 92) put it, 'our product, the product of the society which consumes it'. It is impossible to talk about film as a social practice without talking about its audiences.

Admittedly, film audiences are not what they were. As we saw in Chapter 1, no longer is it the case that a family sees an average of one film a week, or that the same family finds most of the material available suitable for every one of its members, no matter what their age or tastes. After the major decline in movie attendances that just preceded the spread of television in the late 1940s, a number of trends emerged over the latter decades of the twentieth century which signalled a major shift in the constitution of the cinema audience. First, as we noticed in Chapter 1, cinema audiences got younger. The majority of those who attend movies in the USA, the UK, and Australia (the three markets into which I have enquired, but the trends will be replicated elsewhere) are between 12 and 24 years of age. It is in this age group where knowledge of the latest movies, their stars, technologies and other details is of most social, cultural or subcultural significance. This dimension has gained in importance over the last decade or so as a result of the increasing amount of media content devoted to celebrity gossip – much of which, of course, involves those who work in the film industry.

Second, cinema audiences have fragmented, becoming more difficult to address and secure. Although one age group may dominate the potential 'mass' audience for films, it is important for the big event movies to also attract those smaller segments of the market. In most cases, these smaller segments need to be addressed directly by the marketing strategies employed, if they are going to be coaxed into the cinema. An example would be the multiple segments which go to make up the audience for *The Lord of the Rings* films – from the original fans of the novels (that is, nerdy and literary types) to those hard-core fans of film spectaculars who relate to them as a special effects-fest and to whom the novels are irrelevant (or, perhaps, even unknown). Each film must build its own market by recognizing the need to address the various segments to which it might appeal. The industry has had to adapt to the fact that it is only among teenagers that going to the cinema has retained something of its ritual status. There are, it is true, some segments of the market where the ritual has survived – the 'art-house' buffs, for instance – but, importantly, in this case it is almost because it explicitly *excludes* mainstream mass-market movies from its agenda. In general, the modern audience has developed very specific requirements for the films it chooses and it is unlikely to return to the habit of going to the movies regardless of the title showing.

While we might know such things, it is important to stress that the relationship between the industry and its audience is sufficiently complex to make it impossible to determine precisely how changes in audience taste engender changes in production decisions – or the reverse. (As we saw in the discussion of genre in the preceding chapter, there are more than two variables to consider here.) However, we can say that the change in audience demographics – the concentration on the teenage and young-adult groups, and the fluctuation in overall attendances – has closely coincided with changes in the dominant genres of films being produced.

The segmentation of the market has had some contradictory effects. While it has encouraged the industry to invest heavily in those films which do address the mass market, as we have seen, the size of the investment required has also made such films extremely risky to make. As a result, relatively few blockbusters get made. The release of those that are made tends to be compressed into key periods when a saturation campaign is most likely to maximize the box-office returns: holiday periods, such as the long summer break, or Christmas. (These key periods vary according to which hemisphere one is in: Christmas is *the* peak period in Australia as it coincides with summer and the long school holiday, whereas in the US it is the summer break in July and August.) Industry strategies during the 1990s did seem to focus on the smaller, highly targeted movie: organized around a tightly defined genre, a particular star or director, or around a topical selling point (examples include *The Full Monty*, *Chasing Amy* (1997), *Shine* (1996), and *JFK* (1991)). Indeed, many argued these had become the staple for the industry during this decade. That pattern has declined significantly in the last few years and the hegemony of the special effects blockbuster has become more entrenched.

All of this would seem to indicate a shrinking market and a decline in the richness and variety of films now available to the cinema audience – something that has been a concern in the entertainment press over the first years of the twenty-first century. In that context, then, it is important to emphasize that the nature of the cinema experience can vary. The audiences for *The Rocky Horror Picture Show* (1975) are now noted for turning up dressed in character, and participating in the screening/performance of the film by singing along, dancing in the aisles, or even climbing on to the stage in front of the screen. Some cinemas have taken the film on as a regular ritual, screening at midnight on Fridays to a devoted cult audience. Spectators participate not only in the narrative, but in its construction: they scream 'Cut', and 'Close-up', at the appropriate moments. At such occasions, film becomes, more obviously than usual, a performance medium. The ritual quality in film-viewing is generally exposed when audiences see the same film repeatedly – a practice which is relatively common despite the standard theoretical

IT'S SHOCK, HORROR!

By TONY WRIGHT

THE queen of the cult movies, "The Rocky Horror Picture Show", will make a re-appearance in Albury on Sunday night

The decidely weird monster-musical has been around for years, but has retained a bizarre fascination

The movie has been showing continuously in New York and London cinemas since its release six years ago.

Even in staid old Brisbane, "Rocky Horror" has been showing several times daily since July 1976.

The movie grew out of a stage show that became a cult after its debut in a dingy theatre in the low-rent area of Kings Rd, London.

"Rocky Horror" is a pop romp through a tasteless, tacky high-camp tale of transexuality set in a mad castle inhabited by Frank N Furter, pictured.

It is spiced with catchy tunes and outrageous scenes.

But the most extraordinary thing about a visit to a cinema screening the movie is the audience.

The crowd tends to throw itself into the task of becoming part of the film.

With gay abandon, so to speak, true "Rocky Horror" freaks dress up in fishnet stockings and suspender belts, sing along with tunes, throw popcorn, yell advice to the characters on the screen, hiss the baddies, cheer the goodies and generally make whoopee.

The Albury Cinema Centre, which is screening "Rocky Horror" on Sunday night, could be in for a shock.

Weird rocky cult takes over city

15 *The Rocky Horror Picture Show*

assumptions that a film is made to be understood at one viewing. David Lynch's *Wild at Heart* (1990), for instance, often turns up as a midnight screening for regular fans. We are finding that one of the consequences of the increased importance of special effects in contemporary cinema is to also increase the performative dimension of the spectacle on the screen. For the return audience, the sense of power and familiarity is strong: no longer do they wait for the narrative to unfold but they confidently collaborate in its gradual development. This aspect of film – its ritual, performative quality – is often ignored by film scholarship but it is invoked every time someone says to us in a darkened cinema: 'Here it comes, watch this bit!'

Specifying the audience

Contrary to popular wisdom, large audiences are not gulled into attending films by distorting or misleading advertising campaigns. Producers often refer to a film 'finding its audience', and this is a more accurate description of what actually happens. A film needs to specify its audience, not only in its text but also in its advertising campaign; in the series of interviews and promotional performances that may surround it; in the selection of exhibition venues (if there is a choice); even in the selection of the distribution company (again, if there is a choice). It is up to the producers and distributors to agree on how they wish to specify the audiences (or represent the film), and in many cases bad judgements are made. The Australian film, *The Chant of Jimmie Blacksmith* (1978), was a sympathetic and thoughtful study of the plight of a half-caste in rural Australia, as well as a narrative around a true incident involving the mass murder of white settlers by three Aborigines. In the advertising campaign, emphasis was placed on the latter aspect – the logo featured an axe dripping blood – and links were thus constructed with horror films rather than with social-problem films. Already potentially marginal because of its racial subject, it did not 'find its audience' in Australia. One of the reasons given for the box-office failure of the recent blockbuster *Alexander* (2004) is the advance publicity's emphasis on its depiction of a homosexual relationship. Largely a sidebar to the film's primary focus, this has been seen in retrospect as a turn-off for an audience more interested in an uncomplicated adventure spectacular.

I referred earlier to Jon Lewis's distinction (2003) between 'marketable' and 'playable' films. He argues that the industry has become dependent upon films for which a strong marketing campaign can be developed on the basis of their stars, effects, or core concepts – rather than upon those films which audiences will actually find they enjoy (the 'playable' ones). What Lewis is trying to highlight here is the emphasis upon pulling people into the cinema early in the movie's run, rather than trying to make a film that audiences will enjoy and recommend to their friends, thus allowing the box office to build over a period of weeks. As we have seen, this reflects the currently dominant commercial strategy of maximizing the first weekend's box office. The danger of that strategy is that no amount of advertising will continue to pull people into a film they do not find they enjoy and there can be a dramatic drop-off in audiences even after a highly successful first weekend. The history of Hollywood is full of films which cost fortunes, which were expensively promoted, and which lost millions at the box office. *Heaven's Gate* (1980) is a film which many now have heard of simply because it was such a box-office disaster; few have ever seen it. What this highlights is the simple fact that film producers experience great difficulty in predicting how audiences will react to each new production – and in convincing their backers to support any prediction they might eventually make. All they can do is try to specify as carefully as possible just whom this film is going to be for, and then try to ensure – through the release patterns and promotional campaigns – that this audience is reached.

Speaking of classical Hollywood cinema, John Ellis (1982) has said that there were two main ways in which its narrative images could be deployed to specify audiences: through the genre and through the stars. Although the audiences thus 'specified' are perhaps more specific today, this is still largely the case. Audiences choose movies through their representations in the press and on television, and through conversations and other social contacts. These representations are understood in terms of genre – or stars, where they are

16 Publicity still from *Star Wars – Episode III: Revenge of the Sith*

not already enclosed by genre. There is, perhaps, a third set of determinants: the broad cultural context in which the audience and the film are situated. The notion of genre was dealt with in the preceding chapter, so I will concentrate on the latter two categories here.

As suggested in the opening chapter, the context in which any film is released is constituted by a limitless number of components. There are the promotional and 'tied-in' productions – music videos, advertisements, hit songs, merchandise such as t-shirts, interviews, magazine stories, reviews, fan magazine items, and many more. In addition, we might find that particular genres or particular stars have themselves a cultural or subcultural status that is important. There can be other factors as well: the popularity of video and computer games, for instance, has provided a stylistic context and a fan-base for films as different as *Lara Croft* (2001) and *The Matrix* (1999). Attendance at a film can become a statement of membership of a subculture; certainly the cult around *The Rocky Horror Picture Show* supports this.

There are many contextual factors, of course, which are beyond the control of the films' producers. Some films become accidentally newsworthy, or topical, at the time of release. Alan Parker's *Angel Heart* (1987) acquired useful pre-publicity on the basis of an explicit sex scene involving Lisa Bonet, who was then the 18-year-old star of the wholesome American TV family sitcom *The Cosby Show*. (The example reveals how interwoven and comprehensive our cultural networks are.) As a result of the controversy, the film was at least initially constructed as 'explicit' (a small genre in itself) and had a recognizable name even before release. The on-screen depiction of sexual activity has been a favourite means of generating news stories about films before they are released, in fact, and has been one of the means through which European cinema has managed to make itself noticed in Anglophone cultures. In recent years, the depiction of 'actual' (that is, non-simulated) sex in a small number of feature films has also become something of a public controversy with, presumably, positive effects on the box office for the films concerned. However, there are also many instances where such publicity has attracted the 'wrong' audience for the film, resulting in its failure. Those attending Frederic Fonteyne's film *A Pornographic Affair*

(2000), for instance, expecting it to live up to its title would have been extremely disappointed.

In some cases, the context in which a film is released is markedly different from that when it was made. A case in point is Susan Seidelman's casting of Madonna in *Desperately Seeking Susan*. In the period between casting and release, from being a virtual unknown Madonna became an international star. On the one hand, this had the effect of specifying a large, possibly inappropriate audience – Madonna fans. On the other hand, it became very hard for this clever and interesting film not to be seen as an opportunistic star vehicle by some of its critics, or to be ignored by potential audiences who had a less than high regard for Madonna as a pop singer and, especially, as a politically regressive signifier of female sexuality. For what could be seen as a feminist film, this was a critical rather than a commercial problem. Similarly, when films are replayed on TV well after their original run, they may seem entirely different. When Jennifer Lopez co-starred with George Clooney in Stephen Soderberg's *Out of Sight* (1998), she was not fully established as either a singer or an actor; her characterization for the first-run cinema audience, then, was free of many of the contextual complications that would now be available to those who watch it on TV. Furthermore, while her personal following was probably not a major consideration in attracting audiences to the cinema, her subsequent celebrity is very likely to – perhaps inappropriately – influence the audience's decision to watch the film on TV.

The cultural context can be a factor, then, in determining whether or not the film and its audience 'find' each other. However, overwhelmingly, most choices are determined by issues that are essentially generic (as we shall see in Chapter 7, even the problem with *Desperately Seeking Susan* was an argument about genre) or essentially to do with the role of the stars. It is to the cultural function of the star that we turn next.

Stars

It is unexceptional to make the point that film stars are implicated in the film-goers' choice of movie. However, the work of Richard Dyer and others on the 'meaning' of the star has deepened our understanding of just what this process involves. In his book *Stars* (1979), Dyer makes the point that the construction of a star's image within the culture incorporates representations of him or her across an enormous range of media and contexts: fan magazines as well as the mainstream press, TV items and profiles, as well as performances in films, conversations, and hearsay, and personal appearances. The importance of noting this is that the star in a film has a signifying function which may be separate or different from the written character within the film script. Stars are 'signs', not necessarily or entirely subsumed within the character they are asked to play. Since one can conceptualize a star's total image (as distinct from the particular character that he or she plays in a film), the casting of a particular actor has important repercussions on the effect the characterization will have. The casting of John Wayne, for example, was always determined by what *he* signified, the inscription of a particular version of Americanism. His later roles (in *The Shootist* (1976) or *True Grit* (1969)) were self-reflexive in that they commented upon this signifying function by parodying it or self-consciously mythologizing it. (Interestingly, it was only at this point that he was complimented for his acting; only then could we see daylight between the star and the role.)

If we are to consider the meaning of a film we need to dispense with literature-based notions of character as a receptacle into which the star disappears. We need to take account of the meaning of the film's stars and the way those meanings contribute to characterization. Jane Fonda began her career as a sex symbol in the films *La Ronde* (1964) and *Barbarella* (1968) but gradually modified the kinds of characters she played. By altering the nature of the characterizations or representations to which she lent herself, she altered her own meaning to the point where she could play the tortured Bree Daniels in *Klute* (1971). It is important to note, though, that Fonda's meanings were also shaped by activities off-screen, in particular her opposition to the American participation in the war in Vietnam. While these activities would not have informed audiences' readings of her performance in her earlier films, it is easy to see how they might inform an audience's interpretation of her characterization in *The China Syndrome* (1979), where she played an intrepid reporter investigating a nuclear-plant malfunction.

Dyer reveals just how much work the audience (as well as the film-maker) must accomplish in constructing character in films. So much of what constitutes a major character is *already* there to be appropriated to the film's meaning by the audience, and by the film-maker in the act of casting. Casting can be the most important act in the film-maker's construction of a character, since a well-judged piece of casting can mobilize all the meanings carried by a particular star and inject them into the representation of the character on the screen. If we cast Brad Pitt, we do not have to persuade the audience that the character is attractive to women; if we cast Woody Allen, we might have to demonstrate that. (Alternatively, we might have a lot of work to do in any script that cast Brad Pitt to play a neurotic, garrulous, New York intellectual.) Casting Julia Roberts as the repressed and dowdy sister to Catherine Zeta-Jones's selfish diva in *America's Sweethearts* (2001) meant that we spent most of the film waiting for her inevitable emergence as an object of romantic desire. As we track the audience's relationship to a film through the star, we track not only a set of identifications with a star, but a set of meanings already encoded into that star's representation on the screen. Assumptions about the nature of film characterization – as one-dimensional or 'flat' for instance – need to be interrogated by way of an acknowledgement that the face of the star is part of film characterization, too. Often the power of the star to carry contributory meanings relieves the script of the burden of constructing a complex character. The complexity can be achieved visually through the casting of the appropriate performer. Even in apparently light, comedic material, we can see this in action. The casting of Robert De Niro, with his history of playing gangsters, murderers, and other seriously dangerous characters, gave a comic plausibility to his character's secret existence as a closet CIA agent in *Meet the Parents* (2000) and the sequel *Meet the Fockers* (2004).

A further aspect of Dyer's work deals with the wider social meanings of stars. Stars are constructed in contradictory ways that emphasize their typicality *and* their individuality. For the star to attract an audience there must be some representativeness, some apparently recognizable element which audience members can use to link the star with themselves. Mel Gibson spent much of his youth in Australia and commenced his film career there. In films such as *Gallipoli*, and in his public persona, Australian audiences regarded Gibson as a positive representation of the typical Australian male. Yet for him to become a star (both in Australia and internationally) he has had to transcend that representative Australian-ness and generate a richness and individuality. Star status can itself invest the ordinary with mythic status – James Stewart made a career out of depicting the ordinary individual who, blessed only with determination, had the power to affect society. Star status carries with it the potential to individualize and particularize even the most general of social types. Dyer talks of stars 'transcending' their type by being, paradoxically, both representative and unique – both life-like and larger than life. Clearly there are limits to this effect if a film is to be understood, but it does mean that a character which may seem 'flat' in the script can be made 'round' when portrayed by the particularly signifying actor.

The final point to be made about the ways in which an audience will understand the role of the star refers to the social and ideological meanings that he or she carries. Since stars are iconic representations of recognizable social types, they are composed within the field of the dominant and competing definitions of society. Dyer says that one of the types embodied by the star is that of 'the type of the individual himself': he or she embodies 'that particular conception of what it is to be human that characterises our culture' (1979: 111). The depth of affection certain stars excite in their audiences is related to their personal signification as a national type. It could be argued that Hugh Grant has become a signifier of an appealing model of Britishness, for instance. This function of the star is ultimately ideological and is implicated in the relationship between film and the idea of the nation which is taken up in Chapter 6.

Before leaving this topic, it is worth demonstrating the kind of information such an approach produces. Dyer's *Heavenly Bodies* (1986) examines three major Hollywood stars in order to show what they meant to their audiences. His treatment of Paul Robeson, Marilyn Monroe, and Judy Garland reveals both the ways in which the star enacts or mobilizes dominant ideas (of, for instance, sexuality in Monroe's case), and also the ways in which a star can be taken up by sections of the community and given specialized meanings: the gay community's adoption of Judy Garland shows how subcultures can 'make over' even the most mainstream of images to their own use.

In his analysis of Marilyn Monroe, Dyer tries to explain how she came to be *the* sex symbol, probably for all time. First, he makes connections between broader social movements during the 1950s, when Monroe was at the peak of her popularity, and the particular meanings she carried as a star. Sexuality itself, he argues, was an issue at the time:

> [sex] was seen as perhaps the most important thing in life in fifties America. Certain publishing events suggest this: the two Kinsey reports (on men, 1948; on women, 1953), the first issues of *Confidential* in 1951 and *Playboy* in 1953, both to gain very rapidly in circulation; best-selling novels such as *From Here to Eternity* (1951), *A House is Not a Home* (1953) . . . *Peyton Place* (1956) . . . not to mention the thrillers of Mickey Spillane. Betty Friedan, in *The Feminine Mystique*, quotes a survey of Albert Ellis, published in *The Folklore of Sex* in 1961, which shows that 'in American media there were more than 2.5 times as many references to sex in 1960 as in 1950'.
> (Dyer 1986: 24–5)

Dyer does not see Monroe's popularity, or her specific meaning as a sex symbol, as a simple reflection of such trends, however. In fact, he moves away from this kind of broad social analysis and turns to an examination of the 1950s' 'discourses' of sexuality, discourses which are employed in the construction of her meaning as a star. Dyer defines this use of the term 'discourse' as referring to those 'clusters of ideas, notions, feelings, images, attitudes and assumptions that, taken together, make up distinctive ways of thinking and feeling about things, of making a particular sense of the world' (1986: 19). He connects the ways the 1950s had of making 'a particular sense' of sex with the signification of Marilyn Monroe on the screen and in her wider public image as a star.

In Dyer's account, 1950s' America had discovered sexuality as *the* key to the self, and as the central aspect of adult life. Certainly, sexuality assumes a new cultural prominence. For example, with the decline of the family film and the rise of the adult film in response to TV's capture of the family audience, mainstream cinema became more 'daring' and 'explicit' in its treatment of sex. The arrival of *Playboy* is a convenient marker of this new interest in sexuality, and Monroe is herself closely connected with the new magazine as she featured in its first nude centrefold. This created something of a scandal, even though the photo used was from a calendar that Monroe had posed for well before she became a star. Monroe is more than an illustration to *Playboy*, however; according to Dyer, Monroe's image enacted 'as no one else was doing at the time, the particular definitions of sexuality which *Playboy* was proselytising' (1986: 28). These definitions were produced through discourses which represent sexuality as natural, guilt-free, non-exploitative, and as somehow connected with psychological health.

Dyer goes into this at some length (pp. 27–42), but a summary of part of his argument will be sufficient to demonstrate its value. He refers to the scandal over the nude centrefold as a point where Monroe's meaning is clearly available for inspection. When Monroe was challenged by the media about the nude picture (unheard of for a major star at the time), she refused to accept any guilt. 'I've done nothing wrong,' she said, and when asked by reporters what she had on when the photo was taken, replied, 'I had the radio on.' As Dyer says, this is a 'classic dumb-blonde one-liner' which 'implies a refusal or inability to answer the question at the level of prurience at which it was asked'. As Dyer continues to argue, this guiltlessness, naturalness, and the absence of prurience in her attitude to sex, is tied in precisely with the *Playboy* philosophy. *Playboy* represented its sexual discourses as progressive, attacking rigid, bourgeois, and hypocritical sexual values, and recognizing the 'naturalness' of the sex drive. Sexuality was thus disconnected from the sinful temptress image of, say, the heroines of *films noir*, such as Barbara Stanwyck or Joan Crawford, and in its place came a sexually desirable but unthreatening 'natural' sensualist: Marilyn Monroe. Even the apparent dumbness of the 'dumb blonde' was a sign of the natural: if she was 'untouched by the rationality of the world', she was also untouched by its corruption. In Monroe a linkage is established between sexuality and innocence, and this linkage – perhaps more than any other – explains her dramatic power as a popular image.

Dyer does not stop here (although we will). He investigates the meaning of blondeness, of the conventional open-mouthed poses for photo sessions, and of the way in which Monroe was incorporated into popular conceptions of psychology and psychoanalysis of the time. The ambiguity of her image for feminists – an image used to subject women and a person who was herself exploited – is also dealt with. The real value of Dyer's analysis, though, is that it demonstrates how much of the meaning of a film is brought into the cinema *with* its audience and, conversely, the cultural power of the meanings generated by the movies.

The resonance of Dyer's work on film stars has been evident in the related development of the analysis of a broader category of public figure, the celebrity (Marshall 1997; Rojek 2001; Turner 2004). It is now more common to locate a discussion of film stars within this broader context, that of the contemporary proliferation of celebrity across the media. However, among the definitive characteristics of the celebrity is the fact that the primary focus of media interest is on their private lives, rather than on their work or their particular professional achievements. While this is certainly part of how film stars are now celebrated within the media, it is also the case that they are continually producing a body of work which itself contributes incrementally to their public meanings and significance – something which is not true of all forms of celebrity. There is, still, a point in distinguishing between the mode of public visibility the film star acquires, as well as their direct participation in the production of the meanings and pleasures of film texts, and that which is acquired by the media celebrity in general.

17 The ultimate star image: Marylin Monroe

The film experience

Discussion of the relationship between the audience and what it sees on the screen inevitably leads us to re-examine just what it is that constitutes the experience of going to the cinema. In order to differentiate film from television, theorists as well as the industry have talked of film-going as an 'event'. The act of 'going out' is itself intrinsic to the event of cinema-going. The pleasures of the evening are not exhausted by the experience of watching the film, and cinema-going is most often a group activity – rarely do people go to the cinema by themselves. A sense of release and separation from the world is provided even by films which we do not much like. The charge of escapism which is often levelled at film is probably based on the sense of separation from reality, which is highlighted as we leave the cinema, as much as on a close analysis of the content of the majority of films – and indeed, Jackie Stacey (1994) has recovered the notion of 'escape' as a positive term through which to describe the cinema experience.

The specific characteristics of the film experience have provoked a great deal of analysis. We sit in the dark, within a group but still separated from them by the fact that they are not easily visible; we watch realistic images which are nevertheless vastly oversized representations of the real; we sit in comfortable seats, our attention focused on the screen and with no competitors for that attention. The avidity of our gaze is inevitable: the physical structure of the theatre itself implies the strength of the audience's desire to consume the sounds and images which will be projected in front of them. Sociologists such as Andrew Tudor (1974) have argued that the intensity of the image–sound message, the comfort of the viewer, and the heightened sense of occasion, all make the viewer more susceptible to the power of the message. High-culture critics of popular culture have employed this avenue of attack to raise worries about the psychological effects (or, more accurately, the ideological effects) of the medium.

There is certainly an intense vicarious involvement offered to the cinema-goer. Further, that the medium is one of representation rather than an unmediated perception of the real is deliberately buried and effaced by the mechanisms of the medium. Early Cinerama sold itself by its ability to appear to replicate as closely as possible our experience of the real world and then amplify it – to make it *more than real*. The Cinerama rendition of the roller-coaster ride replicated our perceptions of the actual experience so precisely that viewers would feel sick; it created the sensation of speed in the audience as palpably as if they were on the roller-coaster rather than in the theatre. At such moments, the apparatus of the cinema disappears; any thought of mediation is banished by the fact that one's body is telling one that this is *really* happening. The Cinerama image is only an image, but we react to it as if it were more than that.

This blurring of the boundaries between the imaginary and the real is at the heart of the cinema experience. Representation is experienced as perception. Metz (1982) has called the filmed image 'the imaginary signified', referring to the fact that the reality which the filmed images call up is always absent, 'present' only in our imaginations. This recognition has led researchers to examine the similarities between viewing a film and an analogous condition, dreaming. The analogy is very close in some aspects. Dreams don't 'really' happen although we might experience them as if they did; contradictorily, even though the *content* of the dream may not have happened, the *dream experience itself* did. Like films, dreams have the capacity to express thought through images; they also have a tendency towards narrative (even generic) structures, and give the effect of seeming more than real. Jean-Louis Baudry (1974) sees film producing, through the darkness of the theatre, the spectator's relative passivity, and, through the hypnotic effect of flickering light and shadows, what he calls an artificially regressive state. This condition mimics that of dreaming. According to Baudry, cinema, like dreaming, is regressive in that it calls up the unconscious processes of the mind and favours what Freud calls the pleasure principle over the reality principle. Without going into Freudian theories of the structure of the personality, this implies a slip back into the childish, immature version of the self where our wants and desires (the forces behind the pleasure principle) dominate our personalities at the expense of contextual, ethical, and social considerations (the reality principle). In such a formulation, film is dangerous, and this view has been used to support anxiety about whether it is healthy to expose children to the medium.

There is a large literature on these aspects of audience involvement with the image. Metz argues that film narrative itself possesses some of the characteristics of dreams, and that it is dealt with by its audiences in similar, if unconscious, ways. The dream analogy can be a useful one, although it is limited – for one thing – by the fact that films are not only images; they are also sound. Further, the process of decoding film languages is as much conscious and social as it is unconscious and presocial. Indeed, those who draw upon cognitive psychology to explain the nature of the film experience claim that current film theory has underestimated the importance of the spectator's conscious and 'pre-conscious' work (Bordwell 1985: 30). However, there are issues raised by Metz, in particular, which have been followed up.

Metz (1982: 92) says that when he is in the cinema as a member of the audience, he 'watches' and he 'helps'. The cinema audience watches because the image is itself seductive, larger than life, an object of desire. The audience thus concentrates on looking. But the structure of film narrative is such that its meaning has to be actively constructed by the viewers as they watch. The term 'suture' (Dayan 1974), for instance, explains how each shot in a film is continually involved in constructing the relationships which will help the film make sense – relationships between one shot and the next, one sequence and its adjacent sequences, and so on. Because the meaning of one shot is deferred until we see how it is 'fixed' (or stitched together – 'sutured') by its relation to the following shot, cinema is able to hide its method of constructing itself. This deferral of meaning, the closing of gaps by the viewers, means that they drive the narrative forward in order to understand what they have seen. Viewers are diverted from examining the means of construction by concentrating on the meaning.

Film viewers do not know all they need to know until the film ends. This exacerbates the pressure towards completion, towards mastery of the narrative – 'helping'. This mastery is of course always promised and usually delivered since the ending is usually the point at which the film makes sense. But there is a deep contradiction that again reminds one of dreaming, in that spectators are drawn between, on the one hand, their desire for the image, their luxuriating in this amplification of the real and its celebration of the power of their gaze; and, on the other hand, their desire for domination of the narrative, for their achievement of mastery. The result is that we both want the film to end – to gain knowledge of it – and wish that it would continue to offer its objects of desire. Ellis (1982: 81) puts it this way:

> Entertainment cinema offers the possibility of seeing events and comprehending them from a position of separation and mastery. The film is offered to the spectator, but the spectator does not have anything to offer the film apart from the desire to see and hear. Hence the spectator's position is one of power, specifically the power to understand events rather than to change them. This is the position of mastery that can shade into fascination, into the fetishistic desire to abolish the very distance and separation that makes the process of seeing possible.

As he says, the audience desires to 'enter' the film, to disrupt even the minimal boundaries which divide the imaginary and the real in the cinema. This occurs at an unconscious level, and underlines just how essential it is to have some understanding of the unconscious process of watching a film. We need to introduce some of the uses made of psychoanalysis to explain this process.

The film spectator and psychoanalysis

Film theory has had a great interest in psychoanalysis. Of course, psychoanalysis is highly interested in dreams, and the analogies between film and dreams make Freudian theories of the operation of the unconscious an inevitable avenue for researchers to explore. The nature of film's fascination – its collapsing of the boundaries of the real – is a further invitation to psychoanalysis. If Freud held that the gap between the real and the imaginary (what we see and what we might imagine for ourselves) was the location of desire, then film plays across that gap. What most of the responses to these issues have produced is a series of theories about the processes through which the audience identify with what they see on the screen. These processes are seen to be analogous to the ways in which the audience members construct their own identities within society.

Psychoanalytic theory has emphasized the importance of the 'look', the gaze of the audience. This is reflected in its references to the audience as 'the spectator'. The power of the individual's look is important within Freudian and post-Freudian theory since it is part of the individual's self-definition and relationship to his or her environment. So audiences 'look', and they also 'spectate'. Audiences are 'separated' from the film because it represents actions which are going on for their benefit, but as if they were not there. However, as agents for understanding the film, and as observers who can see but not be seen, they are in a position of considerable power. Freudian theory describes such a position as that of the voyeur, who 'makes an object of' those caught unwittingly in the power of his gaze. The voyeuristic look is one of the pleasures an audience finds in the cinema.

This may not be entirely accurate, as we shall see, because our voyeur knows that while the actors may not be present they *do* know that they are to be watched. So they exhibit themselves to the spectator rather than unwittingly reveal themselves. A passage from Christian Metz outlines just how complicated this relationship is:

> The cinema was born much later than the theatre, in a period when social life was deeply marked by the notion of the *individual* (or its more elevated version, 'personality'), when there were no longer any slaves to enable 'free men' to form a relatively homogeneous group. . . . The cinema is made for the private individual and in the spectator's voyeurism there is no need for him to be seen (if it is dark in the cinema, the visible is entirely confined to the screen). . . . It is enough . . . that the actor should behave as though he were not to be seen (and therefore as though he did not see his voyeur), that he should go about his ordinary business and pursue his existence as

foreseen by the fiction of the film, that he should carry on his antics in a closed room, taking the utmost care not to notice that a glass rectangle has been set into one of the walls, and that he lives in a kind of aquarium, one which is simply a little less generous with its 'apertures' than real aquariums.

(1982: 96)

Psychoanalytic theory has taken us some way into this aquarium, and I review some of its achievements and concerns in the following section. The most central of these revolve around the problem we have already introduced – the nature of the audience's identification with the image.

Audience identification

We have always been told that we 'identify with' or see ourselves in characters on the screen. Screen heroes and heroines are widely held to offer some kind of wish fulfilment, and our admiration for one or other of them is assumed to be the expression of a wish we might, even unconsciously, want fulfilled. However, we also know that we do not only enjoy movies which invite this kind of identification; in fact, the film experience in either case is not markedly different. Psychoanalysis has revealed two main categories of audience identification; and neither of them has much to do with conventional identification with the hero or heroine.

First, Metz (1982) and others have argued that the nature of cinema-going is such that the very apparatus of the cinema invites us to identify with it. I have already referred to how the development of the camera was encouraged by an ideology of individualism, and explained how its invention incorporates the view that the individual's perception is the organizing principle of reality. When the camera is received as the viewing perspective on a series of projected images, it becomes a proxy for our eyes. Although there are such things as 'point-of-view' shots, where the camera is clearly presenting a series of images from the point of view of a specific character within the film, in most cases it takes the point of view of the narrating authority – the organizing principle of the film – which we identify as that of the audience (us). Metz argues that if we wish to make sense of the film, to achieve mastery over it, it is this point of view with which we must identify ourselves. The camera (and by extension, the projector) becomes our eyes, and when we wish not to see what it shows us – gore in a horror movie, for instance – we shut our eyes and turn our heads. Our processes of perception are dramatized, made material, in the beam of light from the projector streaming down from behind our heads in the darkened theatre. As we see the film as our perception, rather than someone else's representation, we collapse the distinction between our eyes and the projection apparatus. This may not ring entirely true, since many films and even some genres depend on a degree of separation between the audience and the image. Further, the argument entirely discounts the role of sound. Nevertheless, Metz argues persuasively that we 'identify' with the mechanisms of the cinema because they become, as it were, extensions of ourselves.

The second category of spectator identification with narrative film is more difficult to simplify. This is the spectator's identification with more or less everything that he or she sees on the screen. Not only do we identify with our heroes and heroines, but with all the characters at various points in the narrative. This is a consequence of seeing the screen as if it were, in some respects, a mirror of ourselves and of our world.

The post-Freudian theorist Jacques Lacan developed a most influential description of an aspect of childhood development which he called the 'mirror stage'. This is the point when a young child first recognizes itself in the mirror and realizes it has an identity separate from that of the mother. In recognizing an image of itself, and in forming a fascination for that image, the child begins to construct an identity. However, what children see, what they can only *ever* see, is an image of themselves – a representation. Here begins the process of human misunderstanding and self-delusion: our egoistic identification with the image of ourselves is always in some sense illusory.

Nevertheless, the image of oneself is fascinating, irresistible to the child and to the narcissistic aspects of adult personalities. As Dudley Andrew (1984: 149) has put it:

Our fascination with films is now thought to be not a fascination with particular characters and intrigues so much as a fascination with the image itself, based on a primal 'mirror stage' in our psychic growth. Just as we were, when infants, confronted with the gloriously complete view of ourselves in the mirror, so now we identify with the gloriously complete presentation of a spectacle on the screen.

Despite its highly technologized character, the pleasure film offers is, then, almost primal. There seem to be aspects of the process of identifying with film which emanate from our most basic drives. The various categories into which Freud divides the 'look' in his discussion of the components of human sexuality have their parallel in the pleasures that we obtain from film. There is the narcissistic (seeing oneself reflected on the screen), the voyeuristic (enjoying the power of another's image on the screen), and the fetishistic (a way of exaggerating the power of material things or people in order to deal with one's fear of them). All are expressions of human sexuality, or displacements of desire; all can be argued to offer the means of identification between the film and the audience.

This idea of the mirror stage might seem a little far-fetched, but there are many strong arguments for relating the pleasure derived from film to that primitive pleasure felt in the mirror stage. Of course, the analogy does have its limits; it could be argued that in the cinema one sees everything *but* oneself. Perhaps the real benefit of this analogy is its highlighting of the confusion between perception and reality that is common to the construction of the self and to our understanding of the narrative film. In this commonality we can see an ancient psychic root beneath this most modern of narrative systems.

Psychoanalysis also reveals other pre-cinematic patterns which determine the audience–image relationship. Definitions of human sexuality are clearly of interest here, since this is an area where the notion of voyeurism, for one, requires little demonstration. The deployment of the female form and the adoption of the point of view of the unseen male spectator have marked much Hollywood film; they are central to films as otherwise different as *The Seven Year Itch* (1955) and *Rear Window* (1954), and are explicitly interrogated in, for example, Brian De Palma's films *Dressed to Kill* (1980) and *Body Double* (1984), Phil Noyce's *Sliver* (1993), and many more. Most feminist work on the representation of the female in film has focused, predictably enough, on the commodification of the female body; the exploitation of the female body as a cinema spectacle; and the denial that contemporary cinema has made any significant change to these patterns of representation and exploitation.

Laura Mulvey's work has been particularly influential. She, like Metz, argues that the fascination of film is 'reinforced by pre-existing patterns of fascination already at work within the individual subject and the social formations that moulded him' (1975: 305). She appropriates Freud's definition of the look, and claims that cinema is essentially involved with gratifying the desire to look – 'scopophilia'. But this is not a simple matter. As we have said, cinema constructs the audience as voyeur – offering the pleasure of using another as an object of stimulation through sight – and it also constructs the audience as narcissistic – identifying with the object seen. The first construction explains, for instance, the development of the spectacle of the female body in films for the voyeuristic male audience. The second, however, would appear to contradict the first. Presumably, the male does not identify narcissistically with the female object of his voyeuristic look. Similarly, a female spectator is unlikely to identify with the object of the voyeuristic look. Mulvey argues that the narrative film solves this contradiction by representing the female as the object of desire on the one hand, and as the passive object of the film's action on the other. The audience identifies with the male hero's desire for the female, voyeuristically, and with his active resolution of the narrative, narcissistically. Consequently, women are rarely essential to film plots (as they *are* essential to film spectacle), or represented as able to resolve narrative dilemmas unaided. There is no place for the female character actively to drive the movie's narrative and thus compete for the audience's narcissistic identification. The male view, Mulvey argues, is the only point from which the pleasure of film narrative can be derived, and so the pleasure of female film audiences is phallocentric.

This is only part of Mulvey's extensive critique of Hollywood narratives, but it has been extremely important. It is relatively widely accepted now that much mainstream cinema, and particularly Hollywood cinema, is constructed for 'the male gaze': that is, the dominant viewpoint to which the narratives address themselves is masculine, and film's visual pleasures (including the spectacle of the female body) are primarily for men as well. Most of the work Mulvey's original essay inspired has examined the function of the male gaze in specific groups or genres of films. Linda Williams (1984) shows how many films do indeed recognize women's power and depict them as making use of it, only to then punish them for doing so. A staple of suspense thrillers and horror films (two examples Williams cites are *Psycho* and *Dressed to Kill*) is the moment 'when the woman looks' – when, despite what she knows is likely to be waiting for her, and despite her 'female vulnerability', she dares to look behind 'that' door. At such moments, women might be regarded as attempting to appropriate the male gaze, Williams argues. The consequence is some kind of narrative penalty – often they are made the object of the film's violence or terror unless or until they are rescued by a male. One could think of many further examples of this: from the many Hitchcock thrillers where the woman attempts to free herself from the control of a man by 'looking' for herself (*Suspicion* (1941), *Notorious* (1946), *Spellbound* (1945), or *Rebecca* (1940), for instance), to more recent examples such as *Silence of the Lambs* or *Hannibal* (2001). In her book *The Desire to Desire* (1988), Mary Ann Doane examines what one would expect to be a less masculinist genre, the 'women's films' from the 1940s. Doane discovers that here, too, female characters are continually the object of the controlling gaze of the male characters – as the patients of understanding male doctors, for example, or as endangered females in gothic melodrama. Doane maintains that in such films desire itself is effectively masculine. The women are denied desires of their own, left only with the desire to be the object of masculine desire (the 'desire to be desired') or, at best, yearning to be allowed the 'desire to desire'.

While such work became a central element within accounts of popular cinema over the 1970s and early 1980s, subsequent debates within feminist film theory began to question how comprehensive and uncontested 'the male gaze' actually is. As we saw in

Chapter 4, the strong central characters in the *Alien* series and *Terminator 2* are among the cases where a female does take charge of the narrative without becoming masculinized and without being punished for it. Tania Modleski (1988) takes issue with Mulvey's readings of Hitchcock's films as voyeuristic and sadistic in their treatment of women, by finding in many of his films some limited expression of female desire. Following Teresa de Lauretis' 1984 and Mulvey's own revisions (1989) of her early work, Modleski argues that Hitchcock's films are much more ambivalent than had been suggested: that 'despite the often considerable violence with which women are treated in Hitchcock's films, they remain resistant to patriarchal assimilation' (1988: 3). Gaylyn Studlar (1985) further contested Mulvey's assumption that the only pleasures with which a film spectator might identify are the (masculine and sadistic) pleasures of control, as against the (feminine and masochistic) pleasures of submission. A common element in arguments such as Modleski's and Studlar's is their resistance to an undifferentiated notion of the sense individual female members of the audience might make of the films they see. Simply, they are wary of arguments which assume all women will read these texts the same way. Conversely, Carol Clover's 1992 work, on low-budget horror–slasher films, rejects the related proposition that all male viewers would necessarily view these films the same way; that is, rather than identifying with the sadistic and predatory men at the centre of the action in such films as *I Spit on Your Grave* (1978), she argues, we must accept the likelihood that even the male viewer must narratively identify with the avenging female.

A consequence of such critiques was the development of the possibility that mainstream cinema might also address, albeit in a subordinated manner, a 'female gaze'. This has occasioned a move away from psychoanalytic explanations towards a focus on the socially constructed, active, female reader of texts – the 'female spectator'. Typically, such a focus foregrounds the social, cultural, or historical factors in our understanding of films in order to account for the pleasures female spectators derive from popular cinema. Significantly, these revisionist accounts push towards a more positive valuing of women's experience of popular cinema which breaks not

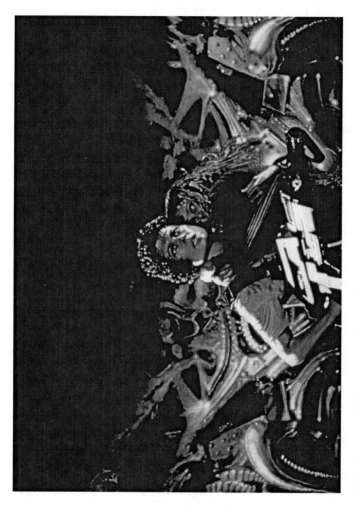

18 Sigourney Weaver as Ripley in *Aliens*

only with the dominant model of psychoanalysis but also with the textual preference for the avant-garde over the popular text. Deirdre Pribram (1988: 5) talks of the importance of emphasizing women's 'presence in, rather than absence from, the "cinematic experience"', and the essays in her collection emphasize the multiplicity of relationships women negotiate with film and television texts. Miriam Hansen (1989: 169) investigates the difference between the 'textually constructed spectator' (the female viewer Mulvey reads from the film text, for instance) and the 'actual' movie-goer (the one who buys the ticket), in order to also counterpose the 'social, collective, experiential dimension of cinematic reception' against exclusively psychoanalytic accounts. In *Babel and Babylon* (1994), her history of female audiences for silent cinema, Hansen claims that women enjoyed the cinema as a space for public collective activity that was very different from that provided in the family. In this space, among other things, they were offered the rare pleasure of gazing upon the male body as a sexual spectacle. Valentino's films, in particular, while certainly aligning the male gaze with sexual and narrative power, also happily displayed the body of the star to the desiring gaze of millions of female fans. Jackie Stacey (1994) has considered the function of the film star for female fans through an ethnographic study of British women's memories of their relationship with Hollywood film stars of the 1940s and 1950s. Stacey's concern takes her beyond the moment of reception examined in theories of the female gaze (that is, when we actually watch the film), and towards a fuller understanding of the more pervasive, and positive, role popular cinema plays within women's everyday lives. As both Hansen and Stacey conclude, their female subjects not only draw pleasure and meaning from viewing films in the cinema, but their enjoyment of a form of fandom also contributes to the construction of their cultural identities.

Importantly, I think, this moves us away from a focus on the film text as the sole location of the film experience. For such theorists as Hansen and Stacey, film does not only happen in the cinema; it is a social practice that affects everyday lives through fandom, gossip, fashion, and the whole range of activities through which cultural identities are formed. Such a focus necessarily foregrounds popular cinema – which still remains the most contentious territory for psychoanalytic theories of identification. Implicit in this theoretical tradition, some critics suggest, is an avant-garde aesthetic committed to resisting the pleasures of popular cinema through a critical account of their destructive political effects (we will come back to this in Chapter 6). Increasingly, this has been recognized as an elitist position which misunderstands popular cinema and undervalues the capacities and interests of its audiences. Yvonne Tasker voices a common criticism that, within the parameters of feminist psychoanalytic criticism, popular texts and pleasures have somehow become subject to analysis 'only in order to be understood, transcended, and moved beyond' (1993: 5). Jacqueline Bobo's 1995 work with black women viewers of Spielberg's film version of Alice Walker's novel *The Color Purple* (1985), suggests there is quite a distance between the actual black audience of the film and the audience presumed by its progressive white critics. Widely attacked by such critics because it was judged to reinforce negative stereotypes of black identity, the film is nevertheless defended by the black women Bobo studied. They found ways of reading this text as positive, and were insulted by what they saw as uninformed assumptions about their vulnerability to the film's supposedly negative messages. These women express their discomfort with the proposition of an undifferentiated female viewer passively consuming films which unilaterally and irresistably position their audiences.

There is now a lengthening line of feminist critiques of psychoanalytic film theory which insist on the need for a greater degree of historical and social specificity, for recognizing that different women will watch the same text in different ways, and for acknowledgement of the multitude of extra-textual factors which influence audience responses to popular film (see, for instance, Barton 2002). In what is now being described as a 'turn to audiences', film studies is also pursuing an interest in extra-textual factors such as the activities of fans or other ancillary popular cultural contexts (Jancovitch 2002).

Desire and the image

It will be clear from the above, then, that the psychoanalytic position is no longer as powerful an influence on film studies today as it once was. Of course, many of the readings these enquiries have produced have remained rich and useful: Barbara Creed's work on the 'monstrous-feminine' in the *Aliens* trilogy is one such instance (1993). However, over the 1990s in particular, the psychoanalytic tradition attracted criticism for its totalizing tendencies and for its displacement of other, alternative, modes of analysis (Shaviro 1993). Judith Mayne suggests that there is a problem with the formulaic character of many contemporary applications of psychoanalysis to film texts:

> How many times does one need to be told that individual film *x*, or film genre *y*, articulates the law of the father, assigns the spectator a position of male oedipal desire, marshals castration anxiety in the form of voyeurism and fetishism, before psychoanalysis begins to sound less like the exploration of the unconscious, and more like a master plot?
>
> (1993: 69)

Certainly, as Bordwell and Carroll have argued (1996), any strong sense of the differences between films, let alone between spectators, tends to disappear before this kind of psychoanalytic theory. The dream analogy also tends to make film simply the bearer of fantasies; just as critics in other art forms have found this position hard to accept, film theorists have produced arguments countering it. The use of the analogy of the dream or the mirror as an explanatory device, as if it were a method of analysis, has been exposed to criticism. It is at the very least reductive to approach the film audience solely through the filter of the unconscious since a single system of signification is thus set aside from the many others which also contribute to the audience's experience of film.

Where psychoanalysis has been most suggestive is in its attempt to describe the audience's desire for the film text. Dudley Andrew, himself a stern critic of psychoanalytic theory, presents a thoroughly psychoanalytic description of the desire for the image:

Desiring to possess the film, we are confined to merely viewing it. Consequently, the successful film can never ultimately satisfy us; rather, it rewards our passion to see by offering us still more to see until we are thrown beyond the bounds of its narrative space and out into the queue waiting for the next film to light up on the screen, to light up the cavern of our psyches.

(1984: 148)

As his closing clauses emphasize, the action which draws us into the cinema is on the screen as well as in our psyches. He emphasizes later (p. 152) that the 'psychic dimension of cinematic meaning is paramount but only as regulated and shaped in cinematic discourse'. The importance of the particular text is not to be overlooked. The specificities of the text add up to what Metz (1982: 92) calls a formula 'for granting a wish that was never formulated in the first place', an admission of the power of the text to call the audience into *its* unconscious, as it were.

It is worth remembering, as we move from this topic, that there are ways other than the psychoanalytic of thinking about pleasure. Roland Barthes (1975), for instance, located pleasure in the body in a much more physical way than did Freud, seeing it as the individual's last defence against the persuasiveness of language and the consensual bullying of ideologies. For Barthes, pleasure is a potentially political force which can be resistant to control. However, neither Freud's nor Barthes's approach seems to have a comprehensive explanatory power. In film, the visceral effects of the car chase, the roller-coaster ride, the coming together of vision and music in a romantic climax (say, in *Titanic*'s clinch on the bow of the ship), occur at moments when the body takes over and dominates our sensation of responding to the film. We experience that take-over as pleasurable. Barthesian notions of pleasure seem inappropriate here: his view of pleasure foregrounds the unconventional, the unpredictable, the ambiguous, and such moments are (at least) a complex mixture of these attributes *and* their opposites.

There are different experiences that we might describe as pleasurable, even in the movies. One frequently forgotten aspect is the pleasure we find in the familiar, in seeing a convention faithfully played out. *Sleepless in Seattle* is overtly constructed around a generic parallel between its narrative and that of *An Affair to Remember* (1957); the more recent film invests significant portions of its time into reminding viewers of the conventions of the earlier film before it faithfully plays them out in the more modern setting. As the commercial success of *Sleepless in Seattle* would indicate, the pleasure of having one's conventional narrative expectations satisfied in familiar ways cannot be underestimated. Alternatively, there are the satisfactions which come from responding to the new, the surprising, or the disruptive in their combination with more familiar intertextual and generic references – the kind of experience richly on offer in Tarantino's *Pulp Fiction*, for instance. Through such interactions, viewers experience the pleasure of confirming, through their mastery of the film, their membership in the culture.

Again, there are other forms of pleasure we tend to forget if we simply concentrate on the workings of narrative. There is the pleasure in watching fashions and images for their own sake (the appeal of the raft of period melodramas set in Tuscany over the last 4–5 years), or as a kind of shopping trip in order to compose one's own representation of oneself (as in the many teen movies aimed primarily at female audiences and built upon the success of *Clueless* (1995)). There is a further pleasure in watching a film or series of films as parts of the continuing development of the star as a sign (*Pirates of the Caribbean*, for Johnny Depp watchers, offers such a pleasure). We should not underestimate the appeal of pure visual spectacle – landscape, action, costume, special effects. As Tasker reminds us, popular cinema 'is as much concerned with visual pleasure as it is with narrative development' and in certain genres – action films for one – 'visual display is elevated to a defining feature of the genre' (1993: 6). Michele Pierson describes the development of a whole new set of visual pleasures among sections of the contemporary film audience, which privileges the display of computer-generated special effects and graphics in the service of a techno-futurist aesthetic (2002: 101).

As we saw earlier on in this book, critical accounts of popular cinema have often been uncomfortable with the pleasures it provides for its audiences, and in some cases have been eager to dismiss them through some form of aesthetic critique. Hence, the need for Tasker, for instance, to argue a case for the analysis specifically of the action film, a critically denigrated but commercially popular genre. Tasker's work is indicative of recent critical trends in the analysis of film, influenced by cultural studies' reclaiming of the importance of popular cultural forms, which have reasserted the importance of popular pleasures. What I have been listing in the preceding paragraphs are all among the characteristic pleasures of popular culture and they are all (potentially) implicated in the audience's decision to see a film and in what they 'do' with the film when they see it. They are social–cultural pleasures, appropriated by individuals for their own use but in no sense originating with each individual. They are pleasures linked to other social practices within popular culture too, and therefore reveal how the social practice of film is enclosed within *other* practices, within other systems of meaning.

Audiences, texts, and meanings

It is clear that we need to be aware of both textual and 'extra-textual' factors in any audience's understanding of a film. The film's meaning is not simply a property of its particular arrangement of elements: its meaning is produced in relation to an audience, not independently. Once we realize this we find it possible to accept that audiences may find a multiplicity of meanings in any one film text; its meaning is not necessarily 'fixed', unchangeable.

One of the results of the break between film studies and a preeminently aesthetic tradition of film appreciation is the abandonment of the idea that there was a core of meaning in a film which the audience had to uncover. Within film studies, and cultural studies generally, it is now more customary to talk of 'meanings' than of Meaning. Furthermore, meanings are seen as the products of an audience's reading rather than as an essential property of the film text itself. Audiences make films mean; they don't merely decode the meanings already secreted in the text.

This does cause problems at the practical level. Most of us watching a film will feel that there is some limit to the kinds of readings to which it might be subjected. Certain sets of conventions, such as those of genre, seem to exist precisely to organize, determine, or otherwise channel the audience's potentially varied responses into a homogeneous, single point of view. There is a degree of dislocation between the theory and the practice of watching a film. On the one hand and in principle, the audience's readings of a film occupy a theoretical field of almost infinite possibility; on the other hand, in practice we find that while the audience's readings may differ, they will still be contained within a relatively discrete range of possibilities. Cultural studies' attempts to deal with this have employed a range of tactics, from recovering the idea that the text is in control of its readers, to the dethroning of the text in order to see it as entirely the product of socially formed reading practices.

Stuart Hall's 1977 work on television and the press is important here. He argued that the formal properties of media texts were organized in order to 'prefer' one way of being read. This 'preferred' reading was also the one which was most in accord with the meanings produced by the dominant ideological systems. This did not preclude there being other ways of reading a text, however. Although audiences might recognize the preferred reading as one that was implicit in the text's formal properties, they could still refuse that reading for an alternative. This could be 'negotiated' (accepting some, but not all, of the principles behind the preferred reading); or it could be an 'oppositional' reading which wholly rejected the preferred reading position. Whatever reading position was adopted, however, it always articulated itself through a relationship to the dominant ideological system. A crude example of this process would be the way audiences might react to a party political broadcast. For one audience member, the speaker might represent the favoured political party and so engender little argument; for another, the speaker might intersect with his or her value systems only at certain points; and for a third, the speaker might typify all that must be resisted and opposed.

I still find the 'preferred reading' a useful concept. But it does present problems. First, the idea of a preferred reading is not totally separable from that of a 'true' meaning. The text is still seen as the ultimate dictator of its readings. What is offered is an account of 'different readings of the same text'. It is important to recognize that if we believe that meaning is to some extent indeterminate, then 'different readings' of a film will actually produce 'different' films. Second, the functioning of ideology through texts and readers is now seen to be a more complex and less determined process than Hall originally suggested. Hall (1982) has himself contributed to changes in the way in which the work of ideology has been defined.

Perhaps the clearest countermove to Hall emerged from what has become a significant tradition of ethnographic research into TV. The beginnings of this tradition are usually located in Charlotte Brunsdon and David Morley's 1978 work on the British magazine programme *Nationwide*. Morley (1980) reverses the relations suggested in the Hall model by seeing social formations such as class, gender, subculture, ethnicity, and occupation as the key determinants of the audience's opinions about *Nationwide*. Extra-textual factors are thus seen to be driving the reading of texts, and there is the sound of a radical explosion of possible readings as we discover more social categories into which we might divide our audiences. While Morley certainly demolished assumptions of a mass, homogeneous audience soaking up TV indiscriminately, he still offered an account of different versions of the 'same text', in conjunction with a reductive view of what constitutes the differences between audience members.

Neither of these approaches is entirely satisfactory, although both remind us that audiences read films through their specific forms *and* through cultural determinants. The difficulty remaining is to get the balance between audience and film, history and text, 'just right', so that we can see texts and readers as 'mutual supports of each other'.

This last phrase is drawn from Bennett and Woollacott's *Bond and Beyond: The Political Career of a Popular Hero* (1987), and it is to their work that I now wish to turn. *Bond and Beyond* examines the James Bond phenomenon (or at least that part of it which had occurred by the time of writing): the books, the films, the stars, the character, the audiences, the production practices, and, most of all, the meanings it has generated. At that time, the authors admit, Bond had become a little *passé*; the film audiences were growing ever younger, and the backlog of novels had almost gone. They did not foresee the second wind the Bond movies were to develop under the influence of CGI special effects, and Pierce Brosnan's highly successful revival of the character. They argue, and this is as true now as then, that the Bond phenomenon is a revealing location for the examination of how a fictional character can become a popular hero through the specific interactions between books and films, magazine interviews and stars, texts and history. Although film study is not its primary aim, *Bond and Beyond* offers benefits for the discipline because it deals at length with the relationships between popular cinema texts and their audiences.

The first move Bennett and Woollacott make is to extend the meaning of a term we have already met: intertextuality. As they point out, this term conventionally refers to the relationships between one text and another. They introduce the term 'inter-textuality' to denote the complex of relationships between texts and the social conditions of their production and consumption. They challenge the idea that the meaning of a film might be fixed, by proving that the meaning of James Bond as a popular hero has never been fixed. The book is largely devoted to chronicling and analysing the changes in the meanings of James Bond – or what they end up referring to as the varied 'reading formations' which contextualize the texts of Bond.

Bond and Beyond presents a clear account of the way that Bond's meanings had shifted; how meanings had been bred, rather than contained, by these texts over Bond's career as a popular hero. Before the films were produced, Bond was an entirely literary figure. He was specifically British, tied into a mythology of nationhood which constructed Britain as the cutting edge of the Western world, and which denied the decline of its empire and influence on world politics. Bond was also politically chauvinistic and sexually exploitative; attacks were made on the gratuitous sex and violence of the novels well before the films were produced.

The first Bond film, *Dr No*, was released in 1962, and this began what Bennett and Woollacott call the 'ideological remodelling' of the hero. First, Bond was extracted from the cold war climate of the novels from the 1950s, and given a context more appropriate to 1960s *détente*. From 1961, Fleming's novels abandoned the hitherto central ideological opposition between the Soviet Union and the West, and pitted Bond against the international criminal organization SPECTRE. The subsequent partial 'depoliticization' was aimed at broadening the hero's appeal for movie-goers, and giving the films (as the producer put it) 'legs worldwide'. Second, Bond's affiliation with a past – Establishment – Britain was attenuated so that he could become the icon of the 'swinging Britain' of the mid-1960s:

> Bond provided a mythic encapsulation of the then prominent ideological themes of classlessness and modernity, a key cultural marker of the claim that Britain had escaped the blinkered, class-bound perspectives of its traditional ruling elites and was in the process of being thoroughly modernised as a result of the implementation of a new meritocratic style of cultural and political leadership, middle class and professional rather than aristocratic and amateur.
>
> (Bennett and Woollacott 1987: 34–5)

Similarly, 'the Bond girls' who partnered the hero were used to represent a new, modern version of female sexuality – 'liberated from the constraints of family, marriage and domesticity'. In many ways, Bond was quite central to popular culture of the time. As the authors put it, he was a 'sign of the times', but a sign that was to shift from one meaning to another.

James Bond was less central to the popular culture of the 1970s. Bennett and Woollacott argue that there is a ritualistic aspect to the figure at that time which was connected to the key element in the films, the demonstration of high technology in action. The equipping of the Aston Martin, for instance, became a conventional ritual in the films while ideological interest in Bond himself became more muted, even secondary. Relations between Bond and his 'girls' were also realigned during this period so that the liberated woman of the 1960s found herself forced to accept domination of one kind or another. There is a regressive impetus behind the structure of gender relations in the Bond films of the 1970s and, as we move into the 1980s, a deal of confusion as to just what the audience expected of Bond and his women. In the 1980s, the authors say, 'Bond no

longer occupied centre-stage within the re-organized system of intertextual relations which characterised the popular culture of the
period' (1987: 39). Bond films were still an institution, but had less
cultural power than before. The hero himself had less power within
the narrative, too. *A View to a Kill* has Grace Jones's May Day
dominating Bond (sexually and professionally) to an unprecedented
degree. As a result, *Bond and Beyond* points out, she dies. But the
shifts in the way the films represent Bond offer hints of a widening
gap between Bond, his producers, and his audience over the 1980s.

This brief summary outlines a history of a set of texts, and a
history of the meanings which have been given to these texts. Bennett
and Woollacott use such histories to make the point that both
films and their audiences are, as it were, culturally operated; what a
film means can and does change. But there are limits to the ways in
which these changes occur. The problem raised at the beginning
of this section – if there is no 'true' meaning why can't we propose
absolutely *any* meaning? – is a problem that actually arises only in
practice. In theory, we might accept that we *could* offer any meaning.
In practice, however, there are at least some determinate properties
of film narratives, and because any audience member is at a particular point in history he or she has a limited set of options through
which he or she might view a film. This may not resolve the initial
contradiction, but it will enable us to engage in critical practice and
examine the ways in which we, as audiences, explore the social
and textual potential for meaning within feature films.

Bennett and Woollacott's book was influential on cultural
studies during the late 1980s and early 1990s, but it has had a more
recent influence on film studies through Janet Staiger's interest in
their idea that there are historically determined reading formations
which shape the reception of texts or groups of texts. Her
Interpreting Films (1992) examines the historical reception of films
as a prelude to arguing for the recognition of context as a fundamental component of the process of interpreting films. *Interpreting
Films* is about the audience's interpretations, not those of the critic,
and the book presents a careful analysis of a range of approaches
to film texts and their reception – including that of Bennett and
Woollacott. Drawing upon communications studies, linguistics,

and television studies, her discussion is unusual within film studies for its disciplinary eclecticism, as well as for her ultimate disinclination to place the film text at the centre of the analysis. Indeed, by the time Staiger wrote her next book *Perverse Spectators* (2000), she was prepared to make some quite bold statements about the relative importance of text, context, and the spectator:

> I believe that contextual factors, more than textual ones, account for the experiences that spectators have watching films and television and for the uses to which those experiences are put in navigating our everday lives. These contextual factors are social formations and constructed identities of the self in relation to historical conditions. These contexts involve intertextual knowledges (including norms of how to interpret sense data from moving images and sounds), personal psychologies, and sociological dynamics. The job of a reception historian is to account for events of interpretation and affective experience.
> (2001: 1)

The text has been moved aside to allow Staiger to focus upon the 'perverse spectators' in the audience.

Such a focus reflects the 'turn to audiences' – or film studies' own 'cultural turn'. Staiger insists on the importance of external influences upon the audiences' 'interpretative strategies' as they consume the film text: these include aesthetic preferences, the knowledges and expectations the audience member brings into the cinema, and their experience in 'the exhibition situation' (2000: 30–1). She also includes within her account of reception such elements as the 'postmovie talk by spectators', and the range of other reception activities which occur after attending the screening – discussion with other spectators, gossip about the performers, writing to the star, attending celebrity events connected to the film, and so on – and which take the practice of reception outside the walls of the cinema.

Cultural identities

Staiger's evolving project has played an important part in taking film studies beyond the boundaries of the movie-going event itself in order to write a history of cinema reception that is overwhelmingly a social and cultural, rather than merely a textual, history. Of particular interest to us here is that she has foregrounded the critical role played by the cultural identities brought with the spectators into the cinema. At its simplest, her work asks us to recognize that what we make of a particular film has to do, in some way, with who we think we are. Of course, 'who we think we are' is neither simple, nor unitary, nor even particularly stable. Also, it often has a great deal to do with who *other people* think we are. We construct our own identities partly in negotiation with what other people think of us and of people like us. These are not necessarily direct negotiations, although that happens too, but they occur through the meanings we produce in response to media and other representations of specific formations of cultural identities. So, representations of cultural identities matter because they are among the raw materials from which we construct our sense of 'who we think we are' at any one point in time.

Consequently, the representations of those who have less access to power in our society – due to their class or economic status, their race or ethnicity, or their gender or sexuality – have become the focus of a great deal of discussion within film and cultural studies over the last twenty years. This is because such representations are seen to play their part in defining such identities, and therefore they also play a part in maintaining and justifying the very processes which support existing social inequalities. (We will return to a closer examination of this process through the discussion of ideology in Chapter 6). Some of these discussions take the form of objecting to particular representations on the screen because of the definitions of identity they project onto specific sections of the community – and the material effects seen to flow from those definitions. Other discussions take the opposite approach and examine the components of the more benign and positive representations which are used to describe the more powerful sections of the community. These examinations, typically, concentrate on revealing the silences and absences which make the representations desirable or credible. There is now a well-developed tradition within cultural and media studies devoted to the examination of the negotiation of cultural identities through popular cultural forms and practices. Although there are many film studies' writers who have been exploring such issues also for many years – bell hooks, for instance, has always discussed cinema from her perspective as an African-American – film studies' original focus upon the form of the text tended to imply that such considerations were of secondary importance. More recently, however, the cultural studies' tradition referred to above has come to exercise a significant influence on the discussion of contemporary cinema.

I have already referred to some examples of work which have focused upon cinema's participation in the production of particular cultural identities: Stacey's study of female cinema audiences, Bobo's account of the black audience's reading of *The Color Purple*, Hansen's histories of the female public sphere in the silent cinema. All of these emphasize the specificity of the cultural identities engaged in reading and producing film texts – as well as their unpredictability or what Staiger calls their 'perversity'. In some cases, whole genres of film have addressed a particular audience. Initially black cinema in the US developed in opposition to Hollywood through an independent sector that was politically aligned with and responsible to the black community. Eventually, however, this dichotomy began to blur as film-makers 'crossed over' by directing the representation of their own social and cultural experiences to a mass audience. The 1970s' so-called 'blaxploitation' films such as Melvin van Peebles *Sweet Sweetback's Baadasssss Song* (1971) addressed a newly politicized black audience in the US, as well as reflecting a downturn in the industry that had given urgency to attracting new sectors of the population to popular cinema. Timothy Lott tells us that these films 'provided a vehicle for getting a younger black audience into the theatres' (1998: 218). As their name implies, however, the blaxploitation films were often regarded as having sold out the black community in order to achieve commercial success. Around twenty years later, there were a number of films which reached a mass audience while dealing with black experiences in ways that were generally regarded as less exploitative: from the teen movie *House Party* (1990) to Spike Lee's confronting *Do the Right Thing* (1989) and the socially conservative *Boyz N the Hood* (1991). Despite their considerable distance from the territory of the blaxploitation picture, however, argument about these films among black audiences still circulates around the extent to which they might be regarded as having been co-opted by a white view of the black community as a means of making their stories attractive to a mass audience.

The objective of such films is to make their identities and their experiences visible, but also to make them count. So, it is important that they do not misrepresent the experience of their community – something that is less relevant for popular films aimed at or depicting dominant cultural identities. The difficulty for film-makers who address marginalized or subordinated community identities is that they must carry the burden of representing that community, as well as telling a story. However, the issue is not merely that such groups need to fight for an appropriately respectful and informed modality of representation. Julien and Mercer (2002) argue that, even when specific ethnicities (Asian migrants in the UK, in the case they consider) are presented accurately and sympathetically in popular films, they are still inevitably placed, by that representation, on the margins of society. The problem is how to move their identities, as Julien and Mercer put it, from 'de margin' to 'de centre'.

Popular cinema certainly does call up minority audiences and places them in the centre of the frame from time to time, but it would be wrong to see this as a fundamental activity. It would be more accurate to see popular cinema as offering the opportunity for subordinated or marginalized identities to articulate their own mode of consumption. Non-whites, gays and lesbians, and other marginalized sectors of the audience have found their own ways of reading popular films – often by going 'against the grain' of the 'preferred' reading of the film. *Boyz N the Hood*, for instance, was read very positively by the mainstream popular press as a powerful critique of the masculinist ideologies ruling black communities. Within the black community there was considerable debate about the film as a well-meaning but socially conservative exploitation of the prevailing stereotypes; Timothy Lott, for instance, was particularly harsh, describing it as just another 'socially unredeeming bad nigga narrative that fundamentally denies community' (1998: 219). In some cases, of course (and I think *Boyz N the Hood* is probably one), the reception of the film reveals anxieties and contradictions that are embedded within the audience members' own identities and which get put to work in a variety of ways through discussion about the film. *Thelma and Louise*, as we have seen, generated dramatically different responses from its cinema audiences because it tapped into particular sensitivities about sexual difference and the power available to women, about the implications of what could be read as a lesbian partnership at the end, as well as about the appropriate genre into which it could be located so that audiences could deal with such discomforts. At the very least, it generated significantly different possibilities of meaning and pleasure for male, female, gay, and lesbian audiences. (For two different readings of the film which demonstrate this, see Cathy Griggers (1993) and Sharon Willis (1993).)

While the critics may argue all they like about what a film 'really' means, it has become conventional now in film and cultural studies to acknowledge that the meaning of any film text is available for appropriation by particular formations of identity. Indeed, where such appropriation occurs, the interpretation can become an empowering political act – making over a mass cultural product to serve an individual's own interests. As a result, community groups such as gays and lesbians have become particularly skilled 'at raiding basically heterosexual texts for their own purposes' (Holmlund 1991: 154). Non-heterosexual readings of popular films (see for instance Chris Straayer's 1984 reading of *Personal Best* or her 1996 book-length study of so-called 'deviant' interpretations) have become an important component of gay/lesbian or 'queer' culture. Interestingly, this has more than an academic provenance. Gay and lesbian formations of sexuality have also become sufficiently integrated into popular cinema's regimes of representation that it is not uncommon now for a popular movie's construction of eroticism or desire to address both heterosexual and gay or lesbian sexualities.

Such tactics have been incorporated into the marketing of popular cinema. The queer audience, while still dissident in relation to the rest of society, is now sufficiently significant commercially that they are addressed as desirable niche markets by film producers. To the extent that this seems unproblematic to the popular audience, it is possible to say that the 'queer' identity is one which no longer has to be concealed or disavowed within popular culture – and certainly in cinema it has become an increasingly important point of address:

> Queer fandom of 'mainstream' or dominant cinema (the legendary affection gay men have for Judy Garland, say) has been a central discourse of gay and lesbian cultural production; more important, queer readings of, or queer presences within, dominant cinema explode the image of commercial narrative cinema as a repressive monster as well as undermine the interpretation of alternative or independent cinema as its necessary (read, liberatory) white knight.
>
> (Tinkcom and Villarejo 2001: 21)

Queer analysis of film is fast becoming a standard component of contemporary film studies (see for instance Dyer 1990 and 2002; and the big Routledge Reader edited by Benshoff and Griffen (2004)). Studies of gender have also been a staple of the field for decades, not only of femininity but also of masculinity. The work of a journal such as *Camera Obscura* has placed gender at the centre of the analysis of all kinds of cinema (and TV) throughout its life. In the US and the UK, the discussion of film's participation in the cultural politics of race and ethnicity also continues to grow in importance.

Such work constitutes quite a significant shift from the canonical and aesthetic origins of the field I outlined in the first chapter of this book. The overwhelming influence of psychoanalysis during the 1970s and 1980s may have delayed recognition of the usefulness of the kind of attention we have been describing – that is, attention to the cultural identities of actual audiences, their difference and 'perversity'. That said, however, the 'cultural turn' we have witnessed in film studies over the last two decades has greatly sharpened the field's focus on the issue of cultural identity and its implication in both the production and the consumption of the movies. While I could continue to review the various constructions of identity within this cultural and representational field, it is probably more useful if I move on – towards considering how such constructions are formed. That question takes us into another arena: cultural identities are bound up with cultural politics, to do with the dispersal and operation of power and, in order to deal with that, we need to consider film as ideology. It is to that topic – to film, culture, and ideology – we turn in the following chapter.

Suggestions for further work

1   The literature on psychoanalysis and the cinema is large and difficult. It is covered in an introductory manner, but at greater length than is possible here, in such introductory film texts as Nelmes's *Introduction to Film Studies* (1996). An excellent account is Judith Mayne's *Cinema and Spectatorship* (1993), while the Gamman and Marshment and Constance Penley collections of essays, *The Female Gaze* (1988) and *Feminism and Film Theory* (1988), are both very useful. For cognitivist critiques of psychoanalytic approaches, see Bordwell and Carroll's *Post-Theory* (1996) and Shaviro's *The Cinematic Body* (1993).

2   For accounts of the movie industry and the battle for audiences, see Tino Balio's *Hollywood in the Age of Television* (1990), his article on Hollywood in the 1990s in Albert Moran's *Film Policy* (1996), and Justin Wyatt's *High Concept: Movies and Marketing in Hollywood* (1994). There is a group of articles (including an excerpt from Wyatt's book) dealing with audiences and consumption in *The Film Cultures Reader* (Turner, 2002).

3   There is a strong tradition of audience research in cultural and TV studies, and it is certainly now growing in film: see the contributions by Stacey (1994), Hansen (1994), and Staiger (1992 and 2000). Early examples of television audience

research from cultural studies include Hobson's 1982 work on the soap opera *Crossroads* and David Morley's 1980 book on the *Nationwide* audience. More recent research includes Morley's *Television, Audiences and Cultural Studies* (1992) and Marie Gillespie's *Television, Ethnicity and Cultural Change* (1995). Such studies reinforce the importance of the cultural determinants of textual readings.

4   The move towards multiplexes has changed the cinema-going experience for us. Do you think it has changed other aspects, such as the variety of films on offer and the range of tastes accommodated within the one cinema complex? Are there advantages for the cinema audience in the multiplex, or solely advantages to the film producer and exhibitor? Examine the schedules for your local multiplex and see which kind of account they would support.

5   The notion that film is a performative medium is one that deserves further thought. When 'set pieces' occur in films they are greeted with affection and pleasure. They are also those moments for which we remember a film. An example would be the in-car lip-synch performance of Queen's *Bohemian Rhapsody* in *Wayne's World*. Is this kind of moment central to film narratives, do you think? What other examples can you think of? Also, are there actors who specialize in producing such moments? (Eddie Murphy, Jim Carrey, Chris Rock, and Robin Williams come to mind here, but there are others.)

6   Examine a promotional campaign for a new film, and see if you can easily detect just what its audience is assumed to be; then have a look at the film itself and see if this campaign has emphasized one aspect more than another. Your task then is to suggest why this has occurred, and if it privileges one 'reading' of the film. This might be a good point to review the notions of meaning and identity canvassed in the last section. Look at a range of films, such as *Sliding Doors*, *Mulholland Drive*, or *Spiderman*, and see if you can uncover different kinds of readings or addresses to different sections of the audience.

Film, culture, and ideology

There have been many attempts at understanding the relations between film and culture. They have occurred under various headings: film and society, film and politics, film and mass culture, for example. Some analyses have focused on the relations between film and trends within popular culture ('gross-out' teen movies and changing sexual mores, for example), while others have used film as documentary evidence of movements within social history. In many cases, such analyses have assumed a more or less 'reflectionist' relationship between film and society. That is, film is seen as a 'reflection' of the dominant beliefs and values of its culture; if American musicals of the 1940s were Utopian and optimistic, then this must reflect the society's optimism. (An example of such an argument would be Richard Griffith's 'Cycles and genres' (1949).) It should be clear from the rest of this book that such an approach is too primitive: we know, for instance, that American society also produced the alienated and cynical genre of *film noir* during the 1940s – which reflection was the accurate one? The metaphor of reflection is also unsatisfactory because it bypasses the process of selection and combination that goes into the composition of any utterance, whether in film, prose, or conversation. Further, between society and this so-called mirror is interposed a whole set of competing and conflicting cultural, subcultural, industrial, and institutional determinants.

Alternatives to reflectionist views have emerged from structural linguistics, structural anthropology, literary theory, and Marxian theories of ideology. All have contributed to situating the relation between film and society within the broader category of the relationship of representations of *any* kind (photographs, paintings, novels, films) to their culture. Film does not reflect or even record reality; like any other medium of representation it constructs and 're-presents' its pictures of reality by way of the codes, conventions, myths, and ideologies of its culture as well as by way of the specific signifying practices of the medium. Just as film works *on* the meaning systems of culture – to renew, reproduce, or review them – it is also produced *by* those meaning systems. The film-maker, like the novelist or the storyteller, is a *bricoleur* – a sort of handyman who does the best she or he can with the materials at hand. The film-maker uses the representational conventions and repertoires available within the culture in order to make something fresh but familiar, new but generic, individual but representative.

The result of cultural approaches to 'film as representation' is ultimately to focus on the relations between film's representational 'languages' and ideology. Nevertheless, before dealing with this, we need to fill out the overview. There are two broad categories of culturalist approach to the relation between film and culture: textual and contextual. The textual approach focuses on the film text, or a body of film texts, and 'reads' from them information about the cultural function of film. For example, Andrew Tudor's work on film movements (1974) is text-based; his initial premiss is that the texts of German expressionism or Italian neo-realism have something in common which can be understood as expressions of particular aspects of those cultures. We can read, for instance, the recurrence of father–son conflicts in the plots of German expressionist films as symbolic representations of the deep political split between the old and the new guard in the Weimar Republic.

Genre criticism is also initially text-based, even though it may attempt to trace changes in genres to their sources within the culture producing them. Will Wright's study of the western (1975), referred to in Chapter 4, follows such a pattern, as does Schrader's work (1972) on *film noir*, or Dyer's 1977 work on the musical. In general, these textual approaches are responding to a set of conclusions about the specific characteristics of the film text(s); then, operating on the assumption of the culture's 'authorship' of the text, they trace the myths or ideologies of the films back to their sources within the culture. So the suspicion of women in *film noir* is traced back to a series of 'causes', and the Utopian myths which structure musicals are outlined in some detail. Often there is a strong structuralist impulse in such work, since the similarities between films are emphasized more than the differences, and the tendency is to work with many 'typical' texts rather than a few 'individualized' texts.

Although there is no hard distinction between the two angles of approach, contextual approaches tend to analyse the cultural, political, institutional, and industrial determinants of – most often – a national film industry. And although there is, again, an interest in film movements which implies a pre-eminent interest in a particular group of film texts, this is not the primary concern of such approaches. It is the process of cultural production rather than the work of representation that concerns these studies. Such works as those of Kristin Thompson and Douglas Gomery in America, John Ellis and Charles Barr in the UK, and John Tulloch and Tom O'Regan in Australia, examine the function of cultural policy, government intervention, censorship, technologies, patterns of ownership within the chain of production–distribution–exhibition, commercial practices within the film industry, public institutions, global aspects of the film industry, and many other factors which affect the textual form of a film (indeed, whether a project *becomes* a film) well before it is ever seen by a critic. Such work often draws on a well-developed tradition in media studies where detailed histories of a TV programme's production and reception are now relatively commonplace. The strong, if not always fashionable, tradition of film history – essentially the proposition of an aesthetic 'great tradition' for the cinema – has been hijacked (by, for instance, Douglas Gomery) to explore film's industrial history. This has been increasingly useful in developing an understanding of film and culture.

The combination of these two approaches – textual and contextual – has enormous explanatory power. (In the US, Bordwell, Staiger, and Thompson's *The Classical Hollywood Cinema* (1985) and, in Australia, Susan Dermody and Elizabeth Jacka's two-volume cultural history of the revival, *The Screening of Australia* (1987), have demonstrated this.) The combination is also very unwieldy. It is simply beyond our capacity to deal with all the determinants necessary to understand fully the cultural relationships which obtain at any particular point in film history. For this reason, most discussion has focused on the structure, or the theoretical composition, of the relationships. Even the primarily historical accounts are valuable for what they tell us of the structure of the film–culture relationship. The common thread, however, which links the textual and the contextual, and makes an understanding of them complementary rather than mutually exclusive, is that both industry and text, the processes of production and of reception, must be in some way related to ideologies.

The term 'ideology' is itself continually being redefined, contested, and explored within all areas of cultural theory. There is no incontestable definition of ideology. Put at its simplest, we can say that implicit in every culture is a 'theory of reality' which motivates its ordering of that reality into good and bad, right and wrong, them and us, and so on. For this 'theory of reality' actually to work as a structuring principle it needs to be unspoken, invisible, a property of the natural world rather than of human interests. 'Ideology' is the term used to describe the system of beliefs and practices that is produced by this theory of reality; and although ideology itself has no material form, we can see its material effects in all social and political formations, from class structure to gender relations to our idea of what constitutes an individual. The term is also used to describe the workings of language and representation within culture which enable such formations to be constructed as 'natural'.

The culture's ideological system is not monolithic but is composed of competing and conflicting classes and interests, all fighting for dominance. The process is, in a sense, replicated in our narratives. In Chapter 4, I used Lévi-Strauss to suggest that narratives set up binary oppositions which are resolved at their end; it was further suggested that the oppositions themselves were composed of representations of competing ideological positions. (I discussed how *Desperately Seeking Susan* explores opposing definitions of marriage, femaleness, and sexuality through the contrasting lifestyles of Roberta and Susan.) If our narratives do work to resolve social contradictions symbolically, what they must deal with are those existing political divisions or inequities between groups, classes, or genders which have been constructed as natural or inevitable within our societies. Films, then, both as systems of representation and as narrative structures, are rich sites for ideological analysis.

Although cultural studies has produced a welter of ideological analyses of film texts (which 'read off' the ideology from the text), it is important to stress that ideologies structure institutions as well as texts. Our legal system, for instance, is biased towards the defence of property. Although the crime of murder suffers the maximum penalty in most Western countries, in general it is true to say that offences such as arson and theft are treated more severely than assault or, until relatively recently, rape. This, we might say, is 'simply historical'. Yet history, too, is constructed: it is the selection and combination of events, sequences, causes, and effects. (We might say that history has a history.) Ideology works to obscure the process of history so that it appears natural, a process we cannot control and which it seems churlish to question. Yet history is the product of competing interests, all attempting to centre their own interests as those of the nation. The history of the institutions of the law reveals discrimination against the poor; the bias towards the protection of property clearly favours those who have most property – presumably, the propertied classes who framed the laws. Yet the institution of the law is normally seen to be above class, above ideology, above politics.

Film institutions have political interests which ultimately determine which films are made, not to mention which films are seen. The examination of the operation of these institutions reveals the nature of the interests they serve, the objectives they pursue, and what their function means for the audiences, the industry, and the culture as a whole.

Considerations of the workings of ideology are relevant to both kinds of cultural approach – the textual and the contextual. I wish to stay with this contextual approach for the moment, in order to look, first, at how a film industry participates in the construction of the 'nation'. The second step is to examine this area of cultural production through an illustrative case, surveying the forces determining the development of the Australian film industry during the revival of the 1970s and beyond.

Film and national culture

These days, as all the talk about globalization and cosmopolitanism encourages us to think of ourselves as 'citizens of the world', it is easy to forget that the nation-state's conventional role as the 'natural' form of political organization is a relatively modern one. It is also very durable. Most people these days still expect our membership of the nation to bind us together, enabling us to achieve more than we could as separate cells or groups of interests. Identification with the nation is often a source of pride and pleasure, too; sporting events, national celebrations of coronations, inaugurations, or holidays such as Independence Day or Remembrance Day, are important and satisfying rituals of cultural membership. But we also know that identifications with 'the nation' can be extremely arbitrary. Post-war reconstructions of European national boundaries cannot have hoped to construct 'national' allegiances easily with a line drawn across a map. Recent political events have revealed how unsatisfactory such strategies have been. The Middle East is a further site of the rejection of what are seen as arbitrary attempts to establish definitions of separate nations. This may be an extreme example, but one could also ask whether the Welsh or the Scottish internalize the same idea of the 'nation' as the residents of England. Are Australian Aborigines part of the Australian 'nation', despite their relative powerlessness and subordination? Are the differences between San Francisco, California, and New Orleans, Louisiana, more substantial than the similarities?

Opponents of nationalism see it as a dangerously effective tool of persuasion; to accept that the good of the nation is pre-eminent is also to accept the possibility of subordination to that good. To accept the possibility is, sooner or later, to experience the reality. The so-called 'war on terror' has raised that issue repeatedly, as citizens of many nation-states are asked to forgo freedoms they have hitherto valued and enjoyed in order to better police the security of the nation. So there are at least two sides to nationalism; it can be a positive political benefit or a real political danger. On the one hand, the idea of the nation is one way of mobilizing the sense of identity without which no social group can survive; the rituals of the nation allow us to celebrate and confirm our membership. On the other hand, it can be used to convince those who are inequitably treated to accept their subordination as being in the national interest. When Dr Johnson famously described patriotism as 'the last refuge of the scoundrel', he referred to the persuasive power unleashed by the invocation of the nation. It is very difficult to place your own interests above those of the nation without seeming to be selfish and unprincipled. Most importantly, the idea of the nation can operate at the most basic levels of meaning and discourse. It becomes an overriding set of priorities which define what is acceptable and what is not, what is normal and what is not, all through defining what is Australian or British or American and what is not.

Identification with the nation is an essential prerequisite for political power. We can see the political parties at election time scramble to identify themselves with the flag, with national values, or with the signifiers of an 'essence' of the nation – be it a colonial war in South America, a national cricket team, or a group of astronauts. Political parties attempt to centre themselves as representative of the nation; by so doing they hope to persuade voters that their interests, the nation's interests, and the voters' interests (as members of the nation) are identical. In wider conceptions of politics – that is, not party politics but power relations generally – the idea of the nation is enlisted in achieving and maintaining hegemony. Hegemony is the process by which members of society are persuaded to acquiesce in their own subordination, to abdicate cultural leadership in favour of sets of interests which are represented as identical, but may actually be antithetical, to their own. The subordinated are persuaded by the ideologies on offer rather than the particulars of their material conditions (which might be the practical result of such ideologies). Hegemony's aim is to resist social change and maintain the status quo.

The regulation and control of definitions of art, of literature, and of the national film industry are also hegemonic in that the imperative is always to restrict and limit the proliferation of representations of the nation. (This is because the proliferation of representations also proliferates different definitions.) Representations of the nation are themselves particularly important since they both produce and reproduce the dominant points of view. This does not mean that we only have one version of the nation – although ideally that is what hegemony could mean. Rather, the various representations will enjoy a different status and will have different meanings. In effect, they will construct a different nation. So the British culture constructed in *Four Weddings and a Funeral* is very different from the British culture constructed in *Lock, Stock and Two Smoking Barrels*. Similarly, if the star is the 'type of the individual' within the culture, the face of Hugh Grant will represent a very different type of the individual from the face of Vinnie Jones. Such differences can be contradictory and therefore threatening; in such cases, the cultural institutions might attempt to limit or control the multiplicity of representations by depicting some as marginal or crass, for instance. But this strategy may be actively inhibited by the audience's thirst for variety and their active toleration of differences. As we shall see in the Australian example, the pressure for hegemony is often met with resistance from the popular 'unofficial' culture.

Like other ideological constructions, representations of the nation are not 'fixed': their political and cultural importance is such that they are sites of considerable contestation. To gain control of the representational agenda for the nation is to gain considerable power over individuals' view of themselves and each other. This is one of the reasons why there is so much concern within so many countries over the domination of film and TV production and distribution by the USA. If we understand our world (or our nation) through its representations, foreign control of the major media of representation does threaten the coherence of the individual's understanding of that world (or nation). The American domination of the mass media has, to some extent, normalized American images of modern society. Residents of Australia have only relatively recently come to accept Australian urban images on their cinema screens and, only a little less recently, Australian accents in advertising, and from radio or TV announcers. The cultural hegemony facilitated by this domination of the mass media has worried many countries, and not only on behalf of their media industries.

There is a degree of exaggeration here that can imply greater cultural/national differences than actually exist; the withdrawal of all American films would not remove all evidence of sexism, for instance, from Australian cinemas, nor the incidence of cultural chauvinism from British cinemas. However, film does serve important cultural functions and those countries which have set up their own industries aim at recovering some local control over these functions. They can at least break the silence often maintained about their own culture from within American cinema. Consequently, for the UK, Australia, Canada, New Zealand, and many Scandinavian,

South American, and European countries, the question for the last forty years has not been 'Should we have a national cinema?' but rather 'What kind of cinema should it be?' Despite the fact that the mainstream feature film is a global industry, and that even the most successful of the national industries are still enclosed within the macro-structures of the American industry, cinema's ideological power has been recognized in the competing, if subordinated, voices of national film industries.

In general, the results of this development have been twofold. First, most countries have set up a network of institutions or government policies to control foreign input and encourage indigenous output. Measures taken include box-office levies (Sweden), income-tax incentives for investors (Australia), maximum quotas on foreign films (Britain), and limitations on vertical integration with multinational companies. The more positive moves include the establishment of a film and TV school (Australia), national film-financing bodies (Canada), grants and subsidies (Britain), and government-funded marketing enterprises of the kind that Britain and Australia have mounted at the annual international marketplace of Cannes. The 'nationalization' of film promotion through such national marketing offices reveals how closely indigenous film production is connected to the representation and dissemination of images of the nation at home and overseas – even where these images are produced by private and independent companies. What we see is not just a commercial enterprise, but a national cultural project (or projection) as well.

This introduces the second aspect. When films act as *representatives*, as well as *representations*, of the nation overseas they become subject to a different regime of inspection. They are assessed, for instance, for their appropriateness as tourist advertisements, or for their 'typicality' as depictions of national life. (This is not something that tends to happen to American films, however, although much of what we think we know about American society does come from their movies.) The ways in which the texts produced by the national industries are patrolled for their images, for their suitability as the national 'touring team', offer another set of determinants of what is produced, what is distributed, and what is positively received by audiences and by critics. And although we are not talking about American mainstream cinema now, it is in such texts and in their conditions of production that we can most clearly see the relationship between film, culture, and ideology. The lessons learnt from such texts and such conditions can easily be applied to any national cinema, including the American cinema.

This brings us full circle, from the context of national cultural production to the film texts themselves. As I said earlier, one cannot hope to do more than chart the intersection of the forces and conditions of film production and reception. But it is illustrative to look at one relatively self-contained example for the lessons it carries about the processes of cultural production. This example is the revival of the Australian film industry, its recovery from near-extinction during the 1970s, and the condition in which it finds itself today.

A national cinema: the Australian revival

Australia was one of the early participants in the development of a film industry. An Australian Salvation Army film, *Soldiers of the Cross* (1901), has some claim to being the first full-length feature in the world, although it was not a continuous film but a mixture of slides, film, music, and the spoken word. *The Story of the Kelly Gang* (1906) has slightly stronger claims to being the longest narrative film to that date in the world. Whatever the validity of such claims, Australian film-makers responded quickly to overseas developments and for the first twenty years of the last century enjoyed significant local success. However, increasingly during the 1920s and certainly with the arrival of sound, the industry languished. The professional quality of the local films gradually declined, vertical integration of the industry froze out all but British and American imports, and by the end of the Second World War Australia had lost its last feature production company. For the next twenty years, almost without exception, Australia was a cheap location for foreign productions (*On the Beach*), British or American co-productions of Australian stories (*The Sundowners* and *Smiley*), and the occasional brave attempt to revive the Australian feature (*Three in One*). Attempts to keep feature production alive dwindled into an attempt to keep the local newsreel industry alive, but when television arrived in 1956 even the newsreel began to disappear.

It is worth noting that encapsulated accounts like the one above make historical processes sound inevitable. They are not, and the failure of the various Australian governments to protect their film industry from foreign competition, or from the discriminatory practices of foreign-owned exhibition and distribution chains, is part of cinema history in Australia, as it is in Britain. However, during the first half of the 1960s, some interest was expressed at government level in determining whether a film industry would be viable in Australia. The future can be changed, if those in power can be persuaded that the change is in their interests. The arrival of television in Australia had highlighted the need for the policing of foreign content on Australian screens, as well as revealing the importance of a film industry in supplying the infrastructure and the work force for developments in televised and theatrical drama. Both areas were just beginning to grow at the time. The film industry also had considerable potential as a feeder industry, supplying work to a wide range of arts-related occupations – writers, set designers, graphic designers, actors, sound engineers, script editors, camera operators, and many others. As Australia had restricted the use of foreign advertisements on television – for the first forty years or so of the television industry, most commercials shown in Australia had to be made by Australians – a small film-production industry had grown up within the advertising sector. Peter Weir (*Picnic at Hanging Rock, The Truman Show, Master and Commander: The Far Side of the World*) and Fred Schepisi (*Jimmie Blacksmith, It Runs in the Family, IQ*) are among the directors who worked on advertisements. The potential of this group was clearly not exhausted by working on commercials. There were, then, many industrial and economic arguments which suggested that an expanded Australian film industry would benefit existing and related industries. By the end of the 1960s, these arguments were reinforced by another factor: an increasingly powerful nationalist mythology that came to regard film as the most desirable medium for projecting an image of the new confidence and maturity seen to mark contemporary Australian culture and society.

In 1969, there were no feature film production companies operating permanently in Australia; there was no film financing from government sources outside the documentary unit, the Commonwealth Film Unit (later called Film Australia); and drama production for Australian TV was very limited. There was still resistance to Australian images and voices in the media. In this context, and as a result of several government inquiries and reports as well as the personal lobbying of the Prime Minister of the day, John Gorton, the government made its first major intervention to encourage Australian film production.

Between 1969 and 1971 a film-financing institution was set up (the Australian Film Development Commission), a training institution was established (the Australian Film and Television School), and a range of other concessions and incentives were introduced to encourage local production. The boost to local production highlighted the problems that Australian films experienced in winning distribution and exhibition. At the time, there were two major distributors in the country, Hoyts and Greater Union – neither of them Australian-owned. An investigation by the Tariff Board – set up to protect local industries from 'unfair' competition – made threatening noises about the need to limit foreign ownership and break up distribution monopolies. As a result of such pressure, a minor distributor, Roadshow, which was primarily Australian-owned, took a more supportive attitude towards the Australian product. However, even Roadshow was dependent upon overseas films (it distributed for Warner Bros), so there was a limit to the help it cared to give Australian films by placing them in the right theatres at the right times. The problem has never really been resolved; Australia still cannot supply the distributors with enough features for them to risk breaking arrangements with the American suppliers and so the key box-office periods – Christmas and Easter, for instance – remain almost the exclusive preserve of Hollywood movies.

The institutional structure established between 1969 and 1975 operated as a large cultural bank. Film-makers approached the Australian Film Development Commission (later called the Australian Film Commission) with outlines of their projects. Their suitability, track record, and viability were assessed at this and

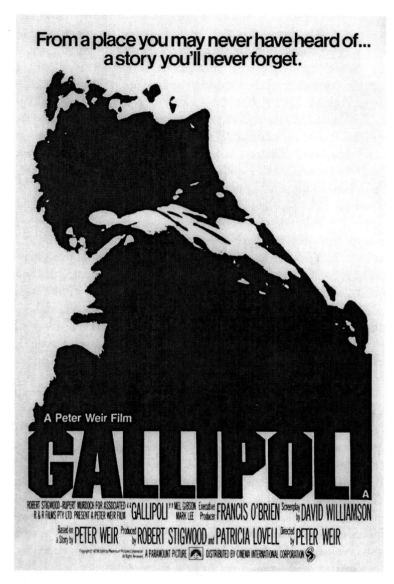

19 The Australian and US posters for Peter Weir's Australian film *Gallipoli*. On the American poster the slogan reads 'From a place you may never have heard of . . . a story you'll never forget' (courtesy of Associated R&R Films)

every subsequent stage. Once the project was favourably assessed, the AFDC/AFC funded further development of the script and the preparation of a budget. Once past this stage, the AFDC/AFC could decide to invest in the project through further seed money, a loan, or a straight grant aimed at completing the film. Apart from exceptional cases such as 1972's *The Adventures of Barry McKenzie*, film-makers had to find the majority of their budgets from private sources – even if this meant mortgaging the family home. (These were not yet Hollywood-style budgets, however: *Picnic at Hanging Rock* was made for less than half a million dollars, which was almost double the average budget for Australian films made in that year, 1975. *Towering Inferno*, an American success of the same year, cost $US14 million.) Between 1969 and 1975, the government film institutions provided as much as 60 per cent of total budgets in some cases, and as little as 20 per cent in others. In the same period, support from the industry itself – that is, the private sector of the TV companies and the distribution and exhibition chains – was derisory; it hit a high of 28 per cent of film budgets in 1970 and dropped to a low of 2 per cent in 1973. They were not prepared to gamble. This is highlighted by the dramatic increase in industry investment, up from 4 per cent to 46 per cent in 1975 – the year of the critical successes of *Picnic at Hanging Rock* and *Sunday Too Far Away*.

This structure was occasionally administered in a bizarre and ad hoc manner (Dermody and Jacka's (1987) book documents this), but it got the industry under way. The first films to catch the attention of the newly delivered Australian audience were the so-called 'ocker' comedies: *Stork*, *Alvin Purple*, and *The Adventures of Barry McKenzie*. The ocker films represented a masculine, populist, and cheerfully vulgar view of Australian society. Australian social practices and idiosyncrasies were celebrated for their own sake rather than for their contribution to world culture, while beer, sex, and bodily functions figured large in the action. The films depended on a very specific definition of Australian-ness.

It is at this point that we can see the ideology behind the film institutions click into place. Initial support for Australian film talked of making 'frankly commercial films' for a local and an overseas market. The ocker films were certainly commercial and at least *Barry*

McKenzie was successful in Britain. But the critics and the funding bodies were appalled by them and by their success. The ocker films dashed all hopes of establishing an image of Australia as a land of sophistication equal to the centres of Europe, with a culture of substance. Instead, Australia looked like the kind of place most of the Eurocentric critics and government film assessors would hate to inhabit. The specificity of the films' depiction of contemporary Australian popular culture was an embarrassment to people who had no commitment to it in the first place, but had rather hoped to help the nation to transcend it.

In a 1975 report on the industry, the supporting rhetoric underwent a crucial change. What Australia needed was 'quality' films which could be the cultural flagships of the nation. Financial capital was not the object any longer (relatively few Australian films made since the revival have returned significant profits). Cultural capital was now the goal.

Although the government film-financing bodies were never organized enough to be in any way conspiratorial, there was a remarkable similarity to the kinds of films which state and federal film commissions supported over the next five years. Instead of more ocker comedies, we had what Dermody and Jacka (1987) have called the 'AFC genre', a national film style determined by the preferences of the funding bodies and greeted critically as a source of national pride. Representative are such films as *Picnic at Hanging Rock* – visually stylish, low-key, highly aestheticized period dramas which offered the visual exoticism of the Australian scenery coupled with moderately symbolic and open-ended narrative forms. Australia was caught in the amber of its history, its present credentials implied by the style and sensibility of its representation of its past. These films deferred to European standards of cinematic taste – the models were the French *nouvelle vague* and the BBC TV's historical drama – rather than to American objectives of entertainment. Beautiful and untroubling films, they were politically conservative and, despite the obsession with history, they said little about contemporary Australia. In the years 1971 to 1977, out of 87 features made, fewer than 10 (if we exclude the ocker comedies) dealt with contemporary Australian society with any degree of seriousness. The obsession with historical drama seemed designed to establish that Australia *had* a history and therefore *was* a culture. Formally, films which moved outside the boundaries of the AFC genre and into Hollywood genres – action or adventure, for instance – were reviled by the critics and spurned by the government institutions (although they did pull in the audiences). *Mad Max* (1979) is relatively unusual for its time because it was made with no government support at all.

It is hard not to see the 'screening of Australia' as a complex exercise involving not only the screening of an image on film, but also a 'screening out' of certain kinds of films; those selected were European in their aesthetic assumptions and constructed Australian-ness through landscape or history rather than through popular cultural forms. In the AFC genre there was a deep ideological resistance to contemporary representations of the nation, perhaps because they almost inevitably celebrated indigenous cultural formations.

It is true that these patterns were less pronounced after 1977. Changes in the funding policies increased film-makers' reliance on private backing, and changes in the tax laws offered substantial incentives (at least until 1987) for investors to use film as a means of writing off high tax liabilities. Further, the burden film carried as the cultural flagship was lightened as the potential of the TV mini-series became apparent. The American success of the Australian mini-series *A Town Like Alice* alerted even the most Eurocentric to the possibilities of the US market and hastened the application of film-funding guidelines to TV production from which they had hitherto been excluded. Predictably enough, during the 1980s history repeated itself, as a parade of AFC genre historical mini-series swept across the nation's TV screens, albeit in competition with the tougher, more critical productions such as Kennedy–Miller's stylish *Vietnam*.

Film critics outside Australia have talked of the Australian revival as a movement with recognizable stylistic characteristics. These characteristics are not just the quirks of certain film-makers, fortuitously working in the same industry at the same time. They are the results of a number of textual and contextual determinants. The dominance of an aesthetic visual style is produced by the ideology of the AFC and other film commissions (and, in turn, the governments overseeing their funding) who saw in it a signification of the sophistication of the culture; such assumptions are nicely overturned when it is noted that the specific performance within that style could be traced to the early training of cinematographers like Russell Boyd in TV advertising. The open-ended narratives emerge from a narrative tradition in Australian prose (see Turner (1986) for an account of this) that is inconclusive and ambiguous, a fashionable interest in *nouvelle vague* existentialism, and the anti-individualist strategy of deferring any ideological narrative resolution on to history. (Many of the films just finish rather than 'end', and seal over this unsatisfying conclusion by the use of historical subtitles, summarizing characters' subsequent fates.) Government intervention in the industry had always constructed the films as cultural products, representing Australia as directly as its career diplomats. The films of this period are almost 'official' in their relation to Australian culture, and the vibrant iconoclasm of the ocker films would have enlivened many of them. The specific texts, then, emerge as the results of complex negotiations between industry, institutions, and national culture, and express a range of accepted ideological definitions of Australia. So the critics approved *Gallipoli*, with its hazy mythologizing of Australian soldiers as innocent and displaced, but decent and robust, descendants from European traditions; but *Crocodile Dundee*'s (1986) construction of the shrewd, potentially criminal (but basically decent), populist proved unacceptable.

While some countries might envy the level of government support given to Australian film during the 1970s – and only the American industry can survive without such support – it is as well to remember that this also binds the industry back into the nation and its representatives. It is ironic to note that as government support became less important to the Australian film industry, and as the influence of private investment became stronger, the variety of Australian films being made widened: ranging from the low-budget art film of Paul Cox's *Cactus* (1986) to the slyly engaging mainstream fare of *Crocodile Dundee*. After 1988, however, there was a further change in the funding structure which again bound producers back into governmental agendas. In an eerie replay of the beginnings of the revival, the 'frankly commercial' rubric was implicitly revived in the requirement that films seeking support from the new film bank (the Film Finance Corporation) find most of their budget from private sources. The tax concessions used to attract private investment earlier in the 1980s were wound back to the point where they no longer served a useful function. The initial effect of this structural change was to privilege the clearly commercial project with a strong likelihood of TV sales over the more idiosyncratic feature film. For a time, fewer features were made and TV mini-series became prohibitively expensive unless they were very likely to achieve major sales overseas. The level of confidence in the industry in the late 1980s and early 1990s reflected the structural uncertainties of the time.

Nevertheless, by the mid-1990s, a measure of confidence had returned to the Australian industry as it had come to terms with the changed funding environment. The clear commercialization of the local industry produced two significant effects. First, it removed some of the pressure on Australian film-makers to produce 'national' films and thus opened the way for more personal and individual projects – what came to be called the 'quirky' films of the 1990s (*Strictly Ballroom* (1993), *Muriel's Wedding* (1994), and *Priscilla, Queen of the Desert* (1994)). Second, it forced a more varied and innovative approach towards the competition with other international cinemas; the Australian industry did not just put its money on the mass-market art film typified by *The Piano* (1993), but it also backed the internationalized special-effects children's film *Babe* (1995), and the virtuoso star vehicle-cum-biopic *Shine*. A consequence of this opportunistic, project-driven, and relatively low-budget strategy was that explicit representations of the idea of 'the national' largely disappeared from Australian film, giving way to more contemporary stories unself-consciously played out within Australian locations. Less pleasing, however, was the outcome for television where the Australian mini-series virtually disappeared; productions in this format are now rare occurrences.

That is not the end of the story as the battles over representation do not end, of course. Controversy developed over *Babe* – how can it be an Australian film when everyone speaks with American or English accents? – which revisited earlier debates about what kinds of film count as Australian. More recently, the increasing number of films being produced in Australia by the major global film companies, and the transnational character of these films and their settings, now threatens to swamp the local industry – raising production costs, occupying limited studio space, and squeezing out the lower budget local productions. As Australia becomes integrated into global Hollywood as a location for so-called 'runaway' productions – a number of blockbusters have been produced there in recent years (*Mission Impossible*, *The Matrix*, the last two *Star Wars* prequels) – there is increasing concern that it might risk losing its local industry entirely. This concern is given added force by the relative failure of recent local productions at the box office, resulting in vigorous debate about the kinds of movies Australian film-makers should be shooting, and the quality of those they are shooting. Furthermore, the government investment in developing an Australian film culture – events, magazines, research, collection policies, and so on as a means of generating an audience for local films – evaporated over 2000–5, and it seems much of the Australian film audience followed suit. Once again, Australian cinema is at a kind of crossroads, and both the production industry and the government is required to think about whether they want such an industry, and what its desired shape and focus is to be.

There are real issues here to do with the structure and viability of a local film industry, but it also needs to be remembered that debates about the national character of film texts are always strategies in the battle to maintain a measure of regulation and control over the images and narratives which represent Australia. That battle is never conclusively won, and we should not forget that this, along with the production of these images and narratives, is the fundamental – ideological – business of a national cinema.

Ideology in the text

From the Australian example we can see that arguments about the aesthetic qualities of specific film texts are never objective or disinterested. Both the production and reception of film are framed by ideological interests, no matter how insistently this might be denied. In this section, I want to examine the workings of ideology in the film text itself. The starting-point is the simple one that ideology is read from film texts, consciously or unconsciously, and the relationship between each text and its culture is traceable to ideological roots.

The problem, however, is how to deal with this. It is impossible to stand outside ideology and talk about it in a language which is itself free of ideology. It is also hard to see things which we like to think are parts of our identity as ideologically constructed. One's tastes, for instance, are formed through ideology, but it is difficult to accept that something as essential to our sense of ourselves is culturally constructed. Just as the concepts themselves can be a little unsettling, ideological textual analysis can have its moments too. It can be, in turns, dizzyingly complex or ridiculously simple. The next two sections – without falling into either of these extreme categories, it is to be hoped – will outline some of the basic assumptions and applications of this mode of representational analysis.

More than any others, ideological considerations allow us to begin to understand the relationship between film texts and their cultural contexts. Importantly, ideological approaches reject the view of the film text as 'unitary' in meaning; that is, as making only one kind of sense, without contradictions, exceptions, or variations in the interpretations made by different members of the audience. Rather, the text is a kind of battleground for competing and often contradictory positions. Of course, this competition usually results in a victory for the culture's dominant positions, but not without leaving cracks or divisions through which we can see the consensualizing work of ideology exposed. Through such cracks, ideological analysis provides the point of entry to an understanding of the film's formal process of construction. These cracks, or gaps, in the text are not simply the inventions of the critic. They are often points where the audience is aware of a weakness in the narrative: where a union between lovers is formed that is 'unconvincing' or where the death of a character might seem unmotivated or arbitrary, or where one might have expected the ending to have a different emotional inflection. Often the formal problems we might discern within a film are traceable to the intransigence of the ideological opposition; an unsatisfactory ending in a film may emerge from the failure to unite the ideological alternatives convincingly.

As the above paragraphs might suggest, generalization is risky in this area. Ideology is a slippery concept since it is not an abstract entity which can be described separately from its workings in a specific act of signification. So we will move to the discussion of an example – a film which highlights the complexities of the working of ideology because it was seen to be explicitly ideological by members of its audience but not by its makers. Fritz Lang's *Metropolis* reveals how unconsciously ideology can work and how it can live in the formal properties of the individual film text.

In 1927, German expressionism was a greatly respected film movement, marked by a strong visual style which employed low-key lighting, geometric shapes, oblique camera angles, and sharp juxtapositions of light and dark. Its narratives were melodramatic, offering gothic and supernatural plots as often as contemporary stories. At the time, the Weimar Republic of Germany was in political disarray, suffering the trauma of defeat in the First World War and the uncertainty of continual changes in government (fifteen different administrations from the beginning of the Weimar Republic until the election of Hitler's National Socialists), and lacking any one political grouping capable of presiding over the reconstruction of the national identity, while a plethora of groups was singled out for special blame and fear: the 'international Jewish conspiracy', the Communists, the dying aristocracy, even the Weimar itself. The film-makers were relatively aloof from this, however, and there are remarkably few direct references to German domestic politics in expressionist films.

It was in this climate that *Metropolis* was made. The film tells the story of a workers' revolution in a futuristic dictatorship. The revolution is actually instigated through a plot hatched between the ruler of Metropolis and a mad scientist, and is intended to discredit a workers' liberation movement which is given the contradictory attributes of both Christianity and Communism. The workers destroy the factory and flood their homes, but stability is reinstated by the end of the film. The ruler's son mediates between the workers and the boss, as Christ mediates between God and Man. Or, as the film has it, he is the 'heart' which guides the co-operation between the 'head' (the ruler) and the 'hands' (the workers). Although the film establishes the oppression of the workers, its final frames show them surrendering their power to a newly humanized ruler.

Lang was not an overtly political film-maker at this point, and certainly had no special admiration for Nazism; he saw the film, as he said later, as a rather 'silly' melodrama. Hitler, however, saw it differently and admired its dramatization of Fascist philosophy. In fact, Hitler was so impressed with Lang, a Jew, that he offered him the post of head of the German film industry and the status of 'honorary Aryan'. Lang, to his credit, fled Nazi Germany for America where he became known for, among other things, his anti-Nazi films during the Second World War.

Ideology is unconscious, as Lang's history demonstrates. He was not a Nazi, nor was he pro-Nazi. Yet his film brought Hitler great satisfaction. This is because Lang, the film-maker/*bricoleur*, used what the culture made available to him – not only its languages but its meanings. These included the dominant images of power as patriarchal, fatherly, and the assumption that political unrest was always undesirable and that reformist politics were either messianic or Marxist. The pentangle (five-pointed star) used to represent the evil of the scientist Rotwang, with its close similarity to the star of David, invokes anti-Semitism. The film's view of the people as gullible and to be saved from themselves is probably also traceable to cultural roots. Most of these assumptions and meanings were appropriated by Nazism as well as by Lang's film. Fritz Lang was not the 'author' of the discourses of *Metropolis*; his culture was.

The ideology of a film does not take the form of direct state-ments or reflections on the culture. It lies in the narrative structure and in the discourses employed – the images, myths, conventions, and visual styles. Even though *Metropolis* is a conventional melo-drama involving a love affair between an individualized hero and heroine, it is not a film which is about character or even about plot. Its most obvious attribute is its portrait of a world. The film's distinctiveness and power arise from its opening series of represen-tations of dehumanizing working conditions, the physical design of the future world, and the depiction of a rigidly hierarchical physical environment in which the people live. These aspects of the film are both prescient and striking. For the contemporary viewer at least, who may find the love interest a little dated, they are the discourses of a pre-eminently social, political film.

This being the case, the ending of the film needs to resolve its social/political conflicts as well as its personal dilemmas – but it does not. It is characteristic of the workings of ideology that they express social or political differences as personal and individual, therefore to be resolved at the personal not the political level, and a sign of *individual* weakness, not the weakness of the social or political *system*. The ending of *Metropolis* resolves the love interest, reunites the father and son, but changes almost nothing in the social or political structure of its world. The powerful early scenes of dehumanized workers being sacrificed to the machines are cancelled out by the workers' capitulation to what is a corrupt and irresponsible deployment of power. By the end, the power of the masses is represented as the real threat, and this legitimates the reinstatement of the fatherly, benevolent dictatorship. The masses need protection from themselves, it seems, and the guardianship of their future is placed safely in the hands of the ruler of Metropolis.

The film is composed of a series of moves and counter-moves which are both narratively and ideologically motivated. Its opening images explicitly connect totalitarianism with capitalism by making the Master of Metropolis an industrialist. However, the socialist alternatives inevitably invoked are not supported. The robot Maria is used as a metaphor for the temptress of revolutionary Communism and her demonic destructiveness articulates a warning against such temptations. The destruction she causes legitimizes the need for a restraining power, for a 'head' who can control the 'hands'. When the Master undergoes a humanizing change of heart, his rule is again benevolent, paternal. This is the only concession required to make the workers surrender their destructive power back to the state. The film is marked by a deep formal and ideological contradiction: the powerful image of the working classes as victims is reversed into an image of the working classes as agents of their own destruction; or to put it another way, the critique of class domination and capitalism

20 The art direction and set design for *Metropolis* still impresses; Ridley Scott's *Blade Runner*, almost sixty years later, owes it significant debts is overcome by a dread of Communism specifically, and generally of uncontrolled social change.

Contemporary audiences certainly find this unsatisfying, as the contradictions are crudely smoothed over with the invocation of loyalty to the father, and his reciprocal love for his people. It is this latter aspect, presumably, which appealed to Hitler – the binding of the group back into the nation, the investment of faith in the mother/father, as well as the melodramatic depictions of alternative political positions.

In order to deal with the film's ideology we have to deal, even in this preliminary way, with the surfaces of the text, the formal systems of signification. (In so doing we have uncovered at least two opposing readings, two sets of signification which might make sense of it for an audience.) The method of analysis drives us further than one might expect into the construction of the text, given that the objective of the analysis is ultimately to move *from* the text back to the culture which produced it.

The final point, before leaving this example, is to qualify one false impression that it may have given. I have already talked of the notion of hegemony. This account of *Metropolis* may imply that hegemonic systems are comprehensively, inevitably, controlling and determining. This is misleading. Films must take on some relation to ideologies but they do not necessarily recycle them. John Ellis (1982: 74) approaches this point in the following way:

> General ideological notions are assumed by narrative films. These assumptions are established through repetition, a char- acteristic of ideological reproduction which leads us to assume things unless they are specifically contradicted. Yet mere repetition alone is not the characteristic of the film text. It may take for granted certain meanings, certain assumptions, but it exists to take risks, to work through ideological problems. Hence the innovatory character of the film in relation to ideological meanings. They are not reproduced so much as refreshed, not so much repeated as reworked.

I would go further, and say that they may actively oppose or subvert dominant meanings. For example, in the Australian ocker films a popular narrative form carries meanings that are subversive of some dominant patterns. The result was that such films were critically squashed, but they *did* get made and they *did* find their audiences.

It is important to see the dynamic nature of ideology. Although culture is subjected to hegemonic constructions, this is a process – not a permanently achieved state. The constellations of hegemonic interests can change. The constituent ideologies can change too. As I suggested earlier, we can see the process being acted out in narrative films where ideologies confront each other as structural opposites in the narrative itself – as good guy and bad guy, as right move and wrong move – to be resolved in the final reel. The film's closure mimics the individual processes of making decisions, taking positions, and making sense of the experiences that we go through every day of our lives.

Issues in ideological analysis

Although it is important to retain a sense of the heterogeneity of the ideological system, the vast majority of the work on film and ideology has concentrated on the ways in which film texts inevitably support existing social conditions, and accept existing explanations of those social conditions. Although the constitution of the ruling interests within culture does change, the function of hegemony does not; it works to maintain the status quo. In film studies, this has provoked elitist critiques of the medium from one side of the argument, but more often it provokes analysis which is aimed at revealing ideologies operating in film and in the culture. Study of ideology in film provides an insight into the meaning systems of the culture and into the ways in which such systems are inscribed into all kinds of social practice.

One target of such studies is the kind of film which seems to be critical of dominant positions – apparently pro-feminist films, for instance, such as *The Contender* (2000) or a film like *The Quiet American* which appears to attack US involvement in Iraq. *Tootsie* (1982) could be seen as having some progressive attributes: it depicts a man experiencing the sexism normally handed out to women. He learns just how difficult men make women's lives. In his persona as Dorothy, Mike Dorsey (Dustin Hoffman) attempts to 'liberate' his/her or her female comrades in the television production company, and ultimately leads the way towards redressing the balance to some extent. On the face of it this might seem to overturn the ideological privileges the male has enjoyed. However, as Judith Williamson (1987) has suggested, this is not necessarily true. Mike Dorsey is still a man even when he pretends to be Dorothy, and the lesson we learn from the film is that men are better at being feminists than women, as well as being better at everything else!

Hollywood has a rich tradition of 'changing places' movies, which seem to be critical of the contexts into which the lead characters move; while that might seem progressive, as the narrative unfolds it becomes clear that the point of the film is often simply to justify the character's acceptance of the status quo. Chris Rock's character in *Down to Earth* (2001), itself a remake of the Warren Beatty vehicle *Heaven Can Wait* (1978), may provide the location for a number of comic–critical observations on American attitudes to race, but its resolution is a conventional one. The point of 'trading places' is usually to find out that what one desired is not necessarily what one really wants; so, trading places with a rich person may teach the protagonist the value of their previous, although less materially comfortable, life. Changing places with a white person, as does Rock in *Down to Earth*, is a slightly different matter, because it invites audiences to trivialize the structural impediments in black Americans' lives. The main character's relief at finding he is black once again (demonstrated by the fact that he can't get a cab to stop for him any more) may work to bring the narrative towards closure, but it also demonstrates that the sharp moments early in the film have very little to do with the ideological position it ends up endorsing.

The point of such comments is not to 'spoil' the film for you, but to show how potentially critical positions can indeed be articulated within the boundaries of ideology, but that they are eventually 'clawed back' into the dominant systems to generate their meanings. The first half of the Australian film *Gallipoli* attacks the rich seam of mythology and cultural chauvinism which surrounds the legend of the Anzac (Australian and New Zealand Army Corps) troops' engagement at Gallipoli during the First World War. The effect of any attack on this legend is to demythologize the Anzac heroes, to claim specifically that they were naive or were duped or misled. *Gallipoli* stops short of carrying through this claim. The second half of the film turns its characters into heroes, as the standard mythologizing framework claws back their individuality and oppositional potential into the conventional legend. The freeze frame at the end of the film – which catches the more idealistic hero at the point of being shot while charging the Turkish trenches – is the filmic equivalent of the commemorative statues of the soldier erected in small towns all over Australia after the war. Its ideology, too, is the same.

The demands of the narrative – the relentless movement forward towards resolution – can serve ideological imperatives also. Moral, political, and social complexities are easily obscured within the tide of narrative. This is particularly true of the recent fashion for highly glamorous gangster films – such as those made by Quentin Tarantino. Sorting out the moral complexities in the *Kill Bill* films, for instance, would seem like a highly inappropriate activity to indulge in on the drive home from the cinema. As long as it is clear to whom our narrative allegiance should go, there is little else for the viewer to decide if they want to go along with the world constructed in the film. On the other hand, it is not unusual for Hollywood movies to acknowledge and foreground alternative or competing readings, even as they come to an end. The ending of *Basic Instinct*, for instance, directly challenges our sense of closure with its close-up of the ice-pick under the bed inviting us to think beyond the ending towards further narrative developments. It is possible to think of such ambiguous endings as the product of their ideological, as well as their narrative, possibilities.

The end of *Working Girl* (1988) is signalled by the triumphal soundtrack as the heroine's attempt to cross the line into an executive role achieves success – an office of her own. The camera pulls back, mythologizing the city in which the heroine is working but also reducing her to the status of one person, one window, among thousands. As the camera pulls even further back we lose sight of her altogether and her story is swallowed up in the spectacle of skyscrapers. As a coda to a moral fable of individualist capitalism (which is one way of seeing the film), this closing shot has a very ambiguous effect since it suggests an opposing view of capitalism – as a dehumanizing and alienating system into which the individual disappears.

Such problems of interpretation, the way in which a viewer is led through the feature film, feed back into a central issue in ideological analysis, that of realism. Realism has acquired a special meaning within this tradition of film analysis. It refers to the dominant mode of narrative film-making, and certainly the dominant mode within Hollywood cinema. Realist film creates a world which is as recognizable as possible; and audiences understand it by drawing analogies between the world of the film and their own world. They are assisted in this process by the lengths that realist film goes to in order to look like real life. The technologies of film production are hidden, so that techniques which might draw attention to the means of construction are kept to a minimum. Editing is as seamless as possible, the *mise-en-scène* is as dense as that of real life, camera movements tend to keep pace with the movement of the spectator's eyes, and perspective is maintained as if there were but one spectator. Technologies are not culturally innocent either, as Richard Dyer has demonstrated in his analysis of the representation of 'whiteness' in the cinema and on TV. In *White* (1997), Dyer argues that photography and the cinema, 'as media of light', lend themselves to privileging white people. Not only that, but the aesthetic which has, for example, organized the conventions of lighting in the cinema serves particular social interests:

> The whole argument here is that the photographic media are centrepieces in a whole culture of light that is founded on two particular notions, namely that reality can be represented as being on a ground of white, and that light comes from above; these notions have the effect not only of advantaging white people in representation and of discriminating between and within them, but also of suggesting a special affinity between them and the light.
>
> (Dyer 1997: 84)

The constructedness of these components of the conventions of realism are revealed when Dyer talks about the difficulty of translating onto black faces the lighting practices used to eliminate shadows on white faces. In a further example of what he calls 'the white-centricity of the aesthetic technology of the photographic media' (p. 97), Dyer records the difficulties faced by the cinematographer working on *The Color Purple* with an all-black cast: all the set interiors and set decorations had be made darker than 'normal' in order for the actors clearly to be seen.

Realism's disguising of the constructed as 'the natural' is a direct parallel to the function of ideology. The power of realist film, however, lies in the efficiency of this disguise, its ability to appear to be an unmediated view of reality. Colin MacCabe (1981) has argued that in realist film, TV drama, and the novel, there is what he calls a 'hierarchy of discourse'. Realist narratives offer problems, dilemmas, deficiencies to be solved or supplied; the reader or viewer makes his or her way through the narrative gaining knowledge about how this is to occur. At the end, the reader possesses full knowledge, the problems are solved, and there is a sense of a satisfying conclusion. MacCabe argues that realist fictions guide the reader very carefully through one set of discourses – a set of values, a narrator, or the control of the perspectives of the camera – which takes on the role of an authoritative narrator. The authority of the narrative 'tells' the reader what to think, closes off questions, and delivers them to the end of the fiction. The realist text does not question reality or its constituent conditions. Since the realist text depends on the reader seeing it as reality, it cannot question itself without losing authenticity.

MacCabe has claimed that realist films are incapable of expressing opposition to or criticism of dominant values or beliefs, because they depend on them in order to make sense. Even realist narratives which represent themselves as critical of dominant values – the texts referred to in these debates are the TV docu-dramas *Days of Hope* and *Boys from the Blackstuff* – have been attacked as simply using history to naturalize social divisions: 'that is the way it is', they are supposed to say, and there is 'little we can do about it'.

This series of proposals needs qualification. The realist debate is a large one, and further reading will bring a greater understanding of it than is possible in this small section. I would like to make the point, however, that realism is a system of signification which still has to work within specific social and representational contexts. In British film, notwithstanding MacCabe's argument, social realism has often been used in ways that are highly discomforting, rather than complacent or consoling. A film such as *The Crying Game* (1992), for instance, would be an example of this. One needs to be wary of simply applying this theory to any film or any culture without closer investigation. One cannot simply read off the ideology of a film from its formal characteristics – such as its having a strong sense of closure. Indeed, such totalizing assumptions have exposed film theory of the last decade or two to the kinds of critique advanced by Bordwell and Carroll (1996). Carroll warns against 'the routine application of some, larger unified theory to questions of cinema, which . . . unsurprisingly churns out roughly the same answers, or remarkably similar answers, in every case'. The result, he says, is 'theoretical impoverishment' (1996: 41). Just as some critiques of psychoanalysis have shifted the interest in ideology from the unconscious to the historical and the social, Carroll's insistence on a more 'piecemeal' approach advises against the enthusiastic embrace of overarching theories which eliminate the necesssity of engaging directly and in detail with the specificity of film texts.

This flags some issues which can be followed up in further reading. As Bordwell and Carroll demonstrate, the comprehensiveness of the claims made by theories of ideology have provoked the proposition of competing theories which, for instance, suggest that the pleasures of the body might offer resistance to the ideological. We have to seriously consider the possibility that some aspects of the film experience may be 'outside' the ideological:

> For example, if we are studying horror films, it strikes me as incontrovertible that filmmakers often play upon what psychologists call 'the startle response', an innate human tendency to 'jump' at loud noises and to recoil at fast movements. This tendency is, as they say, impenetrable to belief; that is, our

beliefs won't change the response. It is hardwired and involuntary. Awareness of this response enables theorists like me to explain the presence of certain audiovisual patterns and effects in horror film, without reference to politics and ideology. Indeed, insofar as the startle response is impenetrable to belief, it could be said to be, in certain respects, beyond politics and ideology.

(Carroll 1996: 51)

While Carroll's 'bracketing' of ideology here has been resisted by some feminist and psychoanalytic theorists, it is worth considering the limits of the concept.

We need to ask if our pleasure at a car chase on film or our day-to-day experience of physical pleasure is constructed in ideology. We might also need to consider if our conceptions of beauty or style are entirely constructed by culture, or if there is something universal and unchanging about such perceptions. One might understand that beauty is culturally coded while still feeling that it would be impossible to see a tropical island as ugly. Even sexual pleasure may be culturally coded; is sexuality a 'realism' that needs to be interrogated? Further, such questions should concern more than just testing the limits to theories of ideology. The notion of pleasure is still, apart from the important progress made within feminist theory, relatively undeveloped in relation to popular cinema. The residue of aesthetic preferences still affects the kinds of films which get talked about, the kinds of problems seen to be of interest in film studies today. Yvonne Tasker refers to the difference between what 'we know' and what 'we enjoy', as a distinction which ideological criticism has attempted to submerge. As she points out, this is a difficult achievement in practice since 'the kinds of fantasy investments at work in the pleasures taken from the cinema cannot be controlled by conscious political positions in the way that some criticism seems to imply' (1993: 136). These conscious political positions may simply be getting in the way of our understanding of the medium and its relation to its audiences. Drawing on her analysis of heroines in action movies, Tasker suggests that feminists' critical disapproval of action heroines in the films she examines comes, in part, from the notion that 'some forms of activity or entertainment are more appropriate to men and some to women'. The designation of 'inappropriate' images derived from a feminist critical tradition ironically coincides, says Tasker, with a more conventional sense of feminine decorum, 'of knowing one's place within a gendered hierarchy' (p. 136). A benefit likely to emerge from interventions such as Tasker's, expressing a more cultural interest in film, is a more concerted attempt to understand the pleasures provided by mainstream genre films – from horror films to teen movies. It is not enough to think of them working solely through the pleasures of a ritual confirmation of ideologies. Stella Bruzzi's (1997) analysis of the function of costume within the feature film offers another fruitful direction for the analysis of pleasure that does not depend upon narrative or character, but upon the spectacular display of fashion and design.

As such questions multiply, and as attentions shift towards the pleasures of Hollywood cinema rather than the unpacking of its ideological agendas, it has to be said that ideological criticism has tended to be pushed to the back of the stove. Where once film studies invested heavily in elaborating the construction of ideologies through particular films, revealing what was often presented as a hidden message buried in the text, this is now a less important component of research and criticism in the field. Taking its place to some extent, and in many ways drawing upon similar theoretical influences, has been the steady development of the attention to how cinema constructs cultural identities – with a particular focus, as we saw in Chapter 5, on the construction of race, ethnicity and gender. To the extent that such concerns have taken on a more central role within the field, the earlier version of ideological analysis looks a little old-fashioned and out of date. That said, it does seem to me, still, to be among the ideas we need to take seriously as a means of understanding how mass-marketed cinema, in particular, generates its meanings as pleasures for a large and varied audience.

A final problem. For many when they first encounter notions of ideology, the argument that they and their identities are culturally constructed is often interpreted as saying that they are not 'real'. It is difficult to get around the sense that there is some genuine reality out there which ideology prevents us getting at. The trick is to realize

21 The action movie: Tom Cruise and *Mission Impossible 2*

that whether that is the case or not is immaterial. Our only access to reality is through its representation. Even as we look at a landscape we do so through cultural filters which actually order what we see. (Early paintings of the Australian landscape make it look just like Europe, its native inhabitants resembling classical statues of Greek and Roman heroes rather than what we now see as the distinctive features of the Aborigines.) Representations of the real world are like any other language system, saturated with ideology. However, this 'real' which culture constructs for us to know and live with is no less material in its effects on our lives and our consciousness. Just because we cannot stand outside our way of seeing the world (to 'see' that way of seeing) does not mean that our relation to the world is in some way false or provisional.

There is no really simple way in which to state this problem. However, Richard Dyer approached a specific aspect of it in his conclusion to *Stars*. Dealing with the notion that beauty is not inherent, even in film stars, and that the pleasure beauty generates is learned rather than being instinctual, even in films, he says: 'while I accept utterly that beauty and pleasure are culturally and historically specific, and in no way escape ideology, nonetheless they are beauty and pleasure and I want to hang on to them in some form or another' (1979: 185).

This is a sensible and instructive reaction to the force of ideology and to the pleasure of film.

Suggestions for further work

1   A good, simple application of theories of ideology to another medium of representation, fine art, is worth searching out: John Berger's *Ways of Seeing* (1972) demonstrates clearly how ideology shapes our view of the world. Much discussion of ideology is extremely complex and jargon-ridden, so this book may help students grappling with the concept. Another text which deals with the topics from a different angle is John Fiske's *Introduction to Communication Studies* (1982), a companion volume to this book in the 'Studies in Communication'

series. Discussion of ideology is to be found in treatments of popular culture – such as Judith Williamson's *Consuming Passions* (1987) or Rosalind Coward's *Female Desire* (1984) – but ideological analyses of films can be found in Nichols's collections of film theory *Movies and Methods* (1976 and 1985), as well as in journals such as *Screen, Jump Cut, Film Quarterly, Camera Obscura, Australian Journal of Screen Theory, Cultural Studies,* and many others.

2   Testing out your understanding of the concept of ideology on some film texts is a good idea. It might be useful, for instance, to turn back to Chapter 4 and examine the evolution of the western as described by Wright (1975) in the light of what you now know about ideology. What changes in ideology might underlie this evolution? (In fact, is the term 'evolution' itself indicative of an ideological position – developmental, always improving, rather than cyclical or revolutionary?)

3   The references to the realism debate are brief; anyone who wishes to follow it further – and it is a key debate – can find the most important articles collected in Bennett *et al.*'s *Popular Television and Film* (1981). As I said in this chapter, ideology has gone off the agenda in recent years, and so many of the key arguments were developed during the 1980s.

4   Ideology is revealed by examining those things we take for granted. Look at a film of your choice and see just what it takes for granted – at the level of dress, décor, and design as well as at the level of the motivations of major characters. Looking at the representations of women in, say, westerns of the 1950s, reveals that the ways in which women are taken for granted have changed. Are there other such instances you can recall, where change has revealed the dynamic process of ideology?

5   For a discussion of ideology and the film industry, Steve Neale's *Cinema and Technology* (1985) is useful and relatively accessible for such a difficult subject; a more challenging account which deals with the political economy of the industry as an ideological formation is Miller *et al.*'s *Global Hollywood* (2001).

6   For a further group of arguments around the notion of pleasure and ideology, see Rutsky and Wyatt (1990) and Noel King (1992).

7   Finally, the reading of ideology in film is an interpretative act. Follow the analyses in Chapter 7 and try to make use of these methods yourself in interpreting films. It is being done skilfully when it does not reduce the films to their constituent ideologies, and when you find as much that is contradictory and conflicting as you find that is unitary and consoling.

Applications

Most students of film find that they can follow the arguments supporting the various theoretical approaches to the subject. Many encounter difficulty, however, when they are asked to apply these theories to a specific film which they watch and then have to talk or write about. This is due partly to an exaggerated respect for theory: many assume that if the process takes so much theorizing it must be hard. The process of reading a film is complex, but the complexity lies in our attempts to understand the process, rather than to employ it. Everyone 'reads' films; film studies tries to understand how this is done. An important first step to applying the theoretical approaches developed in this book is to maintain some confidence in one's own point of view on a film. This chapter, however, may assist in taking the next steps.

It is usually the close 'formal' analysis of a film that appears to be the most arcane and difficult: the extraction of key elements of the narrative or visual style that is so much a staple of film studies' texts and teaching. This chapter presents examples of such close formal analysis in order to demonstrate how it is arrived at. In the first example, an account of the opening scenes of *Butch Cassidy and the Sundance Kid* applies the material on film 'languages' from Chapter 3 and on genre from Chapter 4, incorporates some of the discussion of stars from Chapter 5, and heads towards the ideological concerns of Chapter 6. In the second example, *Desperately Seeking Susan* is subjected to a number of approaches: the analyses proceed from ideas of *mise-en-scène* (Chapter 3), structuralist accounts of narrative (Chapter 4), genre (Chapter 4), audiences (Chapter 5), and ideology (Chapter 6). The intention is to demonstrate what the application of these approaches looks like, and to reveal the kinds of information each approach produces. Finally, these are applications of theory, not full (or even particularly clever) readings of the two films.

Butch Cassidy and the Sundance Kid

Butch Cassidy and the Sundance Kid opens as a silent movie – sepia-toned, flickering, flaring, and unstable. It depicts the exploits of the Hole in the Wall gang, led by Butch Cassidy and the Sundance Kid; the titles tell us they are all dead now but that once 'they ruled the West!' It is not clear if the silent film is a documentary or a dramatic recreation of the gang's activities, but it immediately situates the film in a heroic mode, with the distancing, nostalgic effect of the silent film adding to its mythic dimension. The silent footage introduces and accompanies the credits, occupying the left of the screen, while the credits run on the right. In addition to the whirring sound of the silent projector, a simple nostalgic score establishes the emotional texture of the film. As the credits end, the screen goes to black and the words 'Most of what follows is true' come up. This is to be a western which is about westerns and their mythologies.

The sepia tint and the high contrast between light and dark are maintained for the first two sequences of the narrative. These sequences are specifically contained within the same mythic domain by this device, and many of the meanings of the silent prologue leak into the opening five minutes of the narrative. The prologue is a western within a western, offering us images of the classic 'shoot 'em up' in order to signify the film's self-consciousness and to alert the audience to the degree of participation expected from them. The contrast between the sepia-tinted monochrome stock and the colour-film stock used later on is maintained throughout the film as a contrast between the lost, innocent 'past' of the characters, and the wry, knowing 'present' of the audience. Thematically, the juxta-position of a historical wild west with the modernity of (even silent) film foreshadows the heroes' plight as they become, more clearly as the film progresses, engaging anachronisms. The choice of film stock, then, and its deployment have a thematic function as well as a stylistic or tonal effect.

The first shot of the narrative establishes the door of a grand, western bank, and then we zoom into the interior. Immediately we have an extreme close-up of Butch Cassidy/Paul Newman's face; close-ups of his face will dominate the rest of the sequence. Newman's face is highlighted and attractively modelled by the low-key lighting, which emphasizes the lines of the jaw and the definition of the lips, and which reflects off the famous eyes. The sepia toning is now golden, giving his skin a romantic sheen. Although Butch/ Newman is 'casing' the bank, the focus is almost continuously on his face, briefly intercut with shots of bars, locks, doors, alarms, and finally an armed guard. A montage of close-ups of 'CLOSED' signs and grilles and doors being shut over a soundtrack of farewells tells us that the bank is closing for the day. The first break from close-ups is a medium long shot of Newman as he moves out of the door into the afternoon glare. He says to the guard, 'What happened to the old bank? It was beautiful.' 'People kept robbing it,' says the guard. 'Small price to pay for beauty,' says Butch as he walks out into the light, clearly disgruntled; here is a bank which will be impossible to rob. The joke works because it is anachronistic: it depends on the audience having seen enough westerns to know that Butch is 'casing' the bank and to recognize his remark as parodic of the generic conventions. Also, the play between the present and the past in the silent prologue watched by today's audience is repeated and focused in Butch's remark.

The lighting, the tint in the film processing, and the concentration on the star's face (even while the bulk of the information offered relates to the bank), all serve the scene's main objectives. The star's face, as stated in Chapter 5, is itself a spectacle, a source of recognition and pleasure for the audience. In this opening sequence Newman's face is barely off the screen, and the close-ups are very tight indeed. This is partly to offer the simple pleasure of the star as spectacle, but it also has a narrative function of setting up expectations of toughness and the traditional western hero which are wryly overturned in the exchange with the guard. This will be no ordinary western.

A similar, if more elaborate, procedure occurs in the following scene. The film is still sepia, still a visual blending of myth and history. We move almost immediately to a close-up of the Sundance Kid/Robert Redford's face. He is playing cards at a table, facing the camera which shoots between two other players. These players are occasionally seen in silhouette, but the *mise-en-scène* ensures that the centre of interest is Sundance's face. The lighting is low-key, with most of the light coming from the right side, flaring out in Sundance's hair, but picking up skin textures, the texture of his thick corduroy jacket, and reflecting off one eye when it looks up at his opponents during the card game. Throughout the scene, Redford remains virtually expressionless, but the spectacle of his face varies as he moves in and out of the light, and as his eyes move in and out of the shadows. In a direct parallel with the preceding sequence, his face is offered to the audience for its own sake, although the close-up is less tight, less dependent on an instant recognition of the star's features.

As the card game proceeds, the camera stays on Redford's face but we hear the preamble to, and eventually the delivery of, the charge of cheating against Sundance. Immediately, figures on either side of the screen move out of sight, we hear chairs scraping, and the scenario for the gunfight is set. The accuser stands up, facing Sundance across the table, although we only see past his gun hand as we watch for Sundance's reaction. The card-player dominates Sundance in the frame (Sundance has to look up at him), but he is at the extreme left of the frame, and his face has not yet been seen by the audience. The silence which now falls, and the stillness of Sundance's face, make it a moment of some tension and expectation.

Into this tense moment comes Butch's incongruously cheerful voice: 'We seem to be short of brotherly love around here.' As Butch attempts to intercede, Sundance finally reveals some expression as he insists, childishly, 'I *wasn't* cheating.' Instead of proceeding immediately to the gunfight, the film enters into an affectionate parody of the conventions of the western genre. Butch remonstrates, telling Sundance not to fight, and moves into the frame behind Sundance's shoulder – talking into his ear like an irritating conscience. The camera still holds its close-up on Redford with Newman's face behind him and to one side. Redford is expressionless, even when Newman warns, '*I'm* over the hill, but it *can* happen to you.' The tactlessness of this suggestion just before a gunfight is comic, and the comedy is furthered when Butch starts on the card-player, suggesting a compromise. Sundance's pride has been wounded, and he says he won't leave until the card-player asks him to stay. The perversity of this declaration is underlined when Butch pleads: 'Just ask us to stick around – you don't even have to mean it!' Throughout his intercession with the card-player, the camera stays on Butch's face as it looks up ingenuously. When he is finally pushed away, Butch drops the guise of the genial fool, turns his classic profile, and tells Sundance, 'I can't help you, Sundance.' An immediate cut to the face of the card-player (the first time we see his face) registers his disquiet at the name. This is followed by a medium long shot of the conventional gunfight tableau: the camera is behind the card-player, looking past his gun hand to Sundance who now stands up ready to draw. The tension is built up through a series of cuts between the worried card-player, the cajoling Butch ('Go on, just say it'), and the impassive Sundance. 'I didn't know you were the Sundance Kid,' says the card-player; 'if I draw on you, you'll kill me.' The tide has now turned, and the camera pulls back into the medium long shot of the tableau again as the card-player finally says, 'Why don't you stick around?' Butch grins in an aw-shucks manner and says, 'Thanks, we gotta get going', and the tension is dissipated, the moment made ridiculous by the silliness of the ritual just played out.

However, that is not the end of the sequence. The camera stays with its medium long shot and Butch moves in towards the table to sweep Sundance's winnings into his hat. Meanwhile Sundance walks past the card-player towards the camera on his way out. As he reaches the far left foreground of the screen, the card-player, who is behind him but central, calls, 'Hey, Kid, how good are you?' At this, the sequence explodes into action. Sundance drops into the classic gunfighter crouch, and fires his gun with a speed exaggerated by the quick intercutting of shots of the gun leaving its holster, the card-player's holster being shot from his hip, and his gun spinning across the floor as successive shots hit it. We see Sundance frontally at first, shooting straight at the camera; this magnifies the power of the action. He is then seen from the side, and finally through a close-up of the nonchalant twirl of his revolver as he replaces it in his holster. Throughout, Butch has continued to sweep up the money, and now he walks towards Sundance and the camera. The two move out together as Butch remarks, 'Like I been tellin' ya, over the hill.'

The sequence offers a complicated mixture of mythologizing and parody of the conventions of the western. Just when we see the confrontation averted through the parody of gunfight conventions, the power of the gunfighter is reinvoked, remythologized in the impossible series of shots Sundance is represented as executing. Clearly the film is going to define its own relation to the western genre, and it will be a complex and witty relationship. It is also clear from these sequences that the main characters will be able to have it both ways: they can be witty and self-deprecating, and thus not believe in their own mythologies; but they can also be powerful heroes possessing genuine skills, courage, and coolness. A heady mix, particularly when combined with two stars of the appeal of Newman and Redford.

These opening sequences are an introduction to the film, establishing the main characters and the visual and narrative style. The sequence immediately following depicts the two heroes riding across country to their Hole in the Wall hideout. By the end of this sequence the sepia tones have modulated and disappeared, the most self-conscious of the mythologizing has been done, and the narrative proper can begin. It is an economical and engaging opening, representative of the kind of wit that also informs George Roy Hill's second film with the same stars, *The Sting* (1973).

I have concentrated on the formal elements of the film text up to this point, making minimal references to the role of the audience in understanding this film. It is necessary to point out how actively the audience participates in the generation of the meanings of these two sequences. For a start, the offer of (at least) two viewing positions (one identifying with the nostalgic past and the other with the knowing present) gives the film a semiotic richness in the range of positions from which it can make sense. Further, the film invites the audience to recognize how self-conscious it is. There is a degree of complicity in the relationship between the film and its audience which establishes a nostalgic and affectionate point of view on the outlaws while still gently sending up the mythology of the western outlaw. The competences of the audiences are also tested, even flattered, by the film; as they 'pass' the test they are rewarded with a deeper understanding of the film and of the processes of its construction. Not only is the audience asked to recognize the parodies of the western in order to find the opening sequences comic, but they are also offered the most cryptic of narratives: the card-game sequence depicts a series of actions involving several characters (playing cards, falling still at the challenge to Sundance, pushing their chairs back and leaving) whom we never actually see; we construct this narrative from aural clues alone as the camera stays fixed in close-up on Redford's face.

Again, although my intention here is to focus on the details of the text, it is important to suggest how one might extend the analysis to deal with the film's social and ideological dimensions. The giant close-ups of Newman and Redford in these sequences are excessive, exaggerated, overtly mythologizing. The result is parodic as well as myth-making. *Butch Cassidy and the Sundance Kid* is able to benefit from the spectacle of the star's face while also burlesquing and thus subverting the heroic individualism identified with conventional representations of the western hero. As Wright (1975) has pointed out, the romanticism and individualism of the classic western (which are implicated in the mythologizing close-up) are modified and eventually rejected in such 'professional' westerns as *Butch Cassidy and the Sundance Kid*. The power of the western hero is still exploited visually, but narratively and ideologically it is subverted. The specific sense of anachronism established in the opening sequences of *Butch Cassidy and the Sundance Kid* eventually applies to the western itself; its faith in individual power has little purchase in the film's version of an encroaching twentieth century. Nevertheless, while Butch and Sundance may be fallible and naive, this does not make them less attractive or less interesting; although they have little narrative power (events happen to them), the close-ups ensure that they have enormous power as images.

When I discussed the western in Chapter 4, I referred to Metz's view (1982) that genres ultimately become critical of themselves; that is, films which are recognizably westerns nevertheless set out to attack the conventions and the supporting ideologies of their own genre. It is not difficult to see *Butch Cassidy and the Sundance Kid* in this way. It can self-consciously exploit our nostalgia for these heroic individuals because they have lost their relevance; the film imagines no place for them within contemporary ideological structures. Its sceptical evaluation of Butch and Sundance, and of all they stand for, is acted out in the final freeze frame of the pair facing death optimistically, quixotically, and finally. In *Butch Cassidy and the Sundance Kid* we can see just how the western has changed its meaning, and its relation to dominant ideological positions.

In the last few paragraphs I have moved away from the form of the film text to areas of interaction between the text and the audience, and ultimately the culture. It is important to be aware that meanings do not sit in the text waiting to be recognized – they are produced by the act of reading the film within a specific cultural context. However, from this brief account, it should be clear how the placement of elements within the frame, lighting, film stock, and the soundtrack can contribute to the meaning of a film. This kind of analysis is necessary before any more general conclusions can be drawn, and yet it is also the most straightforward of practices. It simply requires that one be observant and relate what is seen and heard to functions within the narrative. It is, then, a starting-point. We can take a similar starting-point in the next analysis, but we will take it further – exploring other approaches outlined in earlier chapters.

Desperately Seeking Susan

In Chapter 4 I listed the following oppositions as those which structure the narrative in *Desperately Seeking Susan*:

Roberta	*Susan*
conventional	unconventional
bourgeois	anti-bourgeois
suburban	urban
married	unmarried
sexually submissive	sexually aggressive
boring	exciting
constrained	free

I pointed out that these structures shape more than the 'plot': they also determine the ways in which this plot will be represented. So, although this set of oppositions was enclosed within an analysis of the narrative structure, it could as easily have emerged from a close analysis of the representational motifs of the *mise-en-scène*. For example, an account of the *mise-en-scène* at the beginning of the film would make some of the following points.

In the opening sequences, *Desperately Seeking Susan* regularly cuts back and forth between Roberta and Susan in order to introduce the elements of the plot – the stolen earrings, the villain, the central characters. However, the cross-cutting both pairs and juxtaposes Susan and Roberta by comparing and contrasting their lifestyles, their reactions to similar stimuli, and their cultural or subcultural contexts.

The first sequence takes place in a beauty salon, an assembly line of women having manicures or 'beauty treatments', or having their hair styled. Roberta is situated within this world through the framing, the pink tones of the salon's décor and the women's protective smocks, and (ideologically) by her plea to the hairdresser not to do anything 'weird' to her hair. The image of constrained femininity is capped in the following sequence which has Roberta and her sister-in-law framed under the hairdryers – a parody of middle-class suburbia. However, it is in this sequence that we gain our first hint of some resistance in Roberta. She notes the advertisement in the Personals column which is headed 'Desperately Seeking Susan', and reveals that she has been following its story for some time. Her romantic enthusiasm for the word 'desperate' suggests she is ripe for an adventure. After she circles the advertisement we cut to a new location and subject. An establishing shot of an Atlantic City hotel is followed by a slow tracking shot, back from the pink scalloped curtains in Susan's hotel room to Susan herself – lying on the floor taking pictures of herself with a polaroid camera. The pink in the curtains may remind us of Roberta's social world, but in most other respects we are conscious of a radical difference. The room is full of signifiers of pleasure and excess. Susan's clothes are bizarre in design, black in colour, and anything but suburban in their effect. The rich disorder of the room is the antithesis of the a-septic machine-room business of the hairdressing salon.

Despite these contrasts, a link between Roberta and Susan is established as the next move in the plot is made. We find out that Susan is the girl addressed in the advertisement when she recognizes it, and draws a flamboyant heart around it with her eyeliner. She then steals money and the Egyptian earrings from her sleeping mate, packs her things, and leaves by the lift – under the gaze of the villain. When we return to Roberta's world it is through a brief establishing shot of her house, followed by a cut to its interior where her birthday party is in progress. Signifiers of (the 1980s' version of) boring suburbia abound. The plate of hors d'œuvres fills the screen, Carly Simon is playing on the stereo, and one woman is wearing the same dress as Roberta. When her husband Gary calls a halt to the proceedings in order to watch a TV advertisement for his bathroom spa business, we understand the full limits of Roberta's domestic horizon. As the ad plays to the party audience, Roberta walks to the window. The camera follows her out on to the balcony, where she looks at the bridge linking New Jersey to New York. In the background we hear the last line of the spa advertisement: 'Come to Gary's Oasis, where all your fantasies can come true.' We are offered a subjective shot of the magically lit bridge; it is the division between the two worlds and thus an image of escape, or 'desperation' for Roberta. As Roberta looks at it, the music track goes up-tempo and we cut to a bus arriving in New York City carrying Susan and the earrings. Soon, Roberta will drive across that bridge to observe Susan meet her 'desperate' suitor, Jim, and the plot will take off.

This alternating narrative movement establishes what Susan, Roberta, and their respective worlds might be like and what they might mean, by carefully depicting those worlds. All the systems of signification work to construct a network of difference and similarity between the contexts and the characters. An important component, for instance, is the music track. In the opening sequence in the beauty salon we listen to a 1960s 'girly' group, an emblem of old-fashioned romanticism and, less obviously, male domination. When we move to Susan's world it is rock and roll of a more contemporary, unromantic, and insistent kind – the song is *Urgent*. We could follow the parts played by the various systems of signification further, but my essential point here is to establish the connections between the narrative structure and the languages used to represent it.

The preceding discussion of *Butch Cassidy* concluded with the introduction of an ideological reading. We can explore this approach further here. The position that *Desperately Seeking Susan* appears to take towards conventional gender roles (the wife as suburban home-maker, for instance) invites one to see it as a film which foregrounds its social and ideological dimensions.

The ideological invitation into *Desperately Seeking Susan* is sent by the fact that the oppositions described earlier set up a film where Roberta's quest is not so much for a Mr Right as for a member of her own sex who can provide a corrective and progressive role model. Although Roberta finally dumps Gary in favour of the more appealing and less suburban Dez, the audience is by no means certain to see that as the key action of the film. The patterning of oppositions and linkages between Roberta and Susan (the way in which Roberta 'becomes' Susan for Dez, the villain, and for the viewer in her adoption of Susan's jacket, hairstyle, and ultimately name) generates a tension that is only resolved when the two women meet. Although it is not, like *Thelma and Louise*, a female 'buddy' movie, the relations between the women are crucial to the film.

There is a feminist set of ideologies at work in *Desperately Seeking Susan* which enables Susan to be the most powerful and self-possessed of the characters and has the men stand by and watch rather than influence the plot's development. Even when the villain is caught it is Roberta who knocks him out with a bottle. The following scene, in which Roberta and Susan recognize each other, has the structural importance of the lovers' first kiss in a conventional romantic comedy. It resolves and repairs the tensions generated by the rest of the film. But it is understated. Audiences have expressed their disappointment at the lack of a stronger sense of recognition or, even, destiny at this moment. The film seems to deflect the expectations from this meeting by immediately taking us to a more conventional romantic reunion between Roberta and Dez in the projection room of the theatre. This is the second in a series of points of closure to the narrative. It is followed by a third point: a shot of Susan and her boyfriend Jim in the cinema, eating popcorn and enjoying each other's company. The foursome which this establishes would not be out of place in the most conventional romantic comedy. Yet this is followed by still another concluding sequence of newspaper pages announcing the return of the Egyptian earrings, a reward for Susan and Roberta, and a celebratory civic reception. The headline 'What a Pair!' is above a photograph of Susan and Roberta, without Jim and Dez, holding their hands aloft in a victory gesture. In this series of closing sequences we are offered two possibly opposite kinds of closure in that we are asked to celebrate two kinds of 'pairs' – the romantic couple, and 'sisters'.

Why this should matter to the audience is that it raises the possibility that the feminist stance of the film, the concentration on the female protagonists and the depiction of the males as peripheral to the plot, is blurred and defeated by the invocations of conventional romance. Admittedly, the scenes are themselves comic and self-conscious and thus distance themselves from the conventional. However, the repeated moves towards closure are markers of uncertainty, of the width of the ideological gap which has been opened in the film, and which now must be sealed over.

The specific function of the casting of Madonna is worth questioning, too. Although the film is, in a sense, a 'women's film', the ideology of femaleness it constructs is complicated by Madonna. On the one hand, her characterization of Susan represents her as cool, capable, independent, and sexually manipulative – all conventionally masculine attributes. On the other hand, Madonna herself has been offered as a commodity to her male and female fans through the Boy-Toy tag which undercuts progressive notions of the female.

Madonna can be seen as a figure who exaggerates (and therefore makes ridiculous) male expectations of female sexuality; she therefore has a potentially feminist meaning. John Fiske (1987a) examined the 'bundle of meanings' we think of as Madonna and argued that despite her apparent reproduction of a masculine view of women as objects of desire, the way in which she represents herself can be seen as critical and subversive of such masculine points of view. Drawing on interviews with fans as well as textual analysis of her music videos at the height of her fame, Fiske claims Madonna's 'knowing' use of the camera enables her to mock 'the conventional representations of female sexuality at the same time she conforms to them':

> Madonna consistently parodies conventional representations of women and parody can be an effective device for

interrogating the dominant ideology. It takes the defining features of its object, exaggerates and mocks them, and thus mocks those who 'fall' for its ideological effect. But Madonna's parody goes further than this; she parodies, not just the stereotypes, but the way in which they are made.

(1987a: 277)

It is this aspect of her representation of herself, her control of her image rather than her subjection to it, which seemed to strike a chord in her fans. Fiske quotes one fan who can see that the 'tarty and seductive' looks are potentially sexist, but nevertheless feels that 'it's OK with her'. Madonna is seen as the producer of her image, not merely its bearer; that changes the meaning of the image. Paradoxically, the sense of Madonna's personal and sexual independence seems to derive from her explicit appropriation of images of female sexuality; with Madonna, gestures of submission can be double-edged and work as a challenge to the sexuality of the masculine observer. The excessiveness of Madonna's depiction of female sexuality is its most parodic and intimidating aspect and in it we can see a wealth of meanings other than the simple Boy-Toy label; or rather, the label itself becomes ironic, a flippant taunt to the masculine. Who is likely to 'toy' with whom? is the question posed by the image of Madonna.

Fiske's account of the meanings attributable to Madonna would lead us to see her casting as entirely consonant with the film's meanings. Nevertheless, for viewers who do not see Madonna in such a way, her casting must have set up awkward ideological contradictions.

It is worth stressing here that what I have been offering are suggestions towards readings, not any kind of definitive account. Each approach outlined in this book has the potential to produce a different account of the film – in effect, a different film. In my suggestions I have incorporated information made available by the semiotics of stars, by structuralist accounts of narrative, by *mise-en-scène* criticism, by accounts of the female spectator and the 'musculine' heroine, and by ideological theory. The virtue of exploring a number of approaches lies in the fact that the different versions can complement, mirror, or challenge each other. The result is a sense of the complexity of the communication which is occurring, of the film's potential for meaning, as well as of the suspect nature of any claim to definitive or final readings. The ideological argument just mounted, for instance, depends on a number of unexamined assumptions. One is that *Desperately Seeking Susan* is a 'women's film' – itself a category which bears closer interrogation. To see *Desperately Seeking Susan* in this way is to place it in a particular genre, and that demands some argument.

If we consider *Desperately Seeking Susan* through notions of genre we immediately recover a sense of its playfulness and assurance, features that are subordinated in the ideological reading. *Desperately Seeking Susan* plays conflicting generic expectations off against each other, moving from one set of conventions to another with a degree of skill and self-awareness. It may start out as a film which foregrounds the opposition constructed between the worlds and thus ideologies of its main characters, but it quickly tells us that the rules which the narrative will follow are those of genre, not the 'real world'. Roberta's subjection is exaggerated and made comic; her birthday closes with her sitting with the remains of her cake watching a rerun of the archetypal romantic weepie *Rebecca* on the TV. The opposition between her life and Susan's is too stark to require interpretation; rather, it becomes the structural basis for the film's narrative. Similarly, when we follow Susan leaving her hotel room, she spills her belongings on the floor in front of the lift. The lift has just discharged a passenger who looks at Susan for an exceptionally long time, and then slowly walks off, shoes squeaking theatrically. We have just met the villain, and the character's general – if not specific – significance has been signalled by the long take: not in order to imitate reality but to interpellate the audience into the story. Such moments announce that whatever else it is, this is a film which will make use of tension, coincidence, all the paraphernalia of a 'caper' movie or adventure comedy. The device of the knock on the head to produce and relieve amnesia is purely conventional, and to believe it we have to accept its fictionality. So, although the film may resonate interestingly with 'the real', it places itself in the company of the screwball comedy, or the gangster/caper movie, and refers back to classic Hollywood genres as often as it foregrounds its subcultural contemporariness.

This has an effect on the way in which we watch it. It allows us, for instance, to applaud particularly neat moments of narrative transition, like the cut from the cat watching the goldfish to the killer's vigil outside Dez's house. We can enjoy having tricks played on us, or almost played on us, as when we discover the villain at the extreme edge of the frame immediately behind Gary's chair in the final scenes at the Magic Club. This scene is designed to frustrate and prolong the unravelling of confused identities, and the audience are meant to enjoy the series of explicit postponements of the denouement. The way in which characters are moved in and out of locations in this sequence is reminiscent of the way bedroom farce exploits the barest of realistic alibis for the action. Thus, the ideological problems mentioned earlier may seem to be irrelevant in a film that is so careful to present itself as performance, fiction, and entertainment.

The 'women's film' has become something of a genre too, of course. Unlikely to offer itself as fantasy, the women's film usually presents a main female character who learns to find herself (preferably, but not always) without the assistance of a male. Mostly, such films are careful not to mix genres; certainly, they tend not to be easy to mistake for comedies and they are usually loath to risk not being taken as socially truthful by foregrounding their fictionality, their story-telling function. *Desperately Seeking Susan* has important elements of the 'women's film' genre. Roberta is limited and ignored by her husband and depressed by the world in which her marriage has placed her. When she confronts Gary at the Magic Club she accuses him of not 'seeing' her for what she is: 'Look at *me*!' she says, but he turns away. The major change in the situation at the end of *Desperately Seeking Susan* is that Roberta is now more responsible for herself and has recognized her otherness from the Fort Lee housewife she was a week ago. It is not misleading to see the film as an account of her self-realization. If women's film seems to you to be the dominant genre, then the ideological account given above must have carried conviction.

There is still another space the film occupies, however. The world which Susan inhabits, the low-life, rock-orientated, street world of New York City, becomes an image of the normal in *Desperately Seeking Susan*; the suburban world which Gary inhabits is increasingly bizarre, abnormal, and unacceptable. The film then becomes a kind of subcultural film, recommending a lifestyle that few of its viewers will ever taste, let alone adopt, and attacking a lifestyle that most of its audience will eventually aspire to lead – even if they reject its meanings.

It may not be perceptible any longer but there is a very deliberate attempt to place the film accurately within a specific contemporary East Village underground world. Susan Seidelman's earlier film *Smithereens* was about a young girl's adventures in the East Village punk rock scene, and her director's credentials are stronger in this area than in mainstream cinema. In shooting, she chose actual locations; the gritty, street-level feel of the New York scenes reflect this. Despite the fact that New York is represented in a heightened, magical way, as a Wonderland for Roberta's Alice, it is also convincingly realistic. For those members of the audience who belonged to or admired a subculture like this at the time of its release, Seidelman offered some special pleasures. She casts figures from the New York music, art, and film world in cameo roles. Richard Hell, a punk rock singer (from Richard Hell and the Voidoids), plays Meeker, Anna Carlisle (from the cult film *Liquid Sky*) plays Dez's 'ex', and the musician Richard Edson turns up in a short encounter with Susan in St Mark's Place. The film is rooted in the locations and the personalities of the world it is portraying. It is a film which could easily have worn the label 'cult film' in the specificity of its address to a young, style-conscious, urban audience. It is this aspect of the film which endows its depiction of Susan's world with such authenticity; there is no sense that this is a tourist's view of the East Village.

There is, of course, yet another genre into which we could place this film. The casting of Madonna, as mentioned earlier, carried with it the potential to specify a teenage, music-orientated audience whose main objective would be to see a 'Madonna' film. The placement of *Desperately Seeking Susan* within the genre of teen movies would be of some commercial benefit, since this is the largest sector of the cinema market. However, it does seem clear that most

22 Rosanna Arquette and Madonna, *Desperately Seeking Susan*

audiences who were encouraged to see the film as a teen movie or a Madonna film were disappointed. While the film deals with a set of conflicts similar to those of *Risky Business* (1983), *The Breakfast Club* (1985), and other teen movies – conflicts between individual self-expression, say, and social restraints – they are articulated in different ways. In the teen movies, the key constraining influences are parents and school. The hero's or heroine's articulation of independence, or pursuit of pleasure, occurs in spite of and against the ideologies and prohibitions of their family, teachers, or adult advisers. *Desperately Seeking Susan* takes the battle a stage beyond this, to the choice of marriage, examining less specific social pressures towards conformity and compromise. So while one could expect the audience for John Hughes's movies to sympathize with Roberta's plight, they are not likely to identify in the way that they do with the main character in *Risky Business*. *Desperately Seeking Susan* is a film about the difficulties of adulthood and definitions of femininity.

We see films within specific social conditions, and take to them our own set of views of the world. Any reading of a film is only that, one reading. To approach *Desperately Seeking Susan* from one set of assumptions as to what kind of film it is may produce a different film from that perceived by another viewer with a different set of assumptions. There are limits to this process, of course, but the argument about a film's genre is ultimately an argument about what it *is*; it is not surprising that those who disagree on the kind of film they are watching will also disagree on specific details. But divergent or competing readings are not necessarily contradictory of each other. *Desperately Seeking Susan* is, in a sense, many kinds of film. It consciously takes exhilarating risks in order to keep options open, to provide a multiplicity of positions from which it can provide its audiences with the pleasures of cinema. To attempt to reduce that multiplicity to one unitary point of view would be to lose much; also, it would lose sight of the point of this exercise, which is to explore different approaches for their ability to produce a different text. This potential is a benefit, not a threat, to anyone attempting to understand popular cinema and its relations to its audiences.

Conclusion

The readings in this chapter have developed in a circular fashion. We have moved from close analysis of the specific forms of the film text to the reader's decoding of them according to his or her own specific competences and expectations. In the process, we have had to recognize the part played by the reader's competences and expectations in determining the meanings generated for him or her by the text. We have noted the effect of an interaction between the text and what the reader brings to it in producing quite disparate readings of *Desperately Seeking Susan* – in effect, producing a multiple text. We should also remember that the viewing of one film will affect the viewing of subsequent films; what the audience sees in any one visit to the cinema is added to (and will rearrange, modify, or confirm) their experience of films, of genres, of stars, of cinema's pleasures. This experience will go with them into the next movie they attend. The simple point to be taken is that film is not passively understood, nor are its meanings textually 'fixed'; as we saw in Chapter 5, meanings are generated by an interaction between the audience and the text. The relations between a film and its audience, and between film and culture, are relations we need to see as paramount in our understanding of the form and function of the feature film. Understanding a movie is not essentially an aesthetic practice; it is a social practice which mobilizes the full range of meaning systems within the culture.

This book has been aimed at making just that point. As outlined earlier on in the book, the influence of aesthetic principles of film analysis on academic and institutional interest in the medium displaced the social and cultural aspects of film-making, film viewing, film-promotion, and film criticism. As the more cultural studies inflected accounts of literature, TV, and popular culture generally have become more widely known and respected, we have also seen a shift in the way in which film studies has developed. It is now possible to argue that film studies has broken with the dominance of aesthetics in order to reconnect films with their audiences, filmmakers with their industries, film texts with society.

Any argument we might make about the interpretation of cultural signs and meanings can be only provisional. We can never understand the whole cultural system and still be contained within it; we can never step outside it and still understand its workings. But the intention behind this book has been to offer an introduction to what now seem the most profitable ways of understanding the place of film within our social existence, the specific nature of the pleasures film offers, and the deep-seated social functions served by its combination of narrative, sound, and image. I hope that this will be the beginning, not the conclusion, of an interest in the social practice of film.

References

Allen, R. C. and Gomery, D. (1985) *Film History: Theory and Practice*, New York: Random House.

Altman, C. F. (1977) 'Psychoanalysis and the cinema: the imaginary discourse', *Quarterly Review of Film Studies* 2 (3), reprinted in B. Nichols (ed.) (1985) *Movies and Methods*, vol. 2, Berkeley: University of California Press.

Andrew, D. (1984) *Concepts in Film Theory*, New York: Oxford University Press.

Arnheim, R. (1958) *Film as Art*, London: Faber.

Balio, T. (1985) *The American Film Industry*, Madison: University of Wisconsin Press.

—— (1990) *Hollywood in the Age of Television*, Boston: Unwin Hyman.

—— (1996) 'Adjusting to the global economy: Hollywood in the 1990s', in A. Moran (ed.) *Film Policy: International, National and Regional Perspectives*, London: Routledge.

—— (2002) 'A major presence in all the world's important markets: the globalization of Hollywood in the 1990s', in G. Turner (ed.) *The Film Cultures Reader*, London and New York: Routledge.

Barr, C. (1977) *Ealing Studios*, London: Cameron & Tayleur.

Barthes, R. (1973) *Mythologies*, London: Paladin.

—— (1975) *The Pleasure of the Text*, New York: Hill & Wang.

—— (1977) *Image–Music–Text*, London: Fontana.

Barton, S. (2002) 'Your self-storage: female investigation and male performativity in the women's psychothriller', in G. Turner (ed.) *The Film Cultures Reader*, London and New York: Routledge.

Baudry, J.-L. (1974) 'Ideological effects of the basic cinematographic apparatus', *Film Quarterly*, 28 (2).

Bazin, A. (1967) *What is Cinema?*, vol. 1, Berkeley: University of California Press.

Bennett, T., Boyd-Bowman, S., Mercer, C., and Woollacott, J. (eds) (1981) *Popular Television and Film*, London: British Film Institute.

Bennett, T. and Woollacott, J. (1987) *Bond and Beyond: The Political Career of a Popular Hero*, London: Macmillan.

Benshoff, H. M. and Griffen, S. (2004) *Queer Cinema: The Film Reader*, London and New York: Routledge.

Berger, J. (1972) *Ways of Seeing*, London: British Broadcasting Corporation.

Bobo, J. (1995) *Black Women as Cultural Readers*, New York: Columbia University Press.

Bordwell, D. (1985) *Narration in the Fiction Film*, London: Routledge.

—— (1989) *Making Meaning: Inference and Rhetoric in the Interpretation of Cinema*, Cambridge, Mass.: Harvard University Press

Bordwell, D. and Carroll, N. (eds) (1996) *Post-Theory: Reconstructing Film Studies*, Madison: University of Wisconsin Press.

Bordwell, D., Staiger, J., and Thompson, K. (1985) *The Classical Hollywood Cinema: Film Style and Mode of Production to 1960*, New York: Columbia University Press.

Bordwell, D. and Thompson, K. (1986) *Film Art: An Introduction*, 2nd edn, New York: Knopf.

Branston, G. (2000) *Cinema and Cultural Modernity*, Buckingham and Philadelphia: Open University Press

Brunsdon, C. (1997) *Screen Tastes: Soap Opera to Satellite Dishes*, London: Routledge.

Brunsdon, C. and Morley, D. (1978) *Everyday Television: Nationwide*, London: British Film Institute.

Bruzzi, S. (1997) *Undressing Cinema: Clothing and Identity in the Movies*, London: Routledge.

Buscombe, E. (1977) 'Sound and colour', *Jump Cut*, 17, reprinted in B. Nichols (ed.) (1985) *Movies and Methods*, vol. 2, Berkeley: University of California Press.

Byron, S. (1979) '*The Searchers*: cult movie of the new Hollywood', *New York Magazine*, 5 March.

Carroll, N. (1996) 'Prospects for film theory', in D. Bordwell and N. Carroll (eds) *Post-Theory: Reconstructing Film Studies*, Madison: University of Wisconsin Press.

Caughie, J. (ed.) (1981) *Theories of Authorship: A Reader*, London: Routledge & Kegan Paul.

Chambers, I. (1986) *Popular Culture: The Metropolitan Experience*, London: Methuen.

Chatman, S. (1978) *Story and Discourse: Narrative Structure in Fiction and Film*, London: Cornell University Press.

Clover, C. J. (1992) *Men, Women, and Chainsaws: Gender in the Modern Horror Film*, Princeton: Princeton University Press.

Collins, J., Radner, H., and Preacher Collins, A. (eds) (1993) *Film Theory Goes to the Movies*, London and New York: Routledge.

Comolli, J. (1977) 'Technique and ideology: camera, perspective, depth of field', *Film Reader*, 2.

Cook, D. (1981) *A History of Narrative Film*, New York: Norton.

Cook, P. (ed.) (1987) *The Cinema Book*, London: British Film Institute.

Coward, R. (1984) *Female Desire: Women's Sexuality Today*, London: Paladin.

Creed, B. (1993) *The Monstrous-Feminine: Film, Feminism and Psychoanalysis*, London: Routledge.

—— (2002) 'The cyberstar: digital pleasures and the end of the unconscious', in G. Turner (ed.) *The Film Cultures Reader*, London and New York: Routledge; reprinted from *Screen*, 41 (1), which appeared in 2000.

Dayan, D. (1974) 'The tutor code of classical cinema', *Film Quarterly*, 28 (1).

De Lauretis, T. (1984) *Alice Doesn't: Feminism, Semiotics, Cinema*, Bloomington: Indiana University Press and London: Macmillan.

De Lauretis, T. and Heath, S. (eds) (1980) *The Cinematic Apparatus*, London: Macmillan.

Dermody, S. and Jacka, E. (1987) *The Screening of Australia: Anatomy of an Industry*, Sydney: Currency.

Doane, M. A. (1988) *The Desire to Desire: The Woman's Film of the 1940s*, London: Macmillan.

Dyer, R. (1977) 'Entertainment and utopia', *Movie*, 24.

—— (1979) *Stars*, London: British Film Institute.

—— (1986) *Heavenly Bodies: Film Stars and Society*, London: British Film Institute.

—— (1990) *Now You See It: Studies in Gay and Lesbian Film*, London: Routledge

REFERENCES

—— (1997) *White*, London: Routledge.

—— (2002) *The Culture of Queers*, New York: Routledge.

Ellis, J. (1975) 'Made in Ealing', *Screen*, 16 (1).

—— (1982) *Visible Fictions: Cinema, Television, Video*, London: Routledge & Kegan Paul.

Erens, P. (1977) '*Sunset Boulevard*: a morphological analysis', *Film Reader*, 2.

Fell, J. (1977) 'Vladimir Propp in Hollywood', *Film Quarterly*, 30 (3).

Fiske, J. (1982) *Introduction to Communication Studies*, London: Methuen.

—— (1987a) 'British cultural studies and television', in R. Allen (ed.) *Channels of Discourse*, Chapel Hill: University of North Carolina Press.

—— (1987b) *Television Culture*, London: Methuen.

Fiske, J., Hodge, B., and Turner, G. (1987) *Myths of Oz: Reading Australian Popular Culture*, Sydney: Allen & Unwin.

Frith, S. (1986) 'Hearing secret harmonies', in C. MacCabe (ed.) *High Theory/Low Culture: Analysing Popular Television and Film*, Manchester: Manchester University Press.

Gamman, L. and Marshment, M. (eds) (1988) *The Female Gaze*, London: Women's Press.

Gillespie, M. (1995) *Television, Ethnicity and Cultural Change*, London: Routledge.

Gledhill, C. and Williams, L. (eds) (2000) *Reinventing Film Studies*, London: Arnold.

Gomery, D. (1976) 'Writing the history of the American film industry: Warner Bros and sound', *Screen*, 1.

—— (1980) 'Towards an economic history of the cinema: the coming of sound to Hollywood', in T. de Lauretis and S. Heath (eds) *The Cinematic Apparatus*, London: Macmillan.

—— (1986) 'The popularity of film-going in the US, 1930–1950', in C. MacCabe (ed.) *High Theory/Low Culture: Analysing Popular Television and Film*, Manchester: Manchester University Press.

Griffith, R. (1949) 'Cycles and genres', in B. Nichols (ed.) (1976) *Movies and Methods*, vol. 1, Berkeley: University of California Press.

Griggers, C. (1993) '*Thelma and Louise* and the cultural generation of the new butch-femme' in J. Collins, H. Radner, and A. Preacher Collins (eds) *Film Theory Goes to the Movies*, New York: Routledge.

Guerrero, E. (1993) *Framing Blackness*, Philadelphia: Temple University Press.

Gunning, T. (1986) 'The cinema of attractions: early film, its spectator and the avant-garde', *Wide Angle*, 8 (3–4).

Hall, S. (1977) 'Culture, the media and "the ideological effect"', in J. Curran, M. Gurevitch, and J. Woollacott (eds) *Mass Communication and Society*, London: Edward Arnold.

—— (1982) 'The rediscovery of ideology: return of the repressed in media studies', in M. Gurevitch, T. Bennett, J. Curran, and J. Woollacott (eds) *Culture, Society and the Media*, London: Methuen.

Hansen, M. (1989) 'Miriam Hansen', *Camera Obscura*, 20–1 (May–Sept.).

—— (1994) *Babel and Babylon: Spectatorship in American Silent Film*, Cambridge, Mass.: Harvard University Press.

Harbord, J. (2002) *Film Cultures*, London: Sage.

Hawkes, T. (1977) *Structuralism and Semiotics*, London: Methuen.

Heath, S. (1980) 'The cinematic apparatus: technology as historical and cultural form', in T. de Lauretis and S. Heath (eds) *The Cinematic Apparatus*, London: Macmillan.

Henderson, B. (1971a) 'The long take', *Film Comment*, 7 (2).

—— (1971b) 'Two types of film theory', *Film Quarterly*, 24 (3), reprinted in B. Nichols (ed.) (1976) *Movies and Methods*, vol. 1, Berkeley: University of California Press.

Hobson, D. (1982) *Crossroads: The Drama of a Soap Opera*, London: Methuen.

Holmlund, C. (1991) 'When is a lesbian not a lesbian? The lesbian continuum and the mainstream femme film', *Camera Obscura*, 25–6 (Jan.–May).

Jancovitch, M. (2002) 'A real shocker: authenticity, genre and the struggle for distinction', in G. Turner (ed.) *The Film Cultures Reader*, London and New York: Routledge; first published in *Continuum*, 14(1), 2000.

Jeffords, S. (2002) 'Can masculinity be terminated?' in G. Turner (ed.) *The Film Cultures Reader*, London and New York: Routledge

Jowett, G. and Linton, J. (1980) *Movies as Mass Communication*, Beverly Hills: Sage.

Julien, I. and Mercer, K. (2002) 'De margin and de centre', in G.Turner (ed.) *The Film Cultures Reader*, London and New York: Routledge.

Kindem, G. (ed.) (1982) *The American Movie Industry: The Business of Motion Pictures*, Carbondale: Southern Illinois University Press.

King, G. (2000) *Spectacular Narratives: Hollywood in the Age of the Blockbuster*, London and New York: I. B. Taurus.

King, N. (1983) 'Changing the curriculum: the place of film in a department of English', *Australian Journal of Cultural Studies*, 1 (1).

—— (1992) 'Not to be an intellectual: Adrian Martin on teen movies', *Cinema Papers*, 89.

REFERENCES

Klinger, B. (1994) *Melodrama and Meaning: History, Culture and the Films of Douglas Sirk*, Bloomington and Indianapolis: Indiana University Press.

Kuhn, A. (1984) 'Women's genres', *Screen*, 25 (1).

Lapsley, R. and Westlake, M. (1989) *Film Theory: An Introduction*, Manchester: Manchester University Press.

Lévi-Strauss, C. (1955) 'The structural study of myth', *Journal of American Folklore* 78 (270).

—— (1966) *The Savage Mind*, London: Weidenfeld & Nicolson.

Lewis, J. (2003) 'Following the money in America's sunniest company town: some notes on the political economy of the Hollywood blockbuster', in J. Stringer (ed.) *Movie Blockbusters*, London and New York: Routledge,

Lindsay, V. (1915) *The Art of the Moving Picture*, New York: Macmillan.

Lott. T. (1998) 'Hollywood and independent black cinema', in S. Neale and M. Smith (eds) *Contemporary Hollywood Cinema*, London and New York: Routledge.

Lund, D. (1982) 'Writing film history: the struggle for synthesis', in S. Thomas (ed.) *Film/Culture: Explorations of Cinema in its Social Context*, Metuchen, NJ: Scarecrow.

MacCabe, C. (1981) 'Realism and the cinema: notes on some Brechtian theses', in T. Bennett, S. Boyd-Bowman, C. Mercer, and J. Woollacott (eds) *Popular Television and Film*, London: British Film Institute.

—— (ed.) (1986) *High Theory/Low Culture: Analysing Popular Television and Film*, Manchester: Manchester University Press.

Marshall, P. D. (1997) *Celebrity and Power*, Minneapolis: University of Minnesota Press.

Mast, G., Cohen, M., and Braudy, L. (eds) (1992) *Film Theory and Criticism*, New York: Oxford University Press.

Mayne, J. (1993) *Cinema and Spectatorship*, London: Routledge.

Metz, C. (1975) *Language and Cinema*, New York: Praeger.

—— (1982) *Psychoanalysis and the Cinema: The Imaginary Signifier*, London: Macmillan.

Miller, T. (2001) 'Cinema studies doesn't matter, or, I know what you did last semester', in M. Tinkcom and A. Villarejo (eds) *Keyframes: Popular Cinema and Cultural Studies*, London and New York: Routledge.

Miller, T., Govil, N., Maxwell, R., and Murria, J. (2001) *Global Hollywood*, London: British Film Institute.

Modleski, T. (1988) *The Woman Who Knew Too Much: Hitchcock and Feminist Film Theory*, New York: Methuen.

Monaco, J. (1981) *How to Read a Film*, New York: Oxford University Press.

Moran, A. (ed.) (1996) *Film Policy: International, National and Regional Perspectives*, London: Routledge.

Morley, D. (1980) *The Nationwide Audience: Structure and Decoding*, London: British Film Institute.

—— (1992) *Television, Audiences and Cultural Studies*, London: Routledge.

Mulvey, L. (1975) 'Visual pleasure and narrative cinema', *Screen*, 16 (3), reprinted in B. Nichols (ed.) (1985) *Movies and Methods*, vol. 2, Berkeley: University of California Press.

—— (1989) *Visual and Other Pleasures*, London: Macmillan.

Ndalianis, A. (2000) 'Special effects, morphing magic and the 1990s cinema of attractions' in V. Sobchack (ed.) *Meta-Morphing: Visual Transformation and the Culture of Quick-Change*, Minneapolis and London: University of Minnesota Press.

Neale, S. (1985) *Cinema and Technology: Image, Sound, Colour*, London: Macmillan.

—— (2003) 'Hollywood blockbusters: historical dimensions', in J. Stringer (ed.) *Hollywood Blockbusters*, London and New York: Routledge.

Neale, S. and Smith, M. (1998) (eds) *Contemporary Hollywood Cinema*, London and New York: Routledge.

Negra, D. (2001) *Off-White Hollywood: American Culture and Ethnic Female Stardom*, London and New York: Routledge.

Nelmes, J. (ed.) (1996) *Introduction to Film Studies*, London: Routledge.

Nichols, B. (ed.) (1976) *Movies and Methods*, vol. 1, Berkeley: University of California Press.

—— (ed.) (1985) *Movies and Methods*, vol. 2, Berkeley: University of California Press.

O'Regan, T. (1985) 'Ocker and the Tariff Board: the politics of import culture', *Australian Journal of Cultural Studies*, 3 (1).

—— (1986) 'A fine cultural romance: aspects of Australian film in the late 1970s', *Australian Journal of Cultural Studies*, 4 (1).

O'Regan, T. and Goldsmith, B. (2005) *The Film Studio: Film Production in the Global Economy*, Lanham, MD: Rowman & Littlefield.

Penley, C. (1988) *Feminism and Film Theory*, New York: Routledge.

Perry, G. (1975) *The Great British Picture Show*, London: Paladin.

Pierson, M. (2002) *Special Effects: Still in Search of Wonder*, New York: Columbia University Press.

Place, J. and Peterson, L. (1974) 'Some visual motifs of *film noir*', *Film Comment*, 10 (1).

Pribram, D. (ed.) (1988) *Female Spectators: Looking at Film and Television*, London: Verso.

Prince, S. (1996) 'Psychoanalytic film theory and the problem of the missing spectator', in D. Bordwell and N. Carroll (eds) *Post-Theory: Reconstructing Film Studies*, Madison: University of Wisconsin Press.

—— (2002) 'True lies: perceptual realism, digital images and film theory', in G. Turner (ed.), *The Film Cultures Reader*, London and New York: Routledge.

Propp, V. (1975) *The Morphology of the Folk Tale*, Austin: University of Texas Press.

Rimmon-Kenan, S. (1983) *Narrative Fiction: Contemporary Poetics*, London: Methuen.

Rojek, C. (2001) *Celebrity*, London: Reaktion.

Rutsky, R. L. and Wyatt, J. (1990) 'Serious pleasures: cinematic pleasure and the notion of fun', *Cinematic Journal*, 30 (1).

Sarris, A. (1962–3) 'Notes on the *auteur* theory in 1962', *Film Culture* (winter).

—— (1976) 'Towards a theory of film history', in B. Nichols (ed.) *Movies and Methods*, vol. 1, Berkeley: University of California Press.

Schatz, T. (1981) *Hollywood Genres: Formulas, Filmmaking, and the Studio System*, New York: Random House.

—— (1993) 'The new Hollywood', in J. Collins, H. Radner, and A. Preacher Collins (eds) *Film Theory Goes to the Movies*, London and New York: Routledge, reprinted in G. Turner (ed.) *The Film Cultures Reader*, London and New York: Routledge.

Schrader, P. (1972) 'Notes on *film noir*', *Film Comment* (spring).

Sergi, G. (2002) 'A cry in the dark: the role of the post-classical film sound', in G. Turner (ed.) *The Film Cultures Reader*, London and New York: Routledge.

Shaviro, S. (1993) *The Cinematic Body*, Minneapolis: University of Minnesota Press.

Silverman, K. (1983) *The Subject of Semiotics*, New York: Oxford University Press.

Sklar, R. (1975) *Movie-Made America: A Cultural History of American Movies*, New York: Vintage.

Sobchak, T. and Sobchak, V. (1980) *An Introduction to Film*, Boston, Mass.: Little, Brown.

Sobchack, V. (2000) (ed.) *Meta-Morphing: Visual Transformation and the Culture of Quick-Change*, Minneapolis and London: University of Minnesota Press.

Stacey, J. (1994) *Star Gazing: Hollywood Cinema and Female Spectatorship*, London: Routledge.

Staiger, J. (1992) *Interpreting Films*, Princeton: Princeton University Press.

—— (2000) *Perverse Spectators: The Practices of Film Reception*, New York and London: New York University Press.

Stam, R., Burgoyne, R., and Flitterman-Lewis, S. (eds) (1992) *New Vocabularies in Film Semiotics*, New York: Routledge.

Stam, R. and Miller, T. (1999) *A Companion to Film Theory*, Malden, Mass.: Blackwell.

—— (2000) (eds) *Film and Theory: An Anthology*, Malden, Mass.: Blackwell.

Straayer, C. (1984) 'Personal Best: lesbian/feminist audience', *Jump Cut*, 29 (February).

—— (1996) *Deviant Eyes, Deviant Bodies: Sexual Reorientations in Film and Video*, New York: Columbia University Press.

—— (2002) 'The hypothetical lesbian heroine in narrative feature film', in G.Turner (ed.) *The Film Cultures Reader*, London and New York: Routledge.

Stringer, J. (2003) (ed.) *Movie Blockbusters*, London and New York: Routledge

Studlar, G. (1985) 'Masochism and the perverse pleasures of the cinema', in B. Nichols (ed.) *Movies and Methods*, vol. 2, Berkeley: University of California Press.

Tasker, Y. (1993) *Spectacular Bodies: Gender, Genre and the Action Cinema*, London: Comedia.

—— (1996) 'Approaches to the new Hollywood', in J. Curran, D. Morley, and V. Walkerdine (eds) *Cultural Studies and Communications*, London: Arnold.

—— (1998) *Working Girls: Gender and Sexuality in Popular Cinema*, London: Routledge.

Thomas, S. (ed.) (1982) *Film/Culture: Explorations of Cinema in its Social Context*, Metuchen, NJ: Scarecrow.

Thompson, K. (1985) *Exporting Entertainment: America in the World Film Market 1907–1934*, London: British Film Institute.

Tinkcom, M. and Villarejo, A. (eds) (2001) *Keyframes: Popular Cinema and Cultural Studies*, London and New York: Routledge.

Todorov, T. (1977) *The Poetics of Prose*, Oxford: Blackwell.

Tudor, A. (1974) *Image and Influence*, London: Allen & Unwin.

Tulloch, J. (1982) *Australian Cinema: Industry, Narrative and Meaning*, Sydney: Allen & Unwin.

REFERENCES

Turner, G. (1986) *National Fictions: Literature, Film and the Construction of Australian Narrative*, Sydney: Allen & Unwin.

—— (2002) (ed.) *The Film Cultures Reader*, London and New York: Routledge.

—— (2004) *Understanding Celebrity*, London: Sage.

Wasko, J. (2003) *How Hollywood Works*, London: Sage.

Williamson, D. (1986) *Authorship and Criticism*, Sydney: Local Consumption.

Williamson, J. (1987) *Consuming Passions*, London: Marion Boyars.

Willis, S. (1993) 'Hardware and hard bodies: what do women want? A reading of *Thelma and Louise*', in J. Collins, H. Radner, and A. Preacher Collins (eds) *Film Theory Goes to the Movies*, New York, Routledge.

Wollen, P. (1972) *Signs and Meanings in the Cinema*, London: Secker & Warburg.

—— (1976) '*North by North-West*: a morphological analysis', *Film Form*, 1 (2).

Wright, W. (1975) *Six-Guns and Society: A Structural Study of the Western*, Berkeley: University of California Press.

Wyatt, J. (1994) *High Concept: Movies and Marketing in Hollywood*, Austin: University of Texas Press.

Index

CPSIA information can be obtained
at www.ICGtesting.com
Printed in the USA
FFOW04n1659091216
30217FF

9 780415 375146